SOME REASONS WHY THIS BOOK AND ITS AUTHOR ARE SO VERY SPECIAL

Whether the subject is a great choreographer like Balanchine ... a creative pioneer like Martha Graham ... legends like Nijinsky, Pavlova, and Isadora Duncan, or modern luminaries like Markova and Ulanova ... classic ballet or modern dance ... the basic elements of style in dance and its relation to other arts and to life itself ... Edwin Denby proves that he is without equal in his field and in his warm and humane genius.

IF YOU LOVE THE DANCE, THIS BOOK IS INDISPENSABLE!

Also by Edwin Denby and available
from Popular Library:

LOOKING AT THE DANCE
04270-2 $2.50

And don't miss the others in Popular Library's
great Dance Library:

THE COMPLETE GUIDE TO MODERN DANCE
08623-8 $2.50

NUREYEV
04015-7 $2.25

A TIME TO DANCE
08453-7 $1.75

WALTER TERRY'S BALLET GUIDE
08621-1 $2.50

MARTHA GRAHAM
08358-1 $1.95

Dancers, Buildings and People in the Streets

by Edwin Denby

with an introduction by Frank O'Hara

POPULAR LIBRARY • NEW YORK

ACKNOWLEDGMENTS

The author acknowledges with gratitude the assistance of Miss Jacqueline Maskey and Mr. Robert Cornfield in the preparation of this book.

He would like to thank those magazines in which some of the articles and essays in this book originally appeared: *Dance Magazine, Dance Annual, Saturday Review, Kulchur, Evergreen Review,* and *Art News.*

"The Bolshoi at the Met," reprinted from the *Hudson Review,* vol. XIII, no. 4 (Winter, 1959-60), copyright 1960 by the Hudson Review, Inc.

"A Midsummer Night's Dream," *Dance 62,* copyright 1963 by Dance Perspectives, Inc.

Thanks also go to Mr. Richard Buckle, The Guggenheim Foundation, Mr. John Becker, The New York City Ballet, and the Festival of Two Worlds of Spoleto, Italy.

DANCERS, BUILDINGS AND PEOPLE IN THE STREETS

CONTENTS

Part Three   Reports

Part Four   On Painting

INTRODUCTION

In *Some Thoughts About Classicism and George Balanchine,* Edwin Denby writes that Balanchine's remarks had suggested to him ". . . the idea, too, of style as something a man, who has spent many years of his life working in an art, loves with attentive pertinacity." This idea, I think, is the basis of Denby's prose and poetry, a style which ". . . demands a constant attention to details which the public is not meant to notice, which only professionals spot, so unemphatic do they remain in performance." They were speaking of ballet performance, but the idea is equally true of Denby's writing performance, and one of the important secrets of its pleasures.

Since Edwin Denby is a good friend of mine, there are other secrets I should reveal. He sees and hears more clearly than anyone else I have ever known. No expressive or faulty quiver in a *battement,* no ingenious or clumsy transition in a musical score (whether Drigo or Gunther Schuller), no squiggle in a painting and no adverb, seems ever to escape his attention as to its relevance in the work as a whole. Having a basically generous nature, he is not at all guilty about pointing out mistakes and, unlike many poets who are also critics, he feels the moral necessity to point them out lest his praise be diminished by an atmosphere of professional "kindness." Most fortunately, his lyrical poetic gifts are tempered by the journalist's concern for facts and information. He works very hard at the above-mentioned "style" so as to give us

7

a whole spectrum of possibilities: what he saw and heard, what he felt, what he thinks the intention was, what the event seemed to be, what the facts surrounding it were, what the audience responded to, leaving open with a graciousness worthy of Théophile Gautier the ultimate decision of the reader pro or contra his own opinion as critic. Thus, he restores criticism to writing, to *belles lettres* if you wish, to the open dialogue of opinion and discussion between writer and reader which is nonaggressive and has faith in a common interest as the basis of intellectual endeavor. Few critics are so happy as he to receive your re-interpretation or correction of what he has already seen or heard and already written about. He is truly and deeply interested, in a civilized, open-minded way.

On the other hand, he will not just put up with anything. Recently, at the première of Balanchine's *Don Quixote,* he was asked what he thought of the new work. Denby said, "Marvelous! I was very moved."

"I was moved right out of the theatre," his interrogator replied.

"That's where you belong, then," Denby said in the gentlest of tones.

He is always there, telling you what he sees and hears and feels and esteems, not caring whether you agree or not, because it is a friendly parlance about matters which are mutually important. The ballet, the theatre, painting and poetry, our life accidentally in co-existence, is a rather large provenance which he tactfully negotiates and notates. As a theatre man he is interested in The Public, and this gives his criticism a broad, general applicability, moral as much as esthetic, for all its special knowledge and expertise. He is interested in his society, and those societies not his, without sentimentality. For our own society, how we act and what we mean, I cannot think that the two *Lectures* ("Forms in Motion" and "Dancers, Buildings") have less than a major pertinence. For other societies Denby's essays have illuminations about us which are not available elsewhere and are admirably understated.

8

Denby is as attentive to people walking in the streets or leaning against a corner, in any country he happens to be in, as he is to the more formal and exacting occasions of art and the theatre. He brings a wide range of experience to the expression of these insights: his acting and adaptations for the theatre here and in Germany (as John Houseman recently pointed out, he was not only the adaptor but also the rear legs of the horse in Orson Welles' version of Labiche's *Horse Eats Hat*); his work as ballet critic on the New York *Herald Tribune;* his acting in the films of Rudolph Burckhardt and other "underground" film-makers; his more personal and more hermetic involvement with his poems; his constant traveling and inquisitive scholarship; all these activities contribute a wide range of reference for comparison and understanding of intricate occasions, as well as of complicated implications in occasions seemingly obvious and general.

Like Lamb and Hazlitt, he has lightness and deftness of tone, and a sharp, amused intelligence, as evident in the method of perceiving as in the subject matter itself. Much of his prose is involved with the delineation of sensibility in its experience of time: what happens, and how often, if at all? what does each second mean, and how is the span of attention used to make it a longer or shorter experience? is Time in itself beautiful, or is its quality merely decorable or decorous? Somehow, he gives an equation in which attention equals Life, or is its only evidence, and this in turn gives each essay, whatever the occasional nature of its subject, a larger applicability we seldom find elsewhere in contemporary criticism.

Frank O'Hara

Part One

Content and Style

Ashton's *Cinderella*

THE BIG HIT of Ashton's *Cinderella* is its pair of Ugly Sisters, Helpmann and Ashton himself, and it is the one Ashton plays, the Second Ugly Sister, who becomes the charmer of the evening. She is the shyest, the happiest, most innocent of Monsters. She adores the importance of scolding, the fluster of getting dressed up—in a rush of milliners, hairdressers, jewellers, violinists. To do a little dance transports her, though she keeps forgetting what comes next. At the Prince's she is terrified to be making an entrance; a few moments later, poor Monster, in the intoxication of being at a party she loses her heart and imagines she can dance fascinatingly—in the way Chaplin at a fashionable tango-tea used to imagine he could slink like a glamorous Argentine. But after the Slipper-test she accepts the truth as it is, she makes a shy state curtsey to the Princely couple, to the power of Romance and Beauty, and paddles sadly off. No wonder such a Monster wins everybody's heart. Ashton does it reticently, with the perfect timing, the apparently tentative gesture, the absorption and the sweetness of nature of a great clown. He acts as if he never meant to be the star of the show and very likely he didn't. He cast Helpmann, England's greatest mime, as the First Stepsister and gave that part the initiative in their scenes; he himself was only to trail along vaguely, with one little solo in the second act. After all, he was busy at the time choreographing the three acts of the piece, his and England's first full-length classic ballet, and doing it in six weeks. Ashton's unexpected triumph on stage is the sort of accident that happens to geniuses.

The farce mime in the ballet is so amusing and so long in each act it is in danger of killing the dance scenes; as choreographer of it, Ashton keeps the clowning gentle and what is more all the pantomime completely comprehensible—a lovely feat. As dance choreographer his great moments are a set of classic variations for girls representing the Four Seasons (the Good Fairy calls each in turn to attend Cinderella), and a number of entrances for the Jester during the Ball. What a Harlequin-Jester was up to in the piece and how he got so big a part I didn't find out till several days later, but I was so delighted with the vitality and style of all he did, I never thought of wondering about it while I watched. The part is Alexander Grant's, the company's most interesting male dancer. Like a jet of force he darts forward in deep plié, in renversé, bent sideways, bent double, leaping down a flight of stairs, springing into the meager dances of the Guests with a smiling threat. In the Jester's leaps Ashton has timed the rhythm to the leap's arrival (instead of to its departure from the ground) and because your ear anticipates the rhythm, the crouching dancer's downward course through the air keeps the beautiful suspense of an animal pounce. More delicately Ashton uses the same device in the feminine "Seasons" variations and there too it gives the dancer an other-than-human presence. These four classic solos in their conciseness and grace of style, their freshness of fancy and purity of evocation are Ashton's masterpiece. They don't look like Petipa or Balanchine and are worthy of either. The Seasons' passage is also the best incident in the score and in the decoration; as if composer, choreographer and decorator each drew a breath of relief at being free for once of the logic of the libretto.

Seasons, Jester, Second Stepsister are Ashton's most expressive figures but they aren't in a position to carry the central action. *Cinderella* is a three-act ballet in the grand manner—it consists of miming, of classic, demi-caractère and character dancing, of processions, line-ups, tableaux

13

and apotheosis, all of them (including farcical female impersonation) traditional elements of the form. Ashton has composed in each style easily, correctly, clearly, without oddity, camp or other subterfuge, each kind true to its nature and function (so he keeps the farce to mime, never extends it to classic steps). Such a piece leads straightforwardly to the entrances of the ballerina, of the ballerina and her partner, as to its moments of intensest poetic illumination around which the piece revolves and reechoes. The critic, delighted with Ashton's openness, is eager for the big climaxes ahead. He wants to love the ballerina not only for her dancing but even more for what the imagery of her dances can tell of her nature as a human heroine. And the libretto of *Cinderella* is so direct her dances have to be logical parts of the story. An anxious critic is willing to excuse that in the first variation early in Act I (she is daydreaming of the Ball at her housework) she looks mostly ornamental and not-quite-naively playful. She doesn't dance again till at the climax of Act II, she enters, meets the Prince, and is in love. They have a pas de deux and each a variation. The two solos are bright and lovely—like youthful talk, the girl's more original, the boy's more amiable; but after this they could still fall in love with someone else. And when they dance together the rhythm is nervous, hasty, the figures crowded but not intimate—two people being obliging in a difficult situation. Aren't they in love? Watching them the eye doesn't catch any luminous movement-image of a dazzling encounter, a magic contact, and release of romance. Even the three-act form hasn't world or time enough for so many preliminaries. After that, when the third act opens and Cinderella in a morning-after variation remembers the Ball, instead of retrieving the situation by a radiant kind of *Spectre de la Rose* recollection, she fiddles with her broom again and offers an adroit, ingenious anthology of bits from Acts II and I. What a cold fish she is! Even here in private she won't give a hint of the marvel she has seen, of the kiss she has felt. Her shy Ugly Sister has more heart than that, and the smouldering, demonic horsey First Stepsister has more vitality. Here they are—

14

wonderful again—with the slipper, and what a lively family scene it becomes with its motley swirl of characters! Poor, silly Prince, of course the slipper fits only his ballerina! But they haven't danced yet in this act, by rights we'll get another pas de deux. Transformation, rapid procession of our old friends the Seasons and attendant Stars—the magic powers of time that create the bloom of beauty, and here we are in the Bridal pas de deux. Noble style, calm rhythm. And here a lovely dance figure—the Prince kneels and she tenderly touching his bent shoulders extends away from him a lovely arabesque—a shy moment of forbearance in contact, a moment of clarity once more worthy of Petipa. Now the ice is broken, they can begin to really dance together—but no, the pas de deux is over, it's all over, they will never get any closer. Bitterly disappointed in them, I watched them get into a galleon the size of a telephone booth and sail off, while the Stars and Seasons and all Beautiful Powers sank back and subsided in a brief sweet pianissimo close like a gentle sigh. Curtain.

From the special standpoint of dramatic impact or drive, *Cinderella* would be more exciting if its central characters were more expressive; if it had a joyous ensemble dance in Act III and a livelier one in Act I. (I even wished the First Stepsister's grim limp at her last exit could be dramatized to a scene of hatred and eternal horror.) The piece's success in impact is the long ensemble dance climax at the Ball and the claustrophobic crowd that ends it during the fatal strokes of Midnight.

But *Cinderella* hasn't the disharmony of a piece that can't do what it wants to, and impact and drive are not its method of being interesting. The fun of the farce keeps relaxing the hold of the central story and in the story the dances don't try for intensity and fail, they don't look silly, they look agreeable. Ashton's sense of character is a true one as far as it finds expression, but he doesn't strain for drama any more than he does for humor. Comfortable in the pace of its developments and transitions, always amusing or attractive to watch, never embarrassing or insistent, the piece succeeds very well in what it chooses to do. In that so to speak domestic key is its harmony, the harmony of an untroubled voice at home telling once more the same fairy tale.

The fact is *Cinderella* lasts two hours and a half and doesn't seem long. The current that carries it is easy and gentle. Its hold on one's attention is so mild that an American like myself is hardly aware of being in the theatre. The spell it creates doesn't crystallize in a climax or a specific dance image but no mean gesture breaks the continuity of it. English in the lightness of its fragrance, the charm it holds is a grace of spirit, an English sweetness of temper. It doesn't excite, it ever so mildly refreshes. To keep in a three-act ballet such a tone, to sustain it without affectation or banality, shows Ashton's power, and he shows this in doing it as simply as possible, by keeping the dancing sweet.

The dance impetus of his piece, mild though it is, is open and confident. The variety of ballet styles blend without a blur, each springing as fresh as the other from the score, and the spell of being inside the imaginary world of music where dancing is natural doesn't break all evening. The processions and line-ups, for instance, don't disturb the dance pulse of the action, nor does the action jump in and out of the music when the ballerina dances right after the mimes have been funny or when a flurry of character dancers dance in the farce scenes. The jokes come easy, and the miming looks free, it isn't stylized or mickey-moused to fit the notes, but it derives its phrasing and the emphasis from the shape and the stress of the musical phrase as spontaneously as the dancing does. Ashton responds to whatever is buoyant in a musical phrase as a whole, he responds to a musical phrase with a dance phrase and he takes the spring and momentum of his lucidly from the precise form of the other. So the score flows easy and clear and the dancers in motion look fresh and airy. They don't exhaust the music nor vice-versa; they can be many or alone, they can stop or continue. Ashton is sometimes too relaxed and then, though the impetus in the trunk still is right, the armshapes and stepshapes don't count for much; but if he is wary of dramatic tension it is that an expression which isn't in the phrasing clutters a dance and depresses it. The drama of his best ones is in their harmony and pulse. Even when his dances are slight they have in passing a spontaneous air of grace. They look on pitch, they make up a tune. He has disciplined his gift to sincerity, to an inability to fake or strain or impress or aggrandize, all of them uncivilized practices, that make successes but take the fun out of dancing. He could reach grandeur, but he is in no hurry to get there. The pleasure he offers is that of ballet classicism, which says what it does say in a tone at once civilized and innocent, a tone which is personal to him. In such a tone even a slight message makes an evening one is glad to have spent at a theatre.

But the fact is too, that for all the pleasure *Cinderella* gives, it is too slight to hold one's interest a second time. It has enough passages, fascinating to see repeatedly, mime effects and dance effects, to make a brilliant one act piece; but they don't make sense by themselves because they are those of secondary figures. In their own secondary range they express the idyllic human message or tone of the ballet; but the rest of it doesn't widen the range of feeling, doesn't make the idyllic feeling more poignant at the climaxes or more ample in the main ensembles. One may say that Ashton has been weak as a dramatist, weak in the contact between figures. But I think his fault has been an uncertainty of emphasis in the structure of many passages. It seems to me that a dance simultaneously with its impetus develops a quality of human motion contained in a phrase of classic movement, a dance does this in the way a piece of music develops its "thought" by developing and refracting an expressive cadence contained in the harmony of music. The spontaneous emphasis of a dance falls at any rate on one phase of movement more than another, an emphasis which makes a momentary look in motion of a thigh or flank or forearm or instep or neck more dramatic as it passes, with an effect like an unconscious characteristic gesture. These transiently emphatic images reverberated in the harmony of their context determine the particular expression of a dance, its poetic character, its human implications. When they appear large, free and clear, a dance is fascinating, it is expressive. (I don't mean that expression is necessarily rationalizable—the *Waltz of the Flowers* in *The Nutcracker,* for instance, is completely expressive.) Though the dances of *Cinderella* are clear in many ways—but the emphasis of them is not always clear—the emphasis doesn't make luminous the special kind of motion that is the dance's subject matter. This is why the ballet seems slight. But because *Cinderella* shows that Ashton, in the many passages where he has expression, has it without oddity, without forcing his gift or his discipline, it shows his natural power and his achieved craftsmanship. I think the piece shows these qualities further developed than *Symphonic Variations* or than *Scènes de Ballet* (his best), though these two are better theatre, more sustained in brilliance. Because of its slightness and its length the good qualities of *Cinderella* are likely to be overlooked when the sameness of its gentleness in everything it does, even in its clowning, begins to make itself felt more strongly than the harmony of its tone. And for people not susceptible to its charming transparency the piece must seem a weak one the first time they see it.

It may be Broadway hawks would find so transparent a piece invisible. For myself, I might have been less open to *Cinderella's* shy spell had I been in an audience less forbearing than that of Covent Garden. Even at the premiere they looked at the ballet so to speak discreetly, almost as one watches family theatricals, as if the dancers weren't professionals. Afterwards in the lobby I was to find that they saw as clearly as any other audience, but while the performers were working they gave the impression of seeing only the good things. The rules of first night sportsmanship are very different in New York and Paris. But at the *Cinderella* opening, the audience's county family serenity (wonderfully exotic so it seemed to me, as a foreigner) was also due to the influence of a local ritual I knew nothing of, of which I became aware only a few days later when I saw another *Cinderella,* this time at the Palladium. Watching my first Christmas Pantomime, with piping children around me and elders beaming at everything, with slapstick clowning Dames and Cinderella in the same costume as Moira Shearer, and a Good Fairy to wave her wand (the same model as at Covent Garden) and start transformation scenes, and with a Harlequin-descended Buttons—and what a good one!—who "placed" for me the Jester in Ashton's piece, I realized how many childhood echoes the ballet awakens in its public which a foreigner can't share. To the British public *Cinderella* is not in a revived ballet form; as soon as the curtain goes up, the travesty Ugly Sisters at their sewing make everyone feel safe at home in the living Pantomime ritual the audience has known all its life.

Thanks to the ritual Ashton was able to use two of the company's three strongest theatre personalities—Helpmann and himself—in long parts which made the ballet's success. Margot Fonteyn, the greatest of the three, was cast for Cinderella, and her presence when she dances again will of course change the value of the central figure. Shearer in Fonteyn's part is lovely to look at, graceful and true in movement and her legs are fine; Violetta Elvin in the same part is more interesting and alive on stage, and while she isn't more proficient she has a grander kind of schooling (a more forceful bearing and thigh action), but she creates at best her own role, she has not the imaginative radiance by which a ballerina creates a world of romance on the stage all around her. Somes is a clean dancer and is unusually vivid at his first entrance. Nerina's "Spring" is charming. No part is done poorly, the whole company is attractive, bright and well-trained (though in too small-stepping a style) and they did all Ashton asked. He could have given them more had they developed in themselves more boldness and vivacity, qualities which involve a love of acting as well as dancing. But their general outlook of honesty, their sense of good manners and their reticent willingness to dance has a touching quality of its own. Helpmann in the piece is a model of generosity and intelligent good taste. He gives everyone, particularly Ashton, every chance, knowing very well he could upset the balance at any moment by a single gesture delivered full force.

The costumes by Malclès are pretty; his decoration though less stiff than the decor of several British ballets I have seen, aims for a homey-timid charm that only partly comes off. The Prokofiev score (played without any cuts except for one forty-minute chunk at the beginning of Act III) is in a homey style too, but not in the least timid. It is much more vigorous theatre than the ballet. It is completely adroit in continuity, always ready with tunes and lively rhythms, never dull or thick and also with no noticeable counterpoint, completely danceable, brilliantly sustained for the Ball. All this can't be praised too highly and it helps Ashton immensely. But a facile and casual irony in it, suited no doubt to the brilliant Moscow production, doesn't suit the quiet London one. The score doesn't ever gather in a non-narrative, a contemplative climax, an expression of the faith in a marvel which a fairy-tale has. It wasn't Prokofiev's intention to repeat what Tchaikovsky had said so well already, but for all the score's large scale vitality its character seems guarded compared to the innocent sweetness of nature of Ashton. Ashton's spontaneity is nearer to Haydn.

So Ashton has made *Cinderella* well and made it fun; it isn't a great ballet but he is a great choreographer, and proves it in this piece; and that it is a complete popular hit is a pleasure too. *(1949)*

The Paris Opera Ballet

I WANTED TO write you an article about ballet at the Maggio Musicale as you suggested, but I couldn't, so I started a letter and then began to rewrite it to find out what I meant; here it is, it turned out to be just about the Paris Opera.

What I most looked forward to at the Maggio was my first sight of Vyroubova. I agree with you about her entirely. After three steps I loved her—delicious figure, limpid style, sweet absorption. To be sure by the time she had done four ballets I didn't love her as much more as I had looked forward to when she first began; but there was no reason either to love her any less.

She has the sweetest Russian-style virtues. A long foot, quick thigh, delicate bust, small head far from the shoulder. The step has edge, the arms are a classicist's dream, the carriage of the head has distinction, the face makes sense. She is unusually accurate and musical. I thought her best number here was that in *Suite en Blanc* (Vaussard's part, I think) which she did with a kind of demi-caractère liveliness in grace that suited the steps perfectly. She did each of her four parts as if it were a different woman dancing, discovering the impersonation in the impetus of the steps, sustaining it without a break from the first move to the last, with no mannerisms of her own showing ever. (Her other ballets were *Mirages*, *Dramma per Musica* and *Divertissement*, all Chauviré parts.) It was adorable to see how she—a dancer of little experience dancing new parts in a company new to her—by instinct at once accepted the complete responsibility for the piece; to see her go straight for the main thing, the reality of her role and of the imaginative world in which it can be real; to see her conceive of the importance of a character not in terms of rank but in terms of purity of motive; and impersonate beauty in the cleanest steps she could make. Her decision on all this was unhesitating. And it gave her that lovelier authority on stage which I am sure Margot has always had.

It's all there, but on the other hand not yet pronounced enough. Her technique is well rounded and sufficient but not virtuoso. Her waist is weak. And the last two nights here she tired. Nor did she show the variety of accentuation, the nuance in phrasing a finished dancer can; in this particular Chauviré was more interesting than she. And Vyroubova, at least here, did not make her parts magnificent with those movements of complete climax, of lovely stillness that a ballerina is born to express. She is a darling, but she should turn into a marvel, a complete marvel. I wish she could join Sadler's Wells and have the benefit of all you discreet idealists; and since she is the brightest hope in Europe for another great ballerina five years from now, in a sense it's your duty. I think too, that in a couple of years Balanchine could make her long legs twice as long and give her a stunning elegance of attack.

Toumanova was here too, just the opposite of all V's virtues, and wonderful. She was at her worst: careless feet, limp and wormy arms, brutally deformed phrasings; in allegro she was a hoyden, in adagio it was a bore waiting for her to get off that stubby toe; she waddled complacently, she beat time, she put on a tragically wronged stare (Second Avenue style—Lower Second Avenue), she took absurdly graceless and completely unconvincing bows. It upset me while I was in the theatre; but the next day it seemed only ridiculous, I'd half forgotten it, and it had no connection with moments I couldn't help remembering the grandeur of: a few terrifying extensions, a few incisive strokes that counted phenomenally. At those moments she had so much vitality she made everyone else look as if they merely crept or scuttled about her while she danced. It wasn't ballet she did, it wasn't any kind of dancing anybody ever heard of, but it was dancing on some sort of grand scale, it was the real thing in that sense.

I liked Renault very much. His acting is naive, his waist wiggles and wrist-flaps are silly, he has learned no distinction (Blasis ports de bras and head positions, effacés and harmonies of contraposto—men look raw without them). But each time the steps grow difficult and strenuous, he forgets his foolishness, and I don't care about his faults. He whirls and leaps in the rush of action, he likes pouring out his strength, he dances on a big scale and the joy of it then is contagious. And when he looks honest, simple and sweet natured.

The season as a whole was received in a friendly way, not with the enthusiasm I had seen here last year for Sadler's Wells.

I enjoyed *Palais de Cristal,* though friends who know the New York version complained bitterly of the slow tempos which they told me disfigured it. Lifar's ugly edition of *Sleeping Beauty (Divertissement)* makes me cringe like a knife scraping on a plate. His own works at their best have a curious antimusical and desperate pound; apart from this personal quality—at its strongest in *Suite en Blanc*—I can see no interest in them that lasts. With poor choreography ballet loses for me its nerve; but usually I am happy anyway watching a good company dance.

As companies go, the Paris Opera one seems to me very good; and here the credit is Lifar's; they looked fresher, better disciplined and better rehearsed than when I last saw them a year and a half ago. I liked them all very much as professionals. They are attractive, well built, loyal and gifted. They believe in doing what they do with attention and individual imagination. When they begin they suggest a kind of glitter of stylishness on stage that fills me with happy expectation. They show at once that they are going to have variety of expression, that they are not going to do the immature juvenile charm act far too many adult Anglo-Saxon dancers do. So I look forward to the dance action to come when their interesting expressions will become an interesting grace of movement, when it will bloom and shed a radiance over the stage as a dancer's expression does in dancing.

Instead, what I see is different. The dance action looks small and constricted and close, it makes the dancers become short-limbed. In the general effect of shrinkage, the dancers keep their pointed expressions, and the result is arch. Affectedly so, it often seems to me. When I see them stepping out gingerly, when I see a large bold step modestly diminished and a stabbing rapid one becomingly blurred, see the girls separate their thighs as if reluctant to do that in public, the world of decent domesticity it conjures up appals me. And when I catch fretful flappings and crookings of elbows, dissatisfied glances of the girls toward each other and irritated ones at the conductor, a fluster of waist-wriggles, wrist-flicks and head-tosses, the expression reminds me of a nervous woman who can't resist tidying up her furniture and her person after the guests have already sat down. The boys seem to take the feminine flurry with a slightly superior or interestingly sullen male detachment; though their own action is not free of what look like fatuous flourishes and they promenade about with a tight bouncy step that looks silly. All this is my first impression and at this point I realize I have misunderstood everything so far and missed the point completely. So I look more closely at what is happening.

The dancers are well built and strong; but I begin to see that the Opera style transforms them according to its own ideas of grace. It makes their figures in action look thick and droopy in the middle, stumpy and brief at the ends. The figure doesn't hold its shape in the air as it moves. Necks shrink in, shoulders hunch, waists sag and bob, thighs seem to take on weight. The step becomes unresilient, timid and short; the tempo spurts nervously and drags. The pulse of the rhythm is weak. The style makes the dancers look like sedentary persons dancing.

They are painstakingly trained to. They do the step correctly, but they do it only from the hipjoint down.

Similarly they do arm motions from the shoulder out. (The ports de bras are altered as a rule from a correct shape into a resemblance to expressive gesture.) The Paris Opera style avoids using the tremendous strength of waist and back to move with, to move the thighs and upper arms freely and equally. The Ballet Russe or Russian-derived style uses the full strength of the back to initiate, to sustain and to reabsorb a movement; as Negro dancing does too. It gives these styles a kind of follow-through effect, an ease in flow; it gives the dancers a straight but not stiff back, a long neck. In ballet without the full strength of the back their figures bunch up awkwardly in motion, they lose the carriage in large steps, they don't deploy fully in the air. They lose their speed, their spring, their impetus, their vigor in resilience. They don't sustain the continuity, they don't reach the large scale virtuosity or the large scale vitality they otherwise would. The Paris Opera dancers don't, not through weakness, but because the style avoids such effects.

The style's idea of musical grace in dancing is as peculiar as its idea of grace of movement, I mean equally puzzling to a balletgoer used to the Russian-derived style. The Opera dancer likes to put the dance stress where the shape of the musical phrase gives it no support; so it gets a petulant look. She likes to begin a shade behind the beat as if prettily taken unaware, and end a little ahead as if in confusion; then she adds a vigorous flip of the wrist on the last note, which by being synchronized makes the wrist suddenly look disproportionately big, as big as a leg. I speak from the standpoint of the Russian style which treats the score like a glorious partner on whose strength the dancers soar and dart and effortlessly end. By contrast the Opera style has the music run along beside the dancer like a stray dog—it keeps shying away from her when she stops and getting underfoot when she goes on again. An accomplished Opera dancer is one who makes one forget what a nuisance it is.

But such a view is based on the assumption that the Paris Opera style is doing worse what the Russian style does better. Looking at it closer, the Opera style indicates on the contrary that its intentions are different to begin with. Its conception of rhythm and of phrasing inclines away from that of the music and toward that of speech. The general effect is not unlike that of speech rhythm. The dancer shapes her phrases by giving them point, as one would in speaking. She selects a step in the sequence and points it up, giving it a slight retard and a slight insistence, and she lets the other step drop around it so to speak casually and a shade hastily, much as a glittering conversationalist stresses the telling word, delivers his epigram and seems to throw the rest of the sentence away. Following the steprhythm as speechrhythm—and as speechrhythm set against music—one can find virtuoso subtleties and ingenuities in the phrasing of an Opera soloist, odd little vivacities, implications, hesitancies, bursts of rhetoric, tiny gusts of inspiration that hurry her onward. We Anglo-Saxons think a dancer looks like a lady when she dances divinely; but that is our lack of realism. The Paris style doesn't mean to transport you so far from the appearances, from the awkward graces and characteristic reserves of normal sedentary city life. The point of unprofessional carriage and unmusical rhythm is to make the dancer look less like a marvelous vision and more like an opinionated Parisian with all her wits about her whom one might meet in a room full of conversation.

Other traits of the Opera style seem to resemble characteristics of French conversation, too. Ranking dancers are expected to dance against each other as acute conversationalists are expected to talk each other down. Agreement is not considered interesting and when everybody dances it's like everybody talking at once. To pause awhile on stage is like keeping still; it's a sign of respect, not of listening. Listening doesn't count, it's nothing to make a point of; and a dancer doesn't make her stillness a part of the rhythm of the general dance—in the way a singer makes her silence as well as her voice a part of the music.

The Paris Opera style has its own view of what a performance is about. The dancers do not present a ballet as though it were a stage drama. There is no collective attempt to create the illusion of a poetic event taking place before our eyes. They don't come on as imaginary characters whose fate is unknown but fore-ordained. They come on instead in their official character as Opera dancers. The ballet is a ceremony which offers them an occasion for the exhibition and the applause suitable to their various ranks. The excitement of the official ceremony is in the suggestion they individually convey of being people it would be delightful to know at home. And that is perhaps why the dancers scatter in all directions a great many of those little shakes, peckings and perks of the head that look so pretty around a Paris dinner table, though coupled to the foot activity of ballet they unfortunately give an effect of witlessness.

I am under the impression that Parisians of taste (who can remember Diaghilev) take the Opera style far less seriously than I have. They are surprised anyone should. They know there is no one on stage who does it with the acuteness of wit, the stylishness of presence it calls for, or with imaginative scope; and that there are many whose airs and graces are more respectable than stylish. The best Opera dancers try to Russianize their dancing, and even the Opera fans encourage them to.

And as for me, I see that by instinct I can hardly be fair to the style. The weak rhythm it has by choice depresses me as I watch. The fun of ballet is in the feet, in the feet and the bearing and the mutual response of the bodies in motion. The spring and edge and lift of ballet is in its relation to the beat—and to the beat in the full variety and extension which the musical animation of a piece of music gives it through musical structure. Of course, dancers are actors too, and their acting gestures can be delightful, noble, even thrilling. But their most wonderful moments of all come when they are in the middle of dancing. Their expression then looks unintentional. The wit or the sentiment it communicates, the ravishing lyric flight or sweeping collective transport is in the impetus of the dancing bodies, in the sustained pulse of their motion in space. The force of the communication, its imaginative scope is in a kind of reverberation with which the resilient pulse of a rhythmic stream enlarges the hint of natural behavior that appears in a momentary movement of dancing; transfiguring it in the exhilaration of sustained buoyancy into a poetic image as innocent as the action of fate. I love the thrill of such a grace in meaning. But large scale vitality in ballet, even apart from any meaning, is also a pleasure, deeper than it seems. The Paris Opera style has too weak a pulse, too weak a dance rhythm for these two kinds of exhilaration.

Poor Lifar. He looks older on stage than Dolin or Massine. He has had the misfortune to put on weight all over him except between knee and ankle. (And he insisted on leaving no doubt in the matter by appearing as a Greek statue.) Dolin and Massine at least have extraordinary stage presences and are able to conceal some of the weaknesses of their dancing. Here in Florence Lifar wasn't able to conceal any weakness of his; but what surprised even more, he had no stage presence at command with which to pull his performance together. He worked harder than anyone and completely in vain. I haven't the heart to blame him, remembering his beauty and his genius; but if one doesn't, one has to blame Hirsch.

And one has to blame Hirsch too for not suppressing the three recent short ballets of Lifar which were shown here, *Pavane, L'Inconnue,* and *Entre deux rondes.* The first might have been devised for an end-of-the-year party at a desperate dancing school. The other two looked just as batty. One was earnest about the Decay of Western Civilization and resembled an apache number; the other was gay about Our Enduring Cultural Values and offered gambols by a Greek Statue and a Degas Ballet Girl. Tudor could have made wonderful little pieces out of both by making them loathsome intentionally.

There was a piece of business in Lifar's *Giselle,* Act Two, which was new to me. Mourning at her tomb he seemed for some time unwilling to part with the flowers he had brought. He held them out, snatched them back, looked at them appreciatively. Mastering his emotion, he sacrificed them and fainted. But Giselle, dead as she was, rushed out from the wings with a much bigger bunch and pelted him with it headlong. So prompt, so sweet of her, so fitting. He lay drowned in flowers. If only the audience had given way to its impulse, had leapt to its feet in rapture and tossed hundreds of bouquets more, aiming them from all over the house, what a perfect moment of art it would have been for all of us to share with him!

Still, I believe Lifar inspires his company. Their devotion to him, their faith in virtues of his no longer visible on stage is touching. A few company mannerisms seem imitations of mannerisms formerly his own as a dancer; that is foolish but not meretricious. Distasteful, however, is the way his choreography keeps making the dancers look pompous. *(1950)*

A Letter about Ulanova

ABOUT ULANOVA. She is a very great dancer, no doubt of
that, even seeing her as we did very awkwardly presented.
What we all saw first was the magnificent schooling and
the admirable personal discipline. You know how
touching that is when you see a dancer not allowing herself to monkey with the rules. What we saw was a wonderful flow of movement sustained and sustained, a sort of
cantilena style of dancing with beautiful legs (marvelously
sharp arabesques of all kinds, and so clearly differentiated
too), and beautiful elbows. The very beginning of a
movement is fresh and quick and almost at once the motion so begun slows down to a strong full velvet flow; and
before the flow has stopped, without any break (like a
fresh current that appears from below in a wide even
stream of water) the new next motion begins, clear and
decisive, and that one too seems to be already flowing
calm and sustained. It isn't the bird or dragonfly
style of dancing, it's a kind of aspiration upwards:
lightness as a longing and a dream rather than as a pos-
session. I can't think of any one dancer we know who has
that particular quality; nor is it one that goes with being a
model pure-classicist: it's romantic. Ulanova makes herself more heavy and more light, too, like a romantic. And
another quality she shows is that of not presenting herself
to the audience, of being like someone who is dancing for
herself, a sort of half-in-shadow-in-the-deep-woods qual-

30

ity. There isn't much conscious response between her and her partner, I mean all those conscious little consciousnesses. In the same way that the pulse of the rhythm is broad and slow, so the characterization or flavor or key of the dance is barely noticeable; it's there but it's only appreciable after a while. There's something covered, a sort of inner life unconsciously revealed, that carries her more than it directs her. (I'm speaking not of her personally but of the kind of stage personality that comes across.) Of course one can fall in love with such a special creature; or else not. Some people were crabby, I mean a few ballet fans I spoke to.

Of course it's nonsense to pass judgment after seeing her dance half-a-dozen numbers with piano accompaniment in front of black curtains, awkwardly costumed, without a company or a ballet to set her off, and with a foreign audience, who probably expected a triumphant beauty and saw instead a modest little-girl-style creature. The general theatre style that was indicated—I mean the kind of over-all performance atmosphere or manner which is different according to whether the dancers are Parisian, Danish, British or from New York—that theatre style was quite different from any of our various ones; which makes a confusion too. Just as what Parisians think pretty, New Yorkers are likely to think affected, and just as Parisians think mechanical what we see as unaffected and friendly, so there was about the Soviet atmosphere a strange absence of *chic* or bite or risk or individualized projection. It struck us who were foreign to it as homey, and goody-goody. And sometimes this tone made Ulanova seem a bit puss-in-the-corner, which I imagine one wouldn't think in a big long piece where she can gradually make the character clear.

Her weaknesses as a dancer seemed at this performance to be: a kind of thickness, a kind of lack of ease at the base of the neck and all round there in the region of the breast and shoulders. This makes her neck look short, and doesn't give her head that queenly port that is so lovely; but then queenliness isn't her style. Her feet aren't delicately placed when she steps, nor are the hands and

31

wrists so good. But the arms don't suffer, and she has a marvelous lightness in the knees. Though her pas de bourrée weren't beautiful, her feet stretched in the air always were. And particularly beautiful were all her poses in lifts. Really beautiful lifts. I liked a few mime gestures she made very much too.

I liked her second number immensely—for the lifts, much more exact than we make them, and more varied. It's practically the *Sylphides* pas de deux. Next best I liked the *Casse Noisette* and *Swan Lake* pas de deux. Number three, to Schumann's "Chopin" from *Carnaval* was a Greek supported adagio with veil, by Chaboukiani, absurd in style to us. The final Rubinstein waltz was an allegro with bunches of flowers and a very pretty saut de poisson, I couldn't find out by whom: but this also looks to us very *démodé* in style. The style it resembles is a sort of super-dinner-dance adagio couple style: of course it's done so very prettily. The *Dying Swan* I liked least, but she got an ovation for it. The choreography of the two new pieces, the Rubinstein and the *Red Poppy* was uninteresting, but the style is too different to judge at a glance.

Perhaps what I missed in Ulanova's dancing was the want of those moments that affect me so, those moments of rest in a dance when a movement resolves for a hairsbreath of time into repose and finishes, and there is like a sense of eternity from which the dancing and the movement re-arise. I didn't see this completion of repose in her dancing.

Her partner, Kondratov, was a pleasant young man, with no intentions to what we think of as style or grace, a trifle musclebound, completely unaffected. He was a marvelously sure partner, and one who could support her on one upstretched hand, and so forth. Her balance wasn't sure at this performance, and his support was both unnoticeable and pleasing. I don't approve of dancers who don't dance like dancers, but it was interesting to see one so well trained and so *simpatico*. The Parisians were utterly dismayed by such an apparition.

The dance accompanists were wonderful as such. (A good deal of rubato, but never noticeable.)

Oh yes, I forgot to mention Ulanova's wonderful lyric entrances and exits, so soft, merging into an infinite continuation.

This is what I saw so far; I'm coming again to her second concert. (I came back from Greece for her, and was so excited the afternoon before she danced I had to go to bed with a fever.) Maybe next time I'll see more calmly. Beryl de Zoete exclaimed afterwards that she'd never seen dancing before, which was the reaction I hoped to have, but didn't. That she belongs with the half-dozen geniuses we know is obvious too. *(1951)*

New York City's Ballet

I HADN'T EXPECTED so intense a pleasure, looking at New York again, in the high white February sunlight, the childishly euphoric climate; looking down Second Avenue, where herds of vehicles go charging one way all day long disappearing into the sky at the end like on a prairie; looking up a side of a skyscraper, a flat and flat and a long and long, and the air drops down on your head like a solid. Like a solid too the air that slices down between two neighbor skyscrapers. Up in the winter sunlight the edge of such a building far up is miraculously intense, a feeling like looking at Egyptian sculpture. Down in the streets the color, the painted colors are like medieval color, like the green dress of the Van Eyck double portrait in the National Gallery, intently local and intently lurid. And New York clothes—not a trace of charm, dressing is ritualistic like in Africa (or the Middle Ages); the boys are the most costumed; dressed men and women look portentously maneuverable; one set looks more dry-cleaned than the other, and those count as rich. New York is all slum, a calm, an uncomfortable, a grand one. And the faces on the street by day: large, unhandsome, lumped with the residue of every possible human experience, and how neutral, left exposed, left out unprotected, uncommitted. I have never seen anything so marvelous. A detachment from character that reminds me of the Arhats in Chinese painting. Women as well as men in middle age look like that, not comforting but O.K. if you believe in marvels, "believe in" in the sense of live with. They have no conversation, but a slum movie put on its marquee: "Sordid"—*Times*; "Unsavoury Details"—*Herald Tribune*. I never saw so civilized an advertisement in Paris. Manners are calm, everybody is calm in New York except where maybe somebody is just having a fit. No one looks dominated. But one minority looks sometimes as though it suffered acutely, the adolescents. They throw themselves about the city, now supersonic, now limp as snails, marvelously unaware of adults or children. Suddenly across their blank faces runs a flash of anguish, of huntedness, of brutal vindictiveness, of connivance—the pangs of reformatory inmates; a caged animal misery. They are known as punks and jailbait and everybody defers to them, everybody spoils them as people do to what they recognize as poetic. They are not expected to make any return. A few years later they have put on weight, whether girls or boys, and the prevalent adult calm has commenced for and closed on them too, and others are adolescent. Another magic thing about New York is that everything you look at by day, people, buildings, views, everything is the same distance away, like in Egyptian sculpture too. When I look about me in New York I feel as if I saw with an eagle's kind of eye; lovely Italy I looked at with a dear *simpatico* horse's eye. But you want me to tell you about the city's ballet company, which I adore.

The day after I arrived, friends took me to see a morning run-through of a new Balanchine that was to open a few days later. The dancers were in practice clothes under the poetic worklight with a piano on stage. You can imagine how eagerly we started to watch. And the pleasure at first was so keen and so peaceable it seemed to me we might easily have been Orientals watching our local court ballet any time during the last millennium or two. As the piece lengthened measure by measure I understood that nowhere in the world could I have seen a more beautiful new one nor anywhere else seen dancers able to perform its fantastic academic ritual with such an air of ease and virtuoso calm; such pretty dancers, almost Oriental in their impersonalness. Not that they behaved in any way but natural New York. That was my first impression of the New York City Ballet and of *Caracole*.

Later in the season I saw the piece several times, and though it had lost some of its delicacy in the glare of performance, the power of it had become more active and stranger. I saw a number of the company's programs and liked a great deal of what I saw. I was interested to find it a non-Diaghilev-style company. Star composers, star painters, star dancers, star poets—the NYC doesn't try to reproduce this famous formula as every other company still does. Stern as Puritan Fathers, Kirstein and Balanchine deny themselves (and us) all but two pleasures: dancers who within the limits they are kept become unique; and choreography which is the best anywhere. Not only the Balanchine pieces. But the best of his are of course for me unmatchable beauties.

The Balanchine ballets in the repertory are of every known variety: dance ballet, drama with plot, drama of atmosphere, comedy of situation, divertissement (musical show number) sentimental or farcical, exhibition grand pas de deux. (A pas de deux I like very much is the *Sylvia* one, with a very beautiful part for the man, canonically danced by Eglevsky.) Of the entire repertory the pieces that fascinate me the most are three dance ballets, *Caracole, Four Temperaments* and *Concerto Barocco*. *Four Temperaments*, overloaded with brilliance like *Caracole,* is its opposite in material. It is full of Beckmesser-ish dance jokes, classic steps turned inside-out and upside-down, re-timed, re-proportioned, re-routed, girls dancing hard and boys soft, every kind of oddity of device or accent, but never losing the connective "logic" of classicism; never dropping its impetus; and developing a ferocity of drive that seems to image the subject matter of its title: internal secretions.

Classicism is extended in these three dance ballets (as generally in Balanchine's work of the last decade) without upsetting the principle of equilibrium, or shifting the terminal points of a step or port de bras—on the contrary; and still the diversity of movement they have, the range

36

they show in setting steps to music and the range in lyric expression are astonishing. It is easy to see they are models of style—easy to see how each step in time is undistorted, distinct, fleet, spontaneous; how phrases, periods and sections flow on unexhausted with a deep powerful impulse. In the earlier of his dance ballets a few pantomime images like bodily *mudras* emerge from the rushing evolutions of steps; later these pointing hands become indistinguishable portions of the constellated configurations of the dancing.

One can take such dance ballets as just fooling of a fanciful kind or one can take them to be beautiful and serious; they look like both. What they show is young people dancing on stage and how lovely the bodies look. The choreography shows them graceful in the way they dance with one another, or look alone as they move, in the way they hear the music or take a climax or present themselves to the public. It makes an image of behavior, and many momentary ones; a sense of instinctive manners and cruel innocence; unconscious images suggested by devices of structure rather than by devices of gesture. So the individual keeps all her natural ambiguity as you see her decide, and see her swept on past the moment in the stream of dancing. And the force of the image comes not from her will but from the rhythm of the company's dancing and from the physical strength of the step. Often these images of unconscious action seem to me grand and intrepid; and what I love so is the undisturbed bloom like in real life that they have as they flash past. But whether Balanchine meant this I have no idea. I naturally think in terms of a story when I get excited; for people who prefer to avoid human interest, I imagine the fantastic ingenuity of the arrangements, the costliest of hypertrophic pleasure-domes built up on nothing, the sweep and the lift of them, is fun enough.

The dance ballets invite you not to bother with a "meaning," but the drama ballets on the contrary have explicitly the meaning that their story has. The drama of them sometimes catches me like off guard. I have watched the beginning, noticing I wasn't much interested, that it was barely holding my attention; and then not noticed if I was interested till, a long time later, transported far from 55th Street, on stage in front of me I saw Destiny striking down a child of mine—a real poet—and I realized suddenly that it was I who had been watching it done, realized it only as I saw the 55th Street curtain come down. And I was too absorbed still in the solemnity of the vision, to wonder then how Balanchine could have circumvented my tense mistrust at the beginning, and made me accept his magic; and grateful to him too, because though I knew what I had seen was real, he at least assured me it was just a trick. Balanchine's gift for seriousness in the theatre is a rare one. While anything happens it looks like ballet, like a step or a joke or a grace; but when it is finished it suddenly can look serious and real. The victim has been struck square. By the time it is over, the immolation has been thorough. Look at it in *Orpheus*, *Prodigal Son* (where it is a conversion), or in *Fairy's Kiss*.

Prodigal Son is told, since it is about good and evil, in two kinds of pantomime: the dry, insect-light, insect-quick elegance and filth of atheism, and the fleshy Biblical vehemence—so Near Eastern and juicy—of sin and of forgiveness, the bitter sin and sweet forgiveness. Still bolder as an image seems to me the leisure in the pacing of the scenes, which transports the action into a spacious patriarchal world, like a life-time of faith. Very different is the ancestral religious Greece of *Orpheus*. The overslow adagio motions at the beginning and again at the close evoke the magic passes and stalkings of ritual—Orphic and Orthodox both. The forest creatures who witness Orpheus's grief appear in this magic slowed-down time from so remote and so pristine a country, it feels like a pre-Homeric Parnassus. (And don't they form a kind of protopediment or roodscreen?) Eurydice writhes at her husband's feet like a mountain lioness in heat, like the Worm of Death, like an eternal image. A pity the Furies' dance in Hell is of no value. But on earth the Maenads shudder possessed, swallow the spurted blood. Different again is the brutal romantic Switzerland of *Fairy's Kiss*. It is a land of fairy tale, reduced from the country of myth by industrial encroachment. Here the poet is only unconsciously a poet, as long as he may he thinks of himself as an average mill-owner boy. Poignant as is the reduction of consciousness, it is in this particular "world" that the image of looking under the bridal veil in horror becomes so grandiose and takes on so many tragic dreams. And the world of the believed-in fairy story is evoked by the nineteenth-century style of *Fairy's Kiss*. It isn't straight classic, but "like a classic": you can see it in the pantomime and the timing of dance steps; though the company isn't likely to distinguish.

Images such as these familiar ones (I mean to suggest) build up an imaginary country in which the story becomes credible; we recognize it as the particular country of our imagination where people would act as they do in the story, would do the deed they do. And the largeness of the images makes it a country wide enough so that the victim could escape, if he chose; like Achilles. But it is the rhythmic power of the dancing, of the dance scenes, that turns the pantomime quality of a gesture into an emblem, into an image with all its own country all around it. Dance rhythm is a power that creates the validity of the grand style. It is not rhythm used as a wow effect; I think it begins instead by quietening the audience; but it collects the audience's magic mind, its imaginative attention; it puts one into another time sense than that of practical action. One can recognize the same use of rhythm in the nineteenth-century classics, and that is I think the reason for their enduring magic. I imagine that many balletmasters and dancers don't know what to try for in preparing the old ballets, and choreographers don't know what to try for in preparing new ones. The weakening of the rhythmic power of a ballet in respect to its story is the defect of West European ballet in general. And Balanchine's effort to restore it choreographically—and also in dance execution—is a matter of interest for balletomanes to consider and discuss. He seems to me the active choreographer who best can give in his story ballets the impact, the truth and the scale of the grand style, the structural devices to be recognized. Or at least he gives critics an opportunity of calling attention to grand values in contemporary choreography.

As for the less grand style ballets of his in the repertory, I'll have to skip them this time. Except for one I want to mention because it's George doing a turn disguised as Dame Ninette: a carload of respectable ideas, props, pantomime, orchestra noises, all of it honest and none of it dancing. It's *Tyl Ulenspiegel* I mean, and I don't mean to praise it, but I enjoyed seeing within its eleven minutes how many kinds of ideas did get across to me—history, economics, sociology, psychology, morals: how changes of pace presented a gesture in its actual as well as in a symbolic meaning; how casually introduced, how cleanly concentrated, how free in untying each situation was in turn. *Tyl* is a hearty Flemish grabbag—dirt and folk and anarchism and Robin Hood-ness, Bosch and I suppose Rembrandt and a Flemish philosophical novel, and the final *dénouement* even offers the concept of the gifted man who from the solitude of intelligence slips gratefully into ordinary human happiness, the progress from the "hero" to "a man." *Tyl* is also charmingly acted by Robbins, and it has a decor by Esteban Francés, who is the company's one discovery as a big-scale ballet painter.

There is another piece too I want to call your attention to, not for its choreography though, but for its score: it's *Bayou. Balanchine* has made it a sort of Dunham number, gently graceful, that needs only a stage surprise near the end to be a divertissement. But he missed the originality of the score, its subtlety in candor, the sense it gives of clear repose in a secret spot. The liquid continuity of the music, the easy breathing of the melody, the transparency of the harmony, the unelliptic, unabridged, so to speak circular or stanzalike forward motion it has, these are peculiarities of structure that might have looked beautiful reflected in dancing. Like the Furies of *Orpheus, Bayou* is a disappointment; because one can see that with better luck it could so well have become an event. Virgil Thomson, the composer, is also the composer of the opera *Four*

40

Saints, a heavenly opera—in score, libretto, and singing—that I hope you saw in Paris; such pretty dancers, too.

Watching Balanchine's choreographic genius pouring out in gifts in profusion in the NYC repertory is as great a pleasure as I can imagine in the theatre. Many fans here enjoy watching his choreography as keenly as if it were dancing itself. They are used to the dancers and to the dance style and you know how much easier that makes seeing the choreography. But I don't think anybody really wants to separate the dancers from the dance; I like ballet best when all about it, decor and music too and the evening's special good or bad luck for that matter, are all mixed up and indistinguishably beautiful. But I am trying in this letter to isolate what I think are the two remarkable features of the NYC, the grand-style choreography and the company dance style. The company dance style is particularly different from what Europeans try for and want and so on this tour it is particularly open to question and remark.

When you see the NYC doing *Concerto Barocco* or *Symphony in C* and see the de Cuevas or the Paris Opera doing them, you realize in how different a direction the dance style of Balanchine's company is headed. And then when you have seen a good deal of the repertory, you see too what the limits are in which the dancers are quite strictly kept at present. These limits no European company would care for or be able to keep, but they do make the Americans brilliant. American ballet is like a straight and narrow path compared to the pretty primrose fields the French tumble in so happily. The NYC style is the most particularized and the clearest defined of all the American ones; the most Puritan in its uprightness. For me an immediate attraction of the NYC's style is the handsomeness of the dancing, and another is the absence of glamor, of glamorization. To have left glamor out is only a negative virtue, but there is a freshness in it to start with.

Handsome the NYC way of dancing certainly is. Limpid, easy, large, open, bounding; calm in temper and steady in pulse; virtuoso in precision, in stamina, in rapidity. So honest, so fresh and modest the company looks in action. The company's stance, the bearing of the dancer's whole body in action is the most straightforward, the clearest, I ever saw; it is the company's physical approach to the grand style—not to the noble carriage but the grand one. Simple and clear the look of shoulder and hip, the head, the elbow, and the instep; unnervous the bodies deploy in the step, hold its shape in the air, return to balance with no strain, and re-deploy without effort. Never was there so little mannerism in a company or extravagance. None either of the becks and nods, the spurts and lags, the breathless stops and almost-didn't-make-it starts they cultivate in Paris, and cultivate so prettily. (On the analogy of painting the French go in for texture, the Americans for drawing.) As clear as the shape of the step in the NYC style is its timing, its synchronization to the score at the start, at any powerful thrust it has, at its close. So the dancers dance unhurried, assured and ample. They achieve a continuity of line and a steadiness of impetus that is unique. And can brilliantly increase the power of it and the exhilarating speed to the point where it glitters like cut glass. The rhythmic power of the company is its real style, and its novelty of fashion. Some people complain that such dancing is mechanical. It seems quite the opposite to me, like a voluntary, a purely human attentiveness.

It is an attention turned outside rather than inside. It is turned not to sentiment and charm, but to perspicuity and action. It suggests a reality that is not personal, that outlives the dancer and the public, like a kind of faith. The company is not trying for an emotional suggestion, it seems to be trying for that much harder thing, a simple statement. A painter who is a very bright critic told me that at the opening of *Symphony in C,* during the rush and surge of the finale, tears came to her eyes because it was all so entirely objective. There the company must have showed exactly what it meant to; and it is no trivial expression. They are tears such as Fonteyn can make one feel. But for a company effect I felt them only once while

I was abroad, at the rehearsal of *Napoli* by the Royal Danish Ballet, for the company's objectivity of miming.

This I think is the general direction the NYC style has taken, and its achievement so far. I don't mean to suggest that it is the only right one in ballet; I like having different styles to look at. I think it is an interesting one, and suited to American physical traits and habits. The limits and limitations of the NYC style were not nearly as much fun to try to identify. I tried on the ground it might be amusing to hear what an American fan finds fault with.

So the NYC dancing its best looks beautiful in the dance ballets. In the story ballets when one looks for miming, for acting too, one sees with surprise the company isn't performing at all. For instance in *Prodigal Son*. By exception this was badly rehearsed and the boys danced it so soggy they looked like a YMCA gym class. But that wasn't the trouble. Robbins was attentive, simple, modest, a touching actor; but no one else acted at all. They were as neutral as in *Concerto Barocco*. The stinging butterfly hue and desert grandeur of the choreography turned into an airless Sunday school monotone. How I wanted to see *Prodigal* done by the Danes. And *Tyl* too. Or *La Valse:* it looked like an orphanage. Fortunate young people at a ball have a hectic, mannered, almost-frivolous way which is correct for stage ballroom-dancing too (it's a character style, it's not classicism). In *Valse* the steps invite this edginess, this over-quickness; it would have made the ballroom vault over us all; and evoked that more and more unbearable, more unfulfillable longing of juvenile self-consciousness and soft mortality in which the mime scene could strike like an exploding thunderclap. LeClercq and Moncion acted the scene well, but without the company to prepare it, it looked like a timid beginning. (And such miracles of rising choreographic climaxes; what a wow this would be done by your Covent Garden dancers, after a year or two of getting accustomed.) *Serenade* is danced even more meticulously than *Valse;* but despite its constant success, I would prefer it danced so to speak demi-caractère, not straight academic. Done as it used to be before the war, with a slight "Russian" retard and dragging in the waltzing, that tiny overtone of acting gave the whole piece a stylistic unity and coherence in which the beautiful gesture images (from the one at the opening to the very last, the closing procession) appeared not extraneous but immanent in a single conception. *Lilac Garden* is more effective too danced here and there with a slight advance before or retard behind the beat.

In *Swan Lake* Tallchief's head positions were a sharp pleasure. The neat, on-the-note timing of several striking steps in the adagio seemed to me of theoretical interest, but not this time interesting on stage. The entire adagio was taken too fast and too soldier-like in cadence to have the beauty and power it can: a développé has no force at this speed. The Quartet was bad. But after the two new beautiful Balanchine Swan dances—a delight in their musical spring, their bird-look, and perfect too in their anonymity of style—after the beautiful long finale they led into—hundreds of birds beginning to take off, swirling in the air all over the stage, a beating of wings as they rise up, these great birds at arm's length—after they had gone and the toy swans were swimming back along the drop and Eglevsky looked at them immobile, and I looked with him, then as the curtain began to drop and applause started, just then I realized with a miserable pang that she had been transformed back into a beast, and that she was lost, lost forever. Lost to me too. It was as real as Danilova and Petrov had been in the adagio. Acting or no acting, it was the drama of the story that Balanchine saved, and I was grateful to Eglevsky too for it.

Maybe the acting in the ballets I mentioned demands some familiarity with European manners. But the NYC has a chance at character dancing without European precedent in the high school jazz style of *Pied Piper*. The Negro dynamics of the jazz style (such as an over-slow follow-through, a razor-sharp finesse in the rhythmic attack, an exaggerated variety of weight in playing with the beat) are special; but the NYC dancers all have shagged from way back. So I was mortified to see them dancing still in the style of *Swan Lake;* dancing the piece wrong
44

and looking as square as a covey of mature suburbanites down in the rumpus room. All but one dancer, LeClercq, who does the style right, and looks witty and graceful and adolescent as they all so easily might have by nature. The piece has a Robbins-built sure-fire finale, and the public doesn't even guess at the groovy grace it is missing.

After concentrating awhile on muffed effects like these I got so peeved with my favorite company that I started looking for mistakes in the part of the company style I like so much—the neutral, classic part; and I found a few. The boys for instance were girlish about the knee. They were pleasing in personality and partnering but what they had for plié was indecently small. Their silhouettes in the air were weak because they didn't lift the knee enough; on the ground they relied too much on their instep in place of the knee, and so were getting to mince; even when they came out to bow. They had no élancé at all. They imitated Magallanes' unobtrusive inactive way (without its singular beauty), rather than the big-scale action of Eglevsky.

In the dancing of both girls and boys, the fault that troubled me seriously was a bluntness in the rhythm, a monotonous singsong or marching style meter; it looked like tiredness at first, but after a while it looked as if it might grow into a habit. The sameness of attack at all times (as the military say) is the danger that the company's beautiful steadiness and continuity create. And the classic, the school kinds of variety of attack, and the steps that train variety were what I next tried to watch for and saw little of. A long-sustained adagio flow where the pulse seems to vanish in the controlled développé movement; the various changes of speed possible in a passé développé; the sudden change from slow to fast in ballonné; the unexpected pause in demifouetté; the change of speed in a plié with ritardando drop and accelerando rise, or a port de bras with ritardando finish in free meter—where steps with possible variations of speed and of meter occur the NYC does them in a regularized athletic one-two one-two meter. But when these steps cease being rhythmic "variables" they lose some of their interest and color; what is more they no longer sharpen the dancer's sense of rhythmic delicacy, her sense of variety of accentuation, her sense of the difference between the artificially prolonged and retarded follow-through of adagio and the plain swing-back of allegro. The classic over-rapid meeting and separating of thighs when they pass one another in an adagio movement is never seen at all; and that is a failure; and I am sure that the classic plié with a quick rise is much better in *Symphony in C,* in the syncopated preparation passages of Reed's section—because I used to see her do them correctly and now see only a mechanical plié in even meter, and the passage has lost transparency and zip in consequence.

No company I ever saw performed such subtleties of technique reliably. A great star might, but a company indicates them often rather roughly under the stress of acting, or of a collective atmosphere, or a surge of group rhetoric; similarly in other companies the boys dance with a slight difference from the girls not through technical differentiation but by getting the habit when they began to study dancing in the character of a boy or man. The NYC however not only does not care for such messy uncertainties but it also does not encourage any character-dance approach. (To be sure, character dancing also involves rhythmic liberties.) So we have reached the limits of the company style; the present ones.

It would be absurd to suppose that so great a dramatist as Balanchine (and so great an actor) is delighted to see dramatic implications of such scope and power as his not realized by his own dancers. If they perform every piece alike in the style of virtuoso finger exercises, it is because he made the choice. But the negative advantages are clear. The company doesn't offer the fake glamor, the vulgar rhetorical delivery, the paltry characterization that often have become the defects of a company that tries to act, to characterize and make personal everything it dances. I have seen companies act in a serious ballet so that they looked the way dressing-room gossip sounds, the same kind of expression except it wasn't even occasionally

46

fun. Better than that is dancing a few years without any "expression," just neutral. That leaves the choreography unsoiled, and also the public. It doesn't spoil the effect of the physical aspect of the grand style the dancers neutrally dance in. And it doesn't begin them in habits of silly acting. The limitation to a neutral company style made it possible to force the bloom, if one may say so, of qualities stronger in Americans than big scale acting is, made possible the company's large and powerful impetus, its large and candid unspecific expression.

Perhaps one can guess something of the latent powers of the company style by looking at the qualities the principals and stars show that don't look out of harmony with the ensemble. There are unnervous and unfake acting performances for instance. In *The Cage* the way Kaye throws away most of her part (throws away the detail for the sake of the large shape she so can give it) is very fine and grand. (She looked exhausted when I saw her but I thought that was because of rehearsals for *La Gloire*.) She and Robbins long ago learned to do without the insistent projection that so often spoils American ballet acting, because it gives everything the same tough edge and so turns every move into a comic gesture. Moncion I saw act too little to speak of any change. Hayden and Laing, formerly very fine in a tense and even overwrought style of acting, now seemed feeling their way toward a calmer and larger kind, such as Kaye and Robbins use. Together with the acting that Tallchief and LeClercq show, it looks as if the NYC would welcome a simple and steady kind of acting whenever it begins to show.

Tallchief, though weak in adagio, strikes me as the most audacious and the most correctly brilliant of allegro classicists. She can lift a ballet by an entrance, and she has flashes of a grand decision that are on ballerina scale. What I missed seeing was that expressive radiance which makes beautiful not only the ballerina herself, but the whole company with her, and the whole drab area of stage space and bright imaginary world of the ballet that visibly and invisibly surrounds her; a gently indomitable radiance that is a classical ballerina's job; and that several times in my life I have seen a dancer accomplish. LeClercq has a heavenly radiance and a lovely adagio, but neither has been trained to spread indomitably. Her New York elegance of person, her intelligence in every movement, the delicacy of her rhythmic attack, we all adore. Adams has a perfect action, the best adagio, a ravishing figure and a sweet manner that is our equivalent of your "county." Wilde has a beautiful Veronese grandeur and plasticity of shape in her dancing, a glorious jump; and Hayden has a Lautrec edge and vehement stab and a strange softness in her she seems to hate: a great actress, I would guess, if she learns calm. They are all in *Caracole* each with a line as pure as a great ballerina's, and as characteristic as a great horse's in a horse show. And intent little Reed with the heart of gold—but individuals isn't what this letter is about, as I said to begin with. I love them all. I went by the air-station when the NYC was off for Spain and when your Juniors were off to London, and how ravishing they looked, the station full of dancers both times; such an elegant and rich habitual way of moving, the little faces green from the farewell parties the night before, but the bodies delicious to watch in their unconscious young feline assurance. So they flew up into the sky.

About some of the other choreographies. Ashton's two are sound workmanship and each has first-rate passages. I find the subject matter of each too magnificent to suit their official-style scores to suit, either, Ashton's own wonderfully intimate and ironic poetic eye. The more trivial the subject, the deeper and more beautiful is Ashton's poetic view of it. *Picnic at Tintagel* has a fine mystery story opening and very pretty indecent lifts in the pas de deux. To me it seemed that Ashton's Isolde behaved like a Potiphar's wife with a willing young Joe. She appeared in the lobby of her Central Park apartment building in her slip, found a big schoolboy there, seduced him instantly, and then again. A couple of bellhops peeked. And King Mark and some flags murdered the poor punk. Whether young Tristan ever noticed what it was he was doing with the lady—that is left in doubt; and that is the little private poignancy of the piece. It has nothing to do with the legend and very little with love; but it is a fact of life, it is true to life in its way. Tudor's *La Gloire* I was disappointed in; it didn't look like a piece to me in any direction, and Beethoven kept trampling madly on the bits of it. I saw Tudor was interested in "aplomb." The people around me however applauded earnestly as if they had seen something interesting; so I leave it at that. The Dollar and Bolender pieces I missed, and Boris's I'm sorry I didn't enjoy.

The Robbins's ones—altogether exceptional of course in their gift for form and their ambition for sincerity—are exceptional too in the way they are unrepetitive, disciplined, driving, sharp-sighted. The dramatic pressure of *The Cage* is extraordinary. It devours the notes, it die-casts the gesture; when the curtain comes down, as Thomson said to me, there isn't a scrap left over. I was fascinated by the gesture—so literally that of the important Broadway people at parties and in offices. Bothered to be caged in with them, I looked around unhappily. No exit. But the murderous power that led to the climax and beyond—I couldn't really sense it in the force, the propulsive force of the gesture, I felt it outside the characters. In *Tintagel* a discrepancy between what the story forces the dancers to seem to do and what it is I see them really doing on stage strikes me as harmless and fun; faced by the much greater dramatic force of *Cage,* if what is gobbling up my attention seems to be a discrepancy somehow, I get confused. No one else was bothered, as far as I could see. But I liked *Ballade* better because it didn't get started in that fascinatingly literal gesture of his that is wonderfully contemporary but so resistant to development, to the spontaneous growth kind of development. I liked it better too because at the end one girl at least discovers a way out of the trap that Robbins evidently intended to catch all of them in; she wasn't sure she wanted to get out, but it was clear she could if she chose. I liked the musicality of *Ballade* very much. And the Aronson decor too, so Debussy and real peculiar.

Something in the development of the subject matter

seems to put me on the defensive. I'll blow up the impression and analyze it in terms of criticism and see where I get. Robbins's method is that of pantomime. The composition draws attention to descriptive gesture, incidental gesture made by peripheral movements; it does not draw attention to the central impulses of the body that dances. The gesture sequence is accentuated in spastic counterrhythm (an insistent device common to modern or Central European dancing, but used too, though ever so gently, by the Paris ballet dancers in inventing mannerisms for themselves). Robbins's dramatic line, the dramatic power of a piece is developed not from the central impulses to dance—in ballet characters normal as breathing—but it is developed by applying an obsessive rhythm to what for the characters is incidental gesture. It is like seeing somebody punished very heavily for a small fault, and the main drama never coming to light. It is as if the characters were not free agents—they act under a compulsion. The effect is that of a kind of pre-hypnotic vortex. It destroys the reality of facts—sex, war, The South, money—and some facts one doesn't want to see destroyed—that is its danger. American writers to be sure very often use this device, but the honest and beautiful one among them is Poe. He is very careful. I think that Robbins's present technique would perfectly suit a "Fall of the House of Usher." (Is this where I got? My God, where's Jerry?)

Robbins makes delightful and perfect ballets for musical shows, but at the NYC he wants to do something more. *Cage* as drama is as good as the best Hollywood or Broadway successes. I would say that ballet when it is more, is something quite different, something freer. What bothers Robbins is that vast size, that space all around off stage of an imaginary world. But I think he takes serious ballet so seriously he is willing to get lost trying to find it; and I like that, I feel that way myself. Balanchine, Kirstein told me, believes in him entirely. So does the public, and the company's first all-Robbins night brought out a crowd of bright people who wanted to express their confidence and appreciation. I liked that too.

I think there are perhaps a few "background" notions about our ballet that we accept unconsciously but that you wouldn't know about.

First, something yours, and ours have in common, a pallor, a whiteness of spirit, a thinness and meagerness of temperament that the French say they are so bored by, in our ballet, and in yours too; I think we had better not stop to sigh over it. Henry James describes the same characteristic in American acting of fifty years ago; he calls it an Anglo-Saxon shiny white hardness, as the French still do. Fonteyn has now for four years been leading a revolution against it in your country, and you were lucky she undertook it; after her ten years of the correctest rule she was the only person with the authority to try a change. I love the decisiveness of her action, and perhaps her new lovely warmth will influence our "Anglo-Saxonism" too, our own much more pronounced athleticism and shame-facedness. But actually the NYC is hardly more than ten per cent Anglo-Saxon, and it is as likely to be as Negro as white in another decade or so. Actually you English are West Europeans and can still enjoy your different classes and you can still have the pleasant characterization and glamor that come from noting the differences of manner; noting them without envy or moral disapproval. We haven't that tradition any more. But what a ballet company needs first is an instinctively homogeneous style, as unconscious character. The NYC is less "theatrical" than Ballet Theatre was at its best; but it seems to me to be more natural in its dance behavior, to be better founded on unconscious local manners.

It may seem odd to you that we over here put up with an absence of glamor in our best ballet company in a way that Europeans never would. The normal American attitude (I recognize it in myself too) is the one expressed recently by a local anthropologist in a book about our character *(The Lonely Crowd):* "Wherever we see glamor in the object of our attention we must suspect a basic indifference on the part of the spectator." Can you imagine a European speaking so slightingly of his own local glamor? It's a Puritan point of view. But considering

51

what a mess American dancers have so often made of glamor and of acting it's quite as well not to force the issue of inventing them both. The balletomanes are tactfully quiet about that aspect of our ballet, and express instead their approval of the simplicity, the openness and honesty of the NYC style. They feel that the company is developing in classic action a larger scale than any other American company so far, and it is a scale they like. They remember the mistake of Ballet Theatre in glamorizing and characterizing our ballet dancing on the European plan.

Massine whipped up Ballet Theatre once and gave it (with Tudor's help) a brief glory. But he couldn't solve the two main troubles: he couldn't unite the ballerinas to the company and he couldn't get the American dancers to open their hearts instinctively to dancing as the Russian ones had done. Massine proposed success as the magic formula to solve these problems. That sounded American. He had success. He had a triumph. But not a thing was solved. Instead everybody just got nervous. So now Balanchine proposes a different magic. He begins with attention on everyone's part to carriage, to correctness, to the score. This makes a kind of objective, non-egotistic focus, and it gives a kind of disinterestedness of expression. Do you see how this might make a basis for collaboration between chorus and principal other than individual applause, and a basis too for pride in one's work and for giving one's best imagination to it. It makes one moral law for all. You may find this attention to the craft of dancing not enough to hold your interest, you luxurious Europeans; but it's not ugly.

Europeans keep forgetting what a poor country America is. We can't afford those enormous, secure, pensioned, resident, officially respected companies you all do. We have no such luxuries as your wonderful Elvin, Nerina and Grant dancing a young life away under the ancestral Petipas, and growing more and more beautiful through the deep decades of peace that prepare their triumphant accessions. The NYC never knows if it will last another season. It is either underpaid or overworked or both.

With so small a company and so large a repertory—about a dozen novelties a year—there is no time for more than a memorizing of parts. How could they work so hard and act too? You can see for yourself how impecunious the company is—so poor it can't even afford to dress all its repertory, and has to run out every now and then in little whatyoucall'ems. Under the circumstances Balanchine and Kirstein might as well give up trying for tiny advantages as the managements of big vested interest must; they can keep in mind the biggest prize of all, the true grand style. (Fortunately in art there are as many first prizes as contestants, even if so very few ever win one.) *(1952)*

Superficial Thoughts
on Foreign Classicism

EVERYBODY KNOWS THAT the principles of classicism are identical the world over. A ballet audience on any continent recognizes the same steps and the same elaborate theatre apparatus, and knows what to expect in *Giselle* or *Swan Lake*. Everybody wants it that way and is proud of it, and with reason. And yet from experience everybody knows too that an American classic company as it dances a ballet has a general look that is not at all the same as that of a British company, and a Paris company is quite different from either. Different again is a Danish company, or an Italian, and further differences appear no doubt, the farther you travel. It bothers the fans, this paradox.

It doesn't bother the general public. When a foreign company comes to a city accustomed to its own local one, the general public loves the exotic note, the picturesque stars, the novel repertory. Not so a fan. You can see him in any ballet capital, just such a real hard-shelled passionate fan hunched up morosely as a visiting troupe performs a piece he knows and loves. He can see that the company has gifts and works hard—but call that classicism! A few seats farther down is the other type of fan, the sociable kind, darting her sharp look brightly all over the stage at the funny foreigners, nudging her girl friend and giggling, "Did you see his face when he offered that rose?"

When I first heard fans abroad bitterly resent our classicism, bitterly and inexplicably, I supposed they were being something like defensive or imperialist or chauvinist about their own; but later when I heard Americans complain as bitterly about European ballet, I realized it couldn't be the reason. The feelings of a fan about ballet anywhere in the world are deeper and sweeter than politics or economics. They are direct, more like the feelings of a passionate coffee-drinker newly arrived in a strange country and for the first time tasting the brew that there is called coffee. Just as the cut of a pair of pants which is sheer heaven to an ardent sharpie in one country is merely risible to the sharpie in another, so the sociable fan can't help giggling at unexpected behavior in a familiar spot.

Unexpected for me was some of the behavior on stage when I saw a piece called *Suite de Dances* at the Paris Opéra. The orchestra was playing a familiar Chopin piano piece, and when the curtain went up I expected some sort of *Sylphides*. Sure enough there was the moonlight and there was a man dressed for *Sylphides*. But instead of his standing in a grove with the demented bevy of girls in white, there were a fountain basin, and steps rising, and platforms, and more steps—and high upstage center on a raised podium in a vivid white spotlight was this man by himself. He executed a few beautiful Fokinesque ports de bras, rose on half-toe, and then, perfectly satisfied with himself, walked off stage on the third floor. Below in the dry fountain basin a huddle of partly grown kids knelt in an undisciplined lineup with one gangling leg extended. A quarter of an hour later when they got up, their little knees had gone stiff. And as they began to dance they kept glancing down at their knees and then out at us with slum-like grimaces of disdain and shrugged up their little shoulders. Finally came a polonaise for all the big girls in white. But they weren't at all Fokine's moony young ladies. These self-respecting Parisian dancers each brought with her her own cavalier to keep her company. To supply so many hadn't been easy, and some of the partners looked neither youthful nor attractive in their walk; one tubby one, to give himself a more romantic

look, had shadowed his cheeks so heavily that he seemed
to have a three-day beard. Each man, regardless of shape,
was dressed in a short *Sylphides* suit and wore a long
page-bob wig of the loveliest hair. The older ones looked
at the audience rakishly. And the audience applauded and
cheered.

Evidently the audience had seen something quite different from what I had. And as I went home I imagined that
to a Paris fan our own *Sylphides* might seem quite as ridiculous. He might point out that without changing a
single sacrosanct step of Fokine's, our Anglo-American
versions have become—God knows how—as respectably
dreamy as a bath-soap advertisement. No, they aren't always, but now and then they are, aren't they? And I went
on imagining a Paris fan's dismay at the sight of our
cleanwashed girls, looking each one as like all the others
as possible, instead of (as in Paris) as *un*like. How can
you tell them apart, he might say—it was exactly what I
had heard in Paris at the first visit of Sadler's Wells—
what fun can it be to be a fan that way? I have heard the
British answer: "*We* are perfectly well pleased, thank
you—so self-indulgent the French, such a pity too, great
institution, the Opéra." As for the Americans, when they
see a huge gifted company on the vast stage in Paris, they
wonder that the Opéra public likes its dance pleasure of
so small a kind; inspected as though through an opera
glass, a limb or a waist at a time. At home we like the
way a company looks dancing as a company, a bold,
large, and sweeping pleasure.

When I told a lady abroad that I thought it strange that
classic dancing should look so different from one country
to another she said: "But everything else looks different
too; it would be very strange if ballet didn't." And when I
returned, I heard Balanchine say: "When I first came to
Paris from Russia, Diaghilev took me to the best restau-
rants, famous for their fine food. The waiter put before
me a little dish with something particular on it. I complained: 'You call this fine food. I want a big plate. And
bring me potatoes and beef and pork and turnips and cab-
bage and more potatoes.' And then I mixed them all up

on the plate, and it was what I was used to. And I ate it and said to Diaghilev, 'Yes, they have very fine food here.' Ballet is like that. People like what they are used to."

And people are used to changes, too. It is changing all the time. Americans used to be used to the Ballet Russe style, now they are used to the American style—though a few fans still object to the change. Champs-Elysées style has modified the Sadler's Wells. I have heard French dancers sigh for the "great teachers" of New York and Americans enthusiastic about schools in Paris. The Danes are delighted to have Vera Volkova teach them a style opposite to their own, the Italians and Turks have imported English teachers, and the English swear by the Cecchetti method.

But an American fan who travels in Europe from one ballet city to another sees, too, that the general look of the different companies in performance, different though it is, is more alike from capital to capital than the general look of a crowd moving in the street in the morning; the movement of the crowd, I mean, differs even more from one country to another. In Copenhagen the crowd has an easy stride, strong in the waist, light on the feet, with a hint of a sailor's roll. As they pass they look at one another briefly and trustingly without moving the face. They enjoy walking. In Paris they hate to walk. Each individual is going in an individual direction, at a different speed. And they hate it, but they refuse to bump. They carry their bodies with respect like a large parcel of dishes: sort of low. They jab their heels at the pavement, in short steps, each person differently; they trip, and strut, and jiggle, and waddle, and trudge, and limp; and every now and then a beauty passes among them sailing like a swan or stalking like a fine flamingo, completely isolated from the others. They notice her at once, but they refuse to look, and as she passes, every individual in the crowd from fifteen years old to sixty-five becomes more intensely himself or herself. That is their form of homage.

All over Italy half the population is constantly walking up and down hills carrying babies or parcels of food, a steady movement like breathing. The other half is in the street, the men leaning or relaxed in harmonious assurance, or lounging; the girls pass by just a little quickly, with an easy delicacy. Everybody enjoys everybody else's beauty—it belongs to everyone who sees it; they enjoy it all their life over and over with the same pleasure. One could guess that they had invented ballet. They know how to lift the waist imperceptibly as they turn half in profile, how to show a back, hold the head, raise an arm, point a foot, or extend a hand; they love doing it and seeing it. And they mistrust a person who won't make a scene; they all make them without getting confused or losing their sweetness; they do by couples, by threes, or by crowds at ticket booths, and breathe more easily for it. The only thing they will not tolerate is hurry and being hurried. They have no love for losing their habits of behavior; it makes them savage.

In London the crowd in the morning walks well, orderly, and the ears look delicious. Looking at the face isn't done. But then the beauties one would want to enjoy are in taxis, down from the country for the day. Truckdrivers and dock-workers have a curious autochthonous color sense—in subtle off-shade combinations—in their workclothes. After midnight, however, gentle monstrous creatures appear from underground, hideously primped and perfectly pleased with themselves, tell each other their secrets, and vanish, as natural to the soil as the creatures of Alice's dream.

As for the New York crowd, we all know it, and it doesn't resemble any of these at all.

How different the more consciously social movements are—coming into a room at a party, shaking hands, behaving at table or sitting in a chair—everybody knows from foreign movies anyway. Dancers who grow up in a city naturally move in the way people around them have moved all their life. And that makes a difference in the over-all or general look of a whole company, even if it doesn't show in one dancer doing a particular step. But classicism is so naked and enlarged a way of moving that any tiny unconscious residue in it of something else than the step—the residue of habit or of character—shows. And sometimes is beautiful. A dancer cannot intend such an unconscious overtone, for it is beautiful only if it is deeper than any intention. But a ballet fan can sense it and be moved. A faint reminiscence of a gesture seen with wonder as a child and long forgotten, an overtone characteristic of a city in the motion of someone one has loved and forgotten, returns sometimes in a dancer's innocent motion and makes its poignancy the more irresistible. Natural enough that an audience feels closest to the dancing of girls and boys of its own country. But the point of classicism is that local color is by an insistent discipline driven deeper and deeper into the unconscious imagination. There it becomes innocent, out of this world, unnationalist, and unsentimental.

I don't believe in an intentional local overtone in classicism. I believe that a good classicist should have less than as little as possible. But I never saw a homogeneous company that—besides tending to show a single style of teaching—didn't also in its general look show a common regional overtone. In a home company a fan becomes used to it and aware only of classicism; but when a foreign company first arrives the same fan is overpowered by its strangeness, its exoticism, and this keeps him from seeing the real classic dancing. It is very annoying. It takes time for this first confusion to wear off. That is why European fans respond more freely to our ballets with a local color subject than to our classic ones: the general American look is plausible to them in an American number; in a classic number they want the unconscious regional overtone they are used to, as well as the conscious school style they are used to, too; that is the note which for them makes classicism plausible. Even Diaghilev, when he first came to Paris, had no success with *Giselle;* everybody adored the Russians when they were "barbaric" and "primitive," but in classicism these qualities seemed disturbing.

But I believe that fans here in New York are more and more ready to accept the initial shock of foreignness in classicism, curious to find out what a peregrine style may contain either of stimulus to our own or else of interest merely to widen a ballet-goer's sense of the scope of international classicism. It was a similar curiosity that took me to Europe a few years ago to look around. Stay-at-home New Yorkers however have been able to see about as much as I. The only important Western company that has not been here is the Royal Danish Ballet, the importance of which I thought was its freshness and straightforwardness in presenting the touching (and soundly built) Romantic ballets of Bournonville, of which no ballet fan can see too many. The choreography is simple, but original; the pace is easy, but sure; the dances are seen with a beautiful clarity; and the sentiment is both real and modest. It is a pleasure to see how simple, how chaste, ballet can be and still go to your heart. A Galeotti ballet of 1786 (*The Caprices of Cupid and the Maître de Ballet*), in which a few steps have been, presumably at a later date, raised to real toe-steps, but no other change has been made, is still alive and amusing as a piece, and even simpler in choreography. Their *Giselle* and *Coppélia* are the best one can see in their mime passages, but I don't care so much for the dance versions. I saw only two pieces of the modern repertory, and one of them, *Etudes,* seemed to me effective and clean, but not very distinguished. I imagine, however, that three full-length Bournonville ballets would have in New York the sort of gentle innocence we never see on stage, and that many of us would be happy not to resist.

But this extraordinary voyage back into the world of Romantic ballet on which the Danish company can take one, refreshing though it is, is not an aspect of contemporary classicism. I wish one of their great mimes, Karstens or Larsen, could teach in New York. But the traditional atmosphere, the quiet ballet studios they work in, are very different from ours. What I wished very much, too, was that we could import the secure financial organization of those great European ensembles, which is founded on the practical experience of ballet as a long-term investment, analogous to the conception of our own cultural foundations. But the more an American looks at ballet abroad, where it is rooted in a city's life, the more he realizes that the most important way to improve our ballet is to keep it steadily and continuously living among us according to our local conditions, our own manners and behavior. In point of contemporary artistic interest our New York City Ballet is now in its own repertoire incomparably more exciting for me than any Western European company, larger and richer though they are, and brilliant though are some of their stars. And to my mind it is also in the dance style that it is close to achieving.

But I see no reason why one should dispute so unnecessary a question—which country's company is better; there is so much in all of them that is a pleasure, and particularly when one gets to know a company in its own home theatre. The home audience responds so differently on points of manners, points that are unintelligible abroad, and that in fact have nothing to do with classic principles, but that become a part of the company's style. I was astonished and delighted watching a Parisian dancer save an awkward passage in performance. She seemed to be saying to the audience, "I'll tell you a secret: this is a passage of no consequence at all, and it doesn't suit my style either, such a stupid choreographer—oops, that elastic—again!—where was I? Oh yes, I'll just sketch in a few steps, I'm delicious at sketching in, you know—and then, just in a moment more, there's a bit—oh really so clever, you'll adore seeing how divine I am in it—ah, here goes now!" "How adorably alive," the audience whispered to its neighbor. A British dancer in a similar situation seems to say more decorously, "I should be happy if this weren't quite so undignified, but we must dance correctly, mustn't we, and it's such fun really, don't you think?" And her audience, staidly touched, breathes back: "Good old girl." I guess an American, when the audience is losing interest goes on with her steps as if she muttered: "Don't bother me, I'm busy." She would seem rude to a foreigner, but, being an American, I know what she means, and I respect her for it. Better of course to go on dancing sweetly and not say anything at all; and I've seen dancers all over the world do that too, great dancers.

When you get to be familiar with any foreign style it becomes as misleading and absurd, as touching and delightful as daily life is abroad too. But I was curious abroad to find out if there were some particular regional style that was accepted as the best, and asking everywhere I found a general unanimity of opinion. The wisest fans were all agreed that, despite a few obvious defects, the one classic style that they felt in their hearts to be the most exciting, the most lovable and beautiful, was the style of their own country. I could not disagree with any of them, for I felt, so to speak, the same way, and so without going into particulars we parted with mutual expressions of sincere regard. *(1953)*

Impressions of Markova
at the Met

ALICIA MARKOVA HAS become that legendary figure, the last of the old-style ballerinas. Her second *Giselle* with Ballet Theatre this fall season broke a box office record at the Metropolitan Opera House. Five people fainted in standing room. She did the contrary of everything the new generation of ballerinas has accustomed us to. With almost no dazzle left, Markova held the house spellbound with a pianissimo, with a rest. A musician next to me was in tears, a critic smiled, a lady behind me exclaimed "Beautiful!" in an ecstatic, booming voice. Her dancing was queerer than anyone had remembered it. A few days later, meeting a balletomane usually far stricter than I, on the street, I asked him what he thought of her this season. "More wonderful than ever," he cried aggressively. When I asked if he thought she had shown this defect or that, he admitted each in turn, but his admiration was as pure as before. This is the sort of wonder a real ballerina awakens, one our young dancers are too modest to conceive of, and that Markova's dancing used to do for me, too. Though I wasn't carried away this time, I found watching her so-different method intensely interesting.

Details were extraordinary—the beautiful slender feet in flight in the soubresauts of *Giselle,* Act Two, how she softly and slowly stretches the long instep like the softest of talons as she sails through the air; or in the échappés just after, how they flash quick as knives; or in the "broken steps" of the mad scene of Act One, when, missing a

63

beat, she extends one foot high up, rigidly forced, and seems to leave it there as if it were not hers. I was happy seeing again those wonderful light endings she makes, with the low drooping "keepsake" shoulders, a complete quiet, sometimes long only as an eighth note, but perfectly still. I recognized too, the lovely free phrasing of the *Sylphides* Prelude, so large, though not so easy as once. Best of all, better than before, I thought her acting in *Giselle* Act One. Surer than I remembered is the dance-like continuity she gives her gestures and mime scenes— all the actions of the stage business imbedded in phrases of movement, but each action so lightly started it seemed when it happened a perfectly spontaneous one. In this continuity, the slow rise of dramatic tension never broke or grew confused. It was the technique of mime in the large classic style.

In classic miming, a sense of grandeur is given by stillness that is "inside" a phrase of movement the way a musical rest is "inside" a musical phrase. Markova's strong continuity of phrasing; the clarity of shape that mime gestures have when they are made not like daily life gestures but like dance movements from deep down the back; and her special virtuosity in "rests"; these give her miming grandeur. But for dancing, her strength is too small for the grand work of climaxes. She cannot keep a brilliant speed, sustain extensions, or lift them slow and high; leaps from one foot begin to blur in the air; her balance is unreliable. In ballet it is the grand power of the thighs that give magnanimity to the action; there is no substitute and a ballet heroine cannot do without it. Once one accepts this disappointment, one can watch with interest how skillfully she disguises the absence: by cuts, by elisions, by brilliant accents, by brio, by long skirts, by scaling down a whole passage so that it will still rise to a relative climax.

A second disappointment for me was that her powerful stage presence (or projection) no longer calmly draws the audience to herself and into her story on the stage. Markova used particularly to practice that art of great legitimate theatre personalities of drawing the public to her into her own imaginary world; she used to be fascinatingly absorbed in that world. But now she often seems like a nervous hostess performing to amuse, eager to be liked; she pushes herself out on the public. It is a musical comedy winsomeness and looks poor in classic ballet. It was, I thought, a serious mistake for a ballerina of such wide experience to make. Another error, a more trivial one, was the absurd way she danced the *Nutcracker* pas de deux—more like a provincial Merry Widow number than the *Nutcracker*—with a shrunken, slovenly action, bad knees, affectations of wrists and face—and for a Sugar Plum Fairy to be carelessly dressed was unfortunate.

But despite even bad mistakes, there remains her phenomenal old-fashioned style of delicate nuances in dancing. The methods she uses showed here and there and it was fun to look. For instance the divine lightness of attack: Merce Cunningham, with whom I was discussing her technique, spoke of the illusion she gives of moving without a preparation so you see her only already fully launched, as if she had no weight to get off the ground (the stretch from plié is so quick). He remarked very vividly that in a leap she seemed at once "on top of her jump, like an animal." He also pointed out how she uses this illusion to disguise the weakness of a développé—she throws the leg up in a flash with knee half extended, but all you become aware of is the adagio motion immediately after that—a slow dreamy extension of the beautiful instep.

Markova achieves her illusion of lightness not by strength—for strength she has only the instep, shoulder and elbow left. But she draws on other virtuoso resources —the art of sharply changing the speed without breaking the flow of a movement; the art, too, of timing the lightning-like preparation so that the stress of the music will underline only the *following* motion, done at the speed of the music, which is meant to be displayed. As in her phrase beginnings and leaps up, so the same transformation of speed from presto to adagio is used for her weightless descents and her phrase endings—though for the latter, it takes her a beat or two more to subside into stillness than it used to. For the full effect of being stilled and immobile, she often brings forward her low shoulders into a droop, a gesture like a folding-in of petals, like a return into herself. This motion softens the precise stop of the feet, because it carries over for an unaccented count like a feminine ending; like the diminuendo effect of a port de bras which is finished a count later than the feet finish the step. Her softening forward droop in the shoulders also alters the look of the next new start since the dancer takes an up-beat of straightening her shoulders, and so seems to lift and unfold into the new phrase. Such nuances of color or breathing or dynamics give to the old-fashioned style its fullness; but they easily become fullsome. One can watch Markova, however, use them to carve more clearly the contour of a phrase, to make it more visible and more poignant. Our current fashion in classicism is to avoid these nuances to make sure that they will not be used to conceal a cardinal weakness.

In contrast to the solid, sharp, professional, rather impatient brilliance of our grand and powerful young ballerinas, the kind of effect Markova makes seems more than ever airy and mild, transparent and still. The dancer seems to begin on a sudden impulse, and to end in an inner stillness. She seems less to execute a dance than to be spontaneously inventing. She seems to respond to the music not like a professional, but more surprisingly, more communicatively. It is an "expressive" style, as peculiar looking in New York as any Parisian one. It is one our dancers look quite clumsy at, and not only our own, who hardly ever try for it, but many Europeans too, who constantly do.

I have wanted to focus attention on the difference, but I don't mean to judge between these two styles. For my part, I enjoy our own new one because the neutral look of it, a sort of pleasant guardedness, seems to suit our dancers better. Some day they will find out how to open up, but in terms of a technique that suits them. Markova happened to learn a style that suited her physique, her temperament, her environment; and a born ballerina, she made the most of it. The public responds to her now, not because of her style, not because it is the right one, but because she is a wonderfully compelling theatre artist. For me she was, this fall, exhibiting her highly elaborated style rather than dancing a dance or a role, and that limited my enjoyment. But for fans who love classic dancing, and because they love it are happy to see as much as they can of its possibilities, of its richness and scope, it is well worth seeing her perform effects no one in our generation is likely to make so lightly and so lucidly. *(1952)*

Caracole

I HAVEN'T YET managed to speak of *Caracole,* and that
was what I most wanted to when I began to write you—
so very interesting. The plebeian costuming of it is a pity
and an indignity to Bérard too. But I think the NYC decor is so bad and so monkish generally that except for all
of us to make fun of it every chance we get, there is no
use in discussing it (I don't mean the extraordinary lighting). And yet I saw few ballet sets in Europe either that I
wanted particularly to see again. They often looked better
dressed than the NYC's and they showed better if a
dancer was forward or back; but they rarely stood up as
architecture for twenty minutes on end, stood up architec-
turally imaginative while the music and the dancers swept
across again and again; no prettiness of backbone. In Europe what I was happy over was the delicious execution
of costumes possible in Paris, and a grace in it sometimes
in Italy (and in Italy a sweet sensibility for lights). No
use getting into all of that. Despite its hard clothes,
Caracole is a heavenly piece to see, and everybody knows
it immediately. At second sight, it has a so-to-speak Miltonic grip in its suavity; and it takes wild Miltonic risks
with having enough air to breathe with—it isn't airy like
Mozartiana.

But fanciful and sudden, ingenious and beautiful, the
ballet is over and over. Densely so in the long Variation's
movement and again in the Andante; in the Introductory
movement amusing and sweet, in the last quick with a

Figaro kind of wit (a little thinness here doesn't hurt); everywhere with a Mozartian current in continuity and a Mozartian lightness in beginnings and endings. Only the Minuet movement seemed mistaken—it struck me as too tight; though the spikey hooflike steps of the girls seemed to be pricking patterns like those on Baroque prints of horse-ballets and carrousels. The Baroque Spanish Riding Academy of the Hapsburgs is meant to be suggested by the word "Caracole," too; and often the girls' light dances evoke an animal power in grace and—even more beautiful—an animal innocence in display. I remembered Belmonte, a Lipizaner who performed *haute école* here on a variety stage ten years ago, how the massive horse enjoyed himself majestically dancing for us, how he glowed and beamed with princely pleasure. Perhaps you've seen him too. The Variations have something of that; the Andante in turn has a lovely suggestion of great mares being led by the bridle, grandly displayed like in Baroque paintings. When you start thinking this way, the quick nods as the curtain rises become horsey, and the flurry of the Finale like the flurry of a race. But you don't have to—nothing in the sequences is literal, or insists on allusion. Strange that graceful academic dancing can evoke the heavy animals; strange to feel these powerful performing beasts related in their play to Mozart's tender intimacy. Strange how they become other images if you look close at the overpoweringly metrical choreography.

If you watch the steps, in the Variations for instance, a single step or brief combination will flash out oversharply visible, so astonishing is the contrast to the step before it. The shape of the step appears unexpected as lightning and, lightninglike, vanishes—or like the pulsating brilliance of a butterfly on the ground, as its wings open and shut. And through these disparate flashings the dancer's impetus never falters. The powerful muscular pelvic thrust that renews her impetus step by step intensifies the image's visual pulsation. The deep dance beat of these powerful flashes strikes the eye sometimes even twice to a bar (like on 1-3-1 or 1-4-1), and it is set to music light, light in its beat, easy and fluid. The meter is strictly identical; it nails the dance to the music; and feeling them nailed fast to one another, the deep divergence between them in the weight of the beat becomes monstrous and ritual-like. But neither voice falters in its onward movement; and how felicitous each is; watching these contours lengthen, their grace covers over the secret between them and seems to obliterate it.

But something as strange as the incommensurableness of the two synchronized beats recurs in the action of the Andante. In this succession of fragmentary pas de deux, a new duet sometimes takes over with the boy changing partner merely on an upbeat, and the shift cuts into the continuity of the melody; you feel the wound of the cut, and yet you see across it the same tender intimacy continue undisturbed as if dreamlike; continue through each shifted pair and across the flowing melodic periods poignantly unbroken as long as the movement lasts; as if there were tenderness enough forever, the beautiful couples dismembered and recoupled, three boys and five girls, with no jealous failure in their lovely awareness. But as if to give no pathos to this image, the dance does not touch any of the "moments of expression" of the music—the young people on stage seem not to by some delicacy of instinct. Apart from the fateful identity of meter, they have another phrasing, another rhetoric and fashion of behavior than the music—the dancers keep a Maryinsky-Byzantine grandeur of deportment, the music a Viennese spontaneity of sentiment; separate ways of enduring. And when the Andante is finished, it is as if you had seen on two separate faces the same brief look of angelic irony; though they seem strangers, you know how close they have been in a secret they will never tell. The closest description of *Caracole* was that of a poet friend who said smiling when the curtain had fallen, "Balanchine probably made it as fast as Mozart did, or only a little slower."

That is what the excitement of the piece seems like to me. Looking at it more objectively, more relaxed, it seems meant to be as sweet as possible. There is not one novel "expressive" gesture to tax your nervous sympathy; not one step is twisted or odd, each limpidly departs from and returns to a neutral equilibrium; everything is academic convention; nothing but the body in plastic motion in beauty—the dancer appearing effortlessly fantastic. And yet stroke by stroke, so much fantasy, so ceaseless a jet, there is too much to watch, it leaves no time to breathe, to assent. It is a dense choreography one can call impossible to dance and to see the way some pieces of music are called impossible to play and to hear; impossible except that everyone recognizes them right away as miraculous. It is overpowering as to some people may be their first sight of the brilliantly peopled heaven of the circus—acrobats and beasts. For me it made me think of how a boy in love hears a man's voice telling what love is like—so much more of it everywhere than anyone cares for, so much more than too much and every bit lucky— the boy believes that what he is feeling for the man is anger; and it seemed to me that the heavy thrust of its pulse was like the sound almost regular year by year of a heart in a breast. I don't mean Balanchine intended any of these ideas, no, no, not at all; only that I found it so innocent and insoluble; and how wonderful to see such a grandiose work come into being on stage in all its glitter and beauty, danced with a sweetness and a clarity that are disarming. *(1952)*

Some Thoughts about Classicism
and George Balanchine

The beautiful way the New York City company has been
dancing this season in the magnificent pieces of its repertory—in *Serenade, Four Temperaments, Symphonie
Concertante, Swan Lake, Caracole, Concerto Barocco,
Orpheus, Symphony in C,* and the new *Metamorphoses*—not to mention such delicious small ones as *Pas
de Trois, Harlequinade,* or *Valse Fantaisie*—made me
want to write about the effect Balanchine's work has had
in developing a largeness of expression in his dancers, and
in showing all of us the kind of beauty classic ballet is by
nature about. Thinking it over, I saw questions arise on
tradition, purity of style, the future of classicism, and Balanchine's intentions in choreography; and I wondered
what his own answers to them would be, or what he
would say on such an array of large subjects. So one evening after watching an excellent performance of *Four
Temperaments,* I found him backstage and we went
across 56th Street together to the luncheonette for a cup
of coffee.

He began by mentioning the strain on the dancers of
the current three month season, dancing eight times a
week and rehearsing novelties and replacements all day.
After it was over, he said smiling, the real job of cleaning
up their style could begin; for the present it was like a
hospital, all they could do was to keep patching themselves up just to continue. I assured him they had just
danced very well indeed, and then told him about my gen-

eral questions. He paused a moment. Then, taking up the issue of style, he answered that there were of course several styles of classic dancing; that he was interested in one particular one, the one he had learned as a boy from his great teachers in Petersburg—classic mime and character as well as academic style. He spoke as a quiet man does of something he knows entirely and knows he loves. He sketched the history of the Petersburg style. Then he took up aspects of other styles he did not care for—a certain sanctimonious decentness in that of Sadler's Wells, a note of expensively meretricious tastiness in that of the Paris Opera—these are not his words, but I thought it was his meaning. He was not denying the right of others to a different taste than his own; nor did he mean to minimize the achievements of these two great bodies, but only to specify points of divergence. He said he believed in an energetic style, even a soldierly one, if one chose to put it that way.

Passing from the subject of style to tradition, he mentioned as an example the dance we know as the Prince's Variation of *Swan Lake*. He told me that it used to be done all in brisés and small leaps, but that one time when Vladimiroff was dancing it in Petersburg this great dancer changed it to big jetés; and now the big leaps are everywhere revered as tradition. I gathered he thought of tradition rather as a treasured experience of style than as a question of steps; it was a thought I only gradually came to understand.

At this point he noticed that Steve wanted to close his luncheonette, and so we went back to the theatre and continued to speak standing in the backstage corridor. We got on the subject of notation. He emphasized the continuity of movement it could reproduce. I asked if *Four Temperaments* had been notated, adding that I felt sure the public in forty years time would enjoy seeing it as much as we do, and would want to see it danced in the form it has now. "Oh, in forty years," he said, "ballet will be all different." After a momentary pause, he said firmly, as if returning to facts, that he believed ballet was entertainment. I realized he meant the word in its large sense of both a social and an attractive public occasion. But he looked at me and added, in a more personal tone, that when one makes a ballet, there is of course something or other one wants to say—one says what one says. He looked away, as if shrugging his shoulders, as one does after mentioning something one can't help but that one doesn't make an issue of in public.

At the far end of the corridor the dancers were now assembling for *Symphony in C,* the final ballet, and he returned to the subject of style and spoke of two ways of rising on toe—one he didn't like, of jumping up on point from the floor, the other rising from half-toe, which he wanted. Similarly in coming down in a step, he wanted his dancers to touch the floor not with the tip of the foot, but a trifle to one side, as if with the third toe, because this gives a smoother flexion. He spoke too of different ways of stretching the knee in relation to flexing the ankle as the dancer lands from a leap, and of stiff or flexible wrist motions in a port de bras. Details like these, he said, were not consciously noticed by the audience, nor meant to be. But to him they were important, and a dancer who had lived all his life in ballet noticed them at once. They corresponded, he suggested, to what in speaking one's native tongue is purity of vocabulary and cleanness of accent; qualities that belong to good manners and handsome behavior in a language one is born to and which one recognizes in it with pleasure. At that point I felt that he had, in his own way, replied to the large questions I had put at the beginning, though he had avoided all the large words and rubbery formulas such theses are likely to lead to. So I thanked him and went back to my seat and to the first bars of *Symphony in C.*

Balanchine had offered no rhetorical message. He had made his points distinctly and without insistence. It was several days before I realized more fully the larger ideas on the subject of style that his points had implied. He had suggested, for one, that style demands a constant attention to detail which the public is not meant to notice, which only professionals spot, so unemphatic do they remain in performance. The idea, too, of style as something a man who has spent many years of his life working in an art, loves with attentive pertinacity. A classic dancer or choreographer recognizes style as a bond of friendship with the great artists he remembers from his childhood and with others more remote he knows only by name. For in spirit classic artists of the past are present at a serious performance and watch it with attention. And as I see Tallchief dance now in *Concerto Barocco,* I feel that they invisibly smile at her, they encourage her, they blow her little Italian kisses. They danced steps that were different but they understand what she means to do; her courage night after night is like theirs. And I think that they find a similar pleasure in the work of the company as a whole. For dancers have two sets of judges—the public and its journalists who can give them celebrity, and the great artists of their own calling who can give them a feeling of dignity and of proud modesty.

The bond between classic dancers is that of good style. But Balanchine in his conversation did not say that style in itself made a ballet, or that the entertainment he believed in was an exhibition of style. On the contrary he said that when he made a piece there was something or other he wanted to say. He was affirming the inner force that is called self-expression. And no doubt he would recognize it as well as an inner force in dancing. But for him there was no contradiction between creative force and the impersonal objective limitations of classic style. He knew in his own life as an artist—and what a wide, rich and extraordinary life it has already been—that his love of style and his force of expression could not be divided; as they could not have been, for others before him, and I am sure will not be for classic dancers of the future either.

That Balanchine expresses a meaning in a ballet is clear enough in those that tell a story. And he has made several striking story ballets even in the last decade. Among them are his recent vivid version of *Swan Lake; Night Shadow,* a savage account of the artist among society people; *Orpheus,* a large ritualistic myth of poetic destiny; and *Tyl,* a realist and anti-fascist farce. It took our bright-eyed young matinee audience to discover how good the jokes are in *Tyl;* and now the children have made it clear, the grownups see how touching are its sentiments.

The subject matter however of the so-called abstract dance ballets is not so easy to specify. On the point of the most recent, *Metamorphoses,* it happened that while it was being rehearsed, I met him and asked if what I had heard was true, that he was making a ballet on the Kafka short story, *Metamorphosis.* He laughed in surprise, and said no. But he added as a matter of fact, about a month before, going down from his apartment one night to buy a paper, there on the sidewalk in the glare of the stand and right in the middle of New York he saw a huge cockroach going earnestly on its way.—As for me, Olympic athletes, Balinese dancers, Byzantine seraphs seem all to have contributed images for this ballet, besides that Upper East Side cockroach. But on stage these elements do not appear with the expression they have in life. In the athlete section the explosive force of stops and speed makes a dazzle like winter Broadway in its dress of lights; hints from Bali are wildly transformed into a whirring insect orgy; the joyous big-scale nonsense of it and then the evanescent intensity of an insect pas de deux are as simple and childlike in their vitality as a *Silly Symphony* cartoon; and the end is a big sky swept by powerful, tender and jubilant wings. What Balanchine has expressed is something else than the material he began with, something subjective; and I so respond to it.

His dance ballets each express a subjective meaning. I feel it as the cumulative effect of the many momentary images they present, dramatic, lyric or choral. And the pleasure of them is seeing these images as they happen; responding to the succession of their brilliant differences that gradually compose into a structure—an excitement rather like reading a logically disjointed but explosively magnificent ode of Pindar. One might say they are dance entertainments meant to be watched by the natives in New York rather the way the natives of other places than this watch a social village dance in West Africa or watch a Balinese kebyar or legong.

76

I am supposing at least that natives take their dance forms for granted and watch instead the rapid images and figures. I like that way of watching best myself; and the closer I so follow a dance ballet, the more exciting I find it; and the more different each becomes. I do not enjoy all of Balanchine's equally, or all entirely. Some, like *Firebird* or *Card Game,* have disintegrated in large sections. Others, despite brilliant dancing and passages I enjoy, do not appeal to me in their over-all expression—*La Valse, Scotch Symphony, Bourrée Fantasque.* So capricious is a subjective taste. And it is unstable too.

There is a perhaps less capricious way of following a dance piece. It is that of watching its formal structure. And the excitement of doing it is a more intellectual one. I am not sure that it is a good way to watch, but I will mention some of the discoveries one so makes, since they are another approach to the meaning of a piece.

An aspect of structure, for instance, is the way Balanchine sets the score, how he meets the patterns in time, the patterns of energy from which a dancer takes his spring. When you listen closely and watch closely at the same time you discover how witty, how imaginative, how keen his response at every moment is to the fixed architecture of the music. *Pas de Trois* or *Symphony in C* are not hard to follow in this double way, and their limpid musical interest helps to give them their light and friendly objective expression. More complex are the staccato phrasings of *Card Game;* or the interweaving of melodic lines and rhythmic accents in *Concerto Barocco;* or the light play—as of counterpoint—in the airy multiplicity of *Symphonie Concertante.* In this piece the so-called imitations of the music by the dancers, far from being literal, have a grace at once sophisticated and ingenuous. The musical play and the play of dance figures, between them, create bit by bit a subtle strength—the delicate girlish flower-freshness of the piece as a whole. But in relation to the score, the structural quality his ballets all show is their power of sustained rhythm. This power may express itself climactically as in *Serenade* or keep a so-to-speak even level as in *Concertante* or *Card Game.* It makes a difference in applause but not in fascination. Taking as a springboard the force of the extended rhythms—rhythmic sentences or periods—music can construct, Balanchine invents for the dancing as long, as coherent and as strongly pulsing rhythmic figures; whatever quality of the rhythm gives the score its particular sweep of force, he responds to objectively in the sweep of the dancing. And this over-all rhythm is different in each piece.

Not that one doesn't recognize rhythmic devices of accent or of climax that he repeats—such as rhythmic turning of palms inside outside; the Balanchine "pretzels" which I particularly like; or "the gate," an opening in the whirling corps through which in dynamic crescendo other dancers leap forward. He likes bits of canonic imitation; he likes the dramatic path of a star toward a climax to be framed in a neutral counter movement by satellite dancers. And there are some devices I don't care for too, such as the star's solo supported attitude on a musical climax, which (despite its beauty in Petipa) sometimes affects me in the way a too obvious quotation does. But to notice devices in themselves apart from the flow of rhythm and of images they serve to clarify tends to keep one from seeing the meaning of a piece.

Quite another surprise in his ballets if you watch objectively is the variety of shapes of steps, the variety of kinds of movement, that he manages to make classic. "Classic" might be said, of course, to include all kinds of movement that go to make up a three-act classic ballet: academic dancing, mime, character, processions, dancers in repose. And as folk and ballroom steps have been classicized in the past in many ways, so Balanchine has been classicizing movements from our Negro and show steps, as well as from our modern recital dance. In his more recent pieces, the shapes of the steps go from the classroom academicism of *Symphony in C* and the academic virtuosity of *Caracole* through ballroom and more or less traditional character dancing to the untraditional shapes of *Four Temperaments* with its modern style jokes and crushing impact, or of *Orpheus;* or of *Metamorphoses* and its innocent stage show style. What an extraordinary absence of prejudice as to what is proper in classicism these odd works show.

But in what sense can all his variety of movement be classical? It is so because of the way he asks the dancer to move, because of the kind of continuity in motion he calls for. For the continuity in all these pieces is that of which the familiar classroom exercises are the key and remain a touchstone. Classic dancing centers movement in a way of professionally called "placement"; it centers it for the advantage of assurance in spring, balance, and visibility. The dancer learns to move with a natural continuity in impetus, and a natural expression of his full physical strength in the thighs—thighs and waist, where the greatest strength to move outward into space naturally lies.

Balanchine's constant attention to this principle develops in his dancers a gift for coherent, vigorous, positive, unsimpering movement; and a gift too for a powerful, spontaneous rhythmic pulse in action. And a final product of it is the spaciousness which their dancing—Tallchief exemplifies it—comes to have. Clear, sure-footed dancing travels through space easy and large, either in its instantaneous collective surges or in its slow and solitary paths. So space spreads in calm power from the center of the stage and from the moving dancer and gives a sense of human grandeur and of destiny to her action. In his conversation with me he had of course only stressed the small details of motion from which the large effects eventually can grow.

The final consistency that classical style gives to a performance comes from its discipline of behavior. Handsome behavior on stage gives to an entertainment a radiance Broadway dancing knows little of. Balanchine often builds it into the dance—even when he works on Broadway—by so timing the action that if it is done cleanly and accurately the dramatic color becomes one of a spontaneous considerateness among the dancers for one another and of a graceful feeling between the girls and boys. Further subtleties of behavior, subtle alternations of contact and neutral presence, are a part of the expression his pieces have. They seem, as is natural to Americans, unemphatic and usually even like unconscious actions.

But where drama demands more conscious relationships these require a more conscious kind of acting. What Balanchine tries for as classic acting is not an emphatic emotional stress placed on a particular gesture for expression's sake. He tries instead to have expression present as a color throughout a dance or a role, sometimes growing a trifle stronger, sometimes less. It is as if a gesture were made in its simplest form by the whole body as it dances. This is a grand style of acting not at all like the usual Broadway naturalism. In ballet a realistic gesture if it is overstressed or if the timing of it makes the dancer dwell on it "meaningfully," gets clammy; the grand style remains acceptable at any speed or intensity; and Tallchief often exemplifies it at a high intensity—in the writhings of Eurydice for instance, or in the quiet lightness of her last entrance in *Firebird*.

What I have tried to say is that the meaning of a Balanchine piece is to be found in its brilliance and exhilarating variety of classical style. There is nothing hidden or esoteric or even frustrated about the expression of one of his dance ballets. The meaning of it, as of classical dancing generally, is whatever one loves as one watches it without thinking why. It is no use wasting time puzzling over what one doesn't love, one had better keep looking and sharply to see if there isn't something one does, because it goes so fast there is always a lot one misses. Pretty people, pretty clothes, pretty lights, music, pictures, all of it in motion with surprises and feats and all those unbelievable changes of speed and place and figure and weight and a grand continuous rhythm and a tumultuous sweep of imaginary space opening up further and forever, glorious and grand. And because they are all boys and girls doing it, you see these attractive people in all kinds of moments, their unconscious grace of movement, and unconscious grace in their awareness of each other, of themselves, of the music, of the audience, all happening instantaneously and transformed again without a second's reflection. That is what one can find to love. That is the entertainment, different in each piece. All these beauties may be gathered in a sort of story, or you may see them held together only by the music. It is up to you to look and seize them as they flash by in all their brilliant poetry. And many people in the audience do.

Classic ballet is a definite kind of entertainment, based on an ideal conception of expression professionally called "style." It does not try to be the same sort of fun as some other kind of entertainment. It tries to be as wonderful as possible in its own beautiful and voluntarily limited way; just as does any other art. What correct style exists for, what it hopes for, is a singular, unforeseen, an out-of-this-world beauty of expression. In our own local and spontaneous terms this is what Balanchine intends. I wish I had found a less heavy way of treating so joyous and unoppressive a form of entertainment; for a tender irony is close to the heart of it. But I hope I have made clear at least that neither classicism nor "Balanchine style" is, as one sometimes hears people say, merely a mechanical exactness in dancing or in choreography, no personality, no warmth, no human feeling. As for his dancers, this season in particular has shown us that the more correct their style the more their individual personality becomes distinct and attractive on stage.

The strictest fans realize that his work in creating a company is still only half done. But though still unfinished, the result is already extraordinary. London, Paris, and Copenhagen have striking stars, have companies excellent in many ways, larger, wealthier, more secure than we know how to make them. This winter the hardworked little New York City Company has shown itself, both in style and repertory, more sound, more original, more beautiful than any you can see anywhere in the Western world.

In the last five years George Balanchine has come to be recognized as the greatest choreographer of our time abroad as well as here. Such a position has its drawbacks. But for my part, though his prestige may add nothing to my pleasure in his work, I have no quarrel with it. *(1953)*

The Nutcracker

THE NEW YORK CITY BALLET'S *Nutcracker* is a smash hit at the Center. It is Balanchine's *Oklahoma*—a family spectacle, large and leisurely, that lasts two hours and sends people home refreshed and happy. A troubled New York poet sighed, "I could see it every day, it's so deliciously boring." The sentiments are those of family life, Christmas Eve, children growing up among adults, a little girl's odd and beautiful imagination. And the miracle is that these familiar sentiments appear on stage without vulgarization or coyness, with brilliant dancing, light fun, and with the amplitude of a child's wonderful premonitions.

The Nutcracker begins its large-scale entertainment pianissimo. Two children are sleeping in an armchair, left alone. Clara, the little girl, wakes up and goes to the door, peers through the keyhole. She wakes her brother Fritz, who pushes her aside and takes the keyhole for himself. In the next room Father and Mother and the maid are trimming the Christmas tree. Guests arrive, children and parents. For the children there are games and gifts, a box of sugarplums; for the grownups, tea and conversation. Little girls behave, boys grow rowdy. An odd guest comes in late, bringing huge packages. He is an inventor, fascinating and a bit frightening, an artist who makes singular clocks and mechanical toys. He brings three that can actually dance; he also brings a wooden-headed nutcracker for Clara. And he brings his nephew, a boy of Clara's age, but with the glamor of being a stranger and of having almost grownup manners. Clara and he get along very well, too well for Fritz. He grabs his sister's nutcracker and stamps on it. But it isn't badly hurt and Clara puts it to sleep in a new doll bed. There is a traditional party dance for everyone and Clara dances with the clock-maker's nephew. Then the party is over, the guests say goodbye. And the room is empty.

Clara steals back in her nightgown to see her wounded nutcracker. But strange things happen. Huge unlikely mice rustle in and frighten her. The Christmas tree grows and grows enormous. The toy soldiers have become as big as she; so has the Nutcracker, with his sad wooden head. To protect her he leads the soldiers to battle against the mice. But the mice are taller and they win. The monstrous Mouseking appears; the Nutcracker himself rolls on the ground. A brave rabbit pulls the royal tail. The King flings around; Clara throws his shoe and hits the Mouseking on the back. As he whirls again to attack her, the Nutcracker leaps up and runs him through. The fight is finished. The victorious Nutcracker walks through the wall into the moonlit snow. And Clara sleeps on his bed as it glides after him outdoors. The bed wanders about the snow-laden forest, gliding to the music, with Clara asleep on it all alone.

Among the moonbright firs the Nutcracker turns into a Prince. He wakes Clara and gives her a crown. They go deeper into the woods. Snowflakes begin to drift—like snowflakes you watch through a windowpane. First one or two dart past, then more come, they skim and scatter, they spin and thicken and vanish, they gather and rush and they rest. Clara and the Prince walk through them to start their night-time journey as the voices of the boys' choir rise once. The first act is over.

The second act is in the Sugar Plum Fairy's gold palace on a pink underground lake. Sailing up in a walnut shell, the Prince and Clara dock at the pier. The Fairy asks the Prince where they are from. "We come from way over there. This is what happened. I was sleeping. The mice attacked. I fought them. I fought the Mouseking. And Clara threw her shoe and saved me. I killed the Mouse-

84

king. That is what happened." The Fairy answers, "You have a brave heart." She tells some angels who are there to bring a throne and something to eat. As they eat, wonderful sweets run out and dance for them. Hot chocolate, bold and pleasant, from Spain; coffee from Arabia, a strong, peculiar, funny flavor; tea, spry and Chinese. There is marzipan, very sweet, crisp to nibble; candy canes with a sharp peppermint bite; a kind of teacosy giantess who keeps under her skirts small precise candies. And there is a big Christmas cake of many layers, with roses on the icing and a transparent silvery sugar dewdrop—so much cake it might be a garden with tunnels. The Fairy then dances with her Cavalier—so light, gliding and quick, so respectful to each other, so easy in their whispering surprises, soft jumps and airy twists. They are like adults at their very best; and wonderfully well-behaved. Everybody dances for a moment more, and then Clara and her Prince say goodbye; we see them a last time in their walnut-shell ship, alone on a wide rippling blue sea, sailing to still other adventures. And that is the end.

The Nutcracker tells the story of a party at home and then of a party at the Fairy's house. The agitations of Christmas Eve lead to a small nightmare, a nostalgic journey, a glorious arrival. At the Fairy's there is everything that is best at home, radiantly clear. But then one leaves; ahead is another journey, still further.

These are the meanings I see as I watch, but the ballet doesn't press them. Nothing is insisted upon. The dances of sweets are straight dances, if you don't want to think of so much candy. But a small boy near me said, "Isn't there any more food or things to drink?" The pantomime too makes its narrative points straight and clear; but it doesn't force them on you. As little Clara was walking grandly with her prince in the snow, a mother ahead of me whispered to another, "Poor thing, look, she's lost a shoe." Her seven-year-old daughter spoke up: "She's lost it; because she threw it at the Mouseking." It was a dramatic point, and she had seen it, and understood it.

The Nutcracker is a fantasy ballet for children, like a toy that a grownup makes with thoughtful care. Grownups watching can slip back into a world they have left. The buried longings of it are there glittering still, but so charmingly, so lightly offered one doesn't have to notice. It is enough to notice the amusing family bits in the party scene, the fun of the transformations, the jokes in the dream, the sweet brilliance of the dancing, the pervasive grace of the music. And there is the pleasure of seeing children on stage who are not made to look saccharine or hysterical, who do what they do naturally and straight.

Of course, there are many more special pleasures. One of them is the novelty of watching so much pantomime; the more you watch, the odder becomes the difference it makes in a classic ballet, and the more interesting. *The Nutcracker* has several kinds of pantomime. There is that of classic gesticulation—the sequence of gestures by which the Nutcracker Prince tells his story to the Fairy. Each has a specific meaning so old nobody invented it. The gesture of revolving the hands one about the other chest-high (as in a muff) means: "This is what happened." It comes from antiquity, and is related to the silent gesture of "Keep on talking, give out with some more" used in radio booths. "Far from here," "sleep," "mouse," "king," "brave heart" are all gestures you can guess.

Stylized pantomime is quite another thing. It invents a dancey movement that intentionally half-resembles or suggests something else. Light touches of it are in the amusing mouse-and-soldier sequences set by Jerome Robbins. Still a third kind of pantomime is in the movement of the people at the family party. Their actions are not stylized at all, not part dancing, part mimicry; they are the plain normal movements everybody employs in daily life. But the pacing of them, the musical stress of the movement, and their relation to other actions add up to a little drama that is individual; they seem to tell it unintentionally.

Such an action is the deadpan shove—deliberately walked up to and away from—that Fritz gives the clockmaker's nephew; also the nephew's watching him walk away, watching steadily. Later, when the party breaks up, you can see two pairs of children who want to stay together, who are parted by their parents in two quite different tempos. The party scene has many details less prominent, which you discover only gradually. But they are all relevant to the story, they tell you the kind of family, the kind of social pressure in which Clara is growing up. The leisurely oppressive pacing of the party is in one sense the token of a responsible ruling class; but in another it creates the large time in which childhood events occur, the amplitude out of which fantasy takes shape. The party unfolds a story of mutual behavior, good manners and bad, those of children, of parents, of grandparents, guests and hosts, of a family servant, an eccentric artist. All these manners sharpen one's eye for the so-to-speak heavenly manners of the Fairy's palace, the graceful behavior of classic dancing. And *The Nutcracker* is also the story of a child's presentiment of handsome conduct, of civilized society; it is no foolish subject, and it gives the ballet its secret radiance.

So the pantomime becomes the dramatic reason why the grand pas de deux appears as a climax of fullfillment. It tops the shining sweep and rush of the Waltz of the Flowers that precedes it by the unexpected intimacy of its grandeur and glitter. The phrases are brief and intertwining; the star is free, but lightly she stays near her partner and swiftly turns as if diving each time in a different way into his supporting hands; leaps and lifts hover at half height; the adagio extensions move between or across the supporting figuration. The Cavalier's movements are clear, grand and supple. And in the Fairy's Variation (her solo) the brilliancy in intimate effects is delicious. The steps play across the pianissimo music in counter-rhythms, counter-phrases inventing feats of instant top-speed and instant rest, miraculously easy, so light do they dart from the spring of the music; ending (one of the times I saw it) in the featheriest of dazzles. The variation suits Maria Tallchief's soft powerful speed to perfection, and she dances it ravishingly. It is the triumph of her career. In the middle of the pas de deux, my four-year-old friend slipped an arm around his father's neck and whispered, "Are the people real?"

George Balanchine is the choreographer of this *Nutcracker*. The libretto is the old one, the steps and pantomime are new, without looking specifically like Balanchine. That much any balletgoer can see; but fans who like to watch more closely will find the original Balanchine contribution which does not strike one at first sight. For the music's sake, he accepted the old spectacle-ballet action—an action that the score wonderfully plans for and paces. He opened a few dance cuts in the score. In the pantomime, he wove several new theatrical details, all of them derived from the E.T.A. Hoffmann story that the libretto is based on (e.g. the keyhole episode, the role of a Nephew, the wandering bed). For the apotheosis, originally "A Hive of Bees" (representing civilization), he substituted a simpler image, but one also derived from the German story.

In setting the pantomime, Balanchine did not force the German 1820 flavor. He made an old-fashioned Christmas, but kept to actions and manners that his company, including the children, could do naturally. In the group dances he tended to steps and figures of Ivanov's time, one might say to steps that Tschaikovsky had seen. Balanchine's dancers liked to use their fine speed and sharpness, their rhythmic flexibility and musical ear; so he gave them the old steps with swifter displacements, in rhythms that are fresh, or in new virtuoso combinations. The dancers everywhere in the piece have an easy spontaneity in an old-fashioned look, a spontaneity which—if you stop to think of it—is astonishing in a long show whose theatre-concept is unfamiliar to us all.

The spontaneity of the new *Nutcracker* is the mark of its originality. It is central to it. Fanciful ornaments, curious details, the usual signs of originality disappear; their absence gives the piece a kind of classic impersonality. Balanchine liked two numbers from Ivanov's second act, knew them accurately, and quoted them unchanged. But there is so little Balanchinism in his own numbers that these quotations pass without a break in style; I took them for his inventions. They are the Prince's mime scene and the Hoop Dance. (Balanchine danced the steps of it thirty years after Ivanov made them; now thirty years later Robert Barnett dances them, and brilliantly too.)

Balanchine uses the modern effect of strikingly contrasted movements in constant succession only in the Marzipan dance and the pas de deux (where, however, they are separated by flashes of rest, and give a sense of close-up). The long Snowflakes Waltz looks as if it used only a dozen elementary steps, but it is one of Balanchine's most magical inventions. The second act dances make a sustained burst or a repeated surge; the power of each grows from only two or three movement motifs. The drama of each is in its striking rhythmic identity. The dances reflect gaiety or joyousness intimately or at a little distance, light and mild or bright and bold. The other sentiments of the score are expressed by the story situation, the timing of scenic effects, by the contrast of child and adult, or pantomime and dancing. In a nostalgic setting the dances are positive and sanguine.

But there is a powerful dramatic expressiveness in the large opposition between the so-to-speak forest-thick pantomime that fills the first act and leads only to a small clearing where snowflakes dance; and the spaciousness of the second act, with its clear dances that appear and disappear as free as shapes in the sky. The choreographic originality of the second act is not (where I had expected to find it) in decorative fancy. It is in the suddenness with which a dance shape, the shape of a dance, appears and vanishes. Each dance is instantly specific, it keeps its solidity as it rushes through the air, and is instantly gone. It has the grandeur of being complete, of asking nothing, of creating around its brief form a sense of airy stillness, of spacious calm. It seems impossible that so complete an image can be produced so suddenly, prolonged at will, and be so suddenly withdrawn. The effect is magical and powerful. And as I was watching it, wondering, my four-year-old friend seemed to feel a similar wonder. Looking at the same dancers I was, he asked his father very seriously, "How do they get out?" (*1954*)

Opus 34

Opus 34, despite its press, is powerful theatre, brilliantly produced and performed. Once more Balanchine has made a striking ballet different from any in the repertory, different from any anywhere. It is a powerful and it is a paradoxical ballet. It looks like modern dance, but it is entirely classical; it shows no sweeping discharge of physical energy, but it generates as much force as if it did; it is frightening in its pantomime, but the effects seem ludicrous. The fact is it combines the ludicrous and the tragic in a magnificent tragic glee. It is the same glee that is so intolerably enormous in *King Lear.* Children like it, but adults shudder. They wish *Opus* were meaningless, or even a joke at their expense; it isn't, its theatre power is exact at every point.

Opus 34 is a piece in two parts not at all similar at first sight, but both set to the same darkly glistening and oppressive Schoenberg score. The first part is straight dancing in a peculiar range; the second is a fairy tale told in pantomime. The audience watches the first part absorbed and impressed; it watches the second fascinated, frightened and giggling. Then the curtain comes down and there is a curious vacuum, the blank state of not knowing what hit you. One tries to get one's bearings; one can't seem to bring all one has seen in focus.

What has happened on stage has been peculiar. When the curtain goes up, thirteen dancers face you, dressed alike in plaster white, each standing alone. They quiver a knee and stop; they lunge forward and stop; they dangle their hands; crouching, they throw a hand wide, slip it between the legs, grab a knee and stop; they turn up their faces to you and stop; they stand erect again. They are not tense, but very alert. The gestures are swift and clear, done without any sentiment; they look a little comical— yet somehow like those of terror. Stops and movements build into phrases, complex classic figurations, sections. The dance develops a powerful rhythm. The dancers touch themselves, each other, sharply and without feeling and go on; groups start and stop in a narrow compass, they scarcely leave the ground, they stretch their strength oddly downward. By flashes the stops give a sudden super-visibility like a film close-up. It looks funny and dreadful, yet the movements are so elegantly done, the rhythm so strong, the variety so surprising, one has a sense of great dynamism. It is as if people were under an oppressive force, meeting it keenly and swiftly, using to the utmost the space left them. But the dancers come to a repeat; as if there were no issue from the trap. Then, very slow, they mysteriously merge into a close clump of people, and together they meet extinction candidly and without complaint. It is an image of strange tenderness.

At once the pantomime begins. A brother and sister stand with their backs to us at the footlights, facing the darkness upstage. They go forward into it, a witch beckons them aside. As they turn toward her, swooping creatures tear them apart, kidnap them, they disappear. Out of the dark comes a fat squad of nurses, two operating tables, a surgeon. An operation is performed. Bandages, bandages, bandages. Dumped off the tables are the brother and sister, horribly altered, dreadfully fascinating to see. They quiver fantastically, grovel in anguish, they reach for and find each other blindly, ludicrously. A slithery heap of something viscous appears, like a wave. The girl steps into it for relief, it slowly mounts, swallows her. A second wave absorbs the boy. In the heaving waves, the victims wriggle, they try to reach each other, they meet wallowing topsyturvy, are separated. The brother is scooped wondrously upward, gone forever. The girl strands ashore and rises. She finds a frightening memento of him, she hoods herself in it, hooded she paces forward to the footlights. She turns, finds herself where the two of them were once together, facing the enormous dark that bears down on her from everywhere. Alone she slowly paces into it. Blinding lights hit her head-on, set fire to her, and erect she paces on into them. Curtain.

The pantomime is clearly a fairy tale—the dark wood, the witches, the cruel wizard, the bewitched waves and lights. The grisly events are vivid but not naturalistic. They appear and disappear in an unnatural black void. And like a fairy tale, as we accept the truth of the story, we find ourselves back safe in a familiar domestic lamplit room, back in the familiar theatre.

What I have described is what anyone sees who watches the stage. The action is lucidly shown and straightforward. The piece has no surrealist ambiguity; there is no mystification, no siding with the monster, no confusion or violation of personality. Still less is it a hoax, a "period" spoof. Both parts move steadily to an heroic ending, a moment of quiet for an image of final courage. Both show people meeting an overwhelming inhuman force with courage, without complaint. The destiny, savage and ludicrous, that they meet seems to be as a friend said, "the end of everything"; but that is merely what none of us escapes.

The tragic horror of *Opus* is not a gloomy fancy the choreographer wants to make a personal point about. It is given by the score. You hear it insistently evoked by the music. And the program notes tell you the story Schoenberg had in mind. It is contained in the titles of the sections of his score: "Threat. Danger. Fear. Catastrophe." The choreographer has dramatized this four word libretto as convincingly as he could and in two parallel ways. He has projected the rising horror it calls for through striking images of savage irony and human heroism. The glee and the tenderness of these make the unescapable catastrophe not a pessimistic defeat, no, they make it lift tragically in the midst of horror. And the dramatic impact it achieves is terrifyingly real.

As for the dramatic device of mingling the ludicrous and the tragic, that has long been legitimate, and even a glory of theatre. Balanchine has used it before: in *Prodigal Son* for instance, and in *Night Shadow;* used it without a story reference in *Four Temperaments.* And he has long hoped to make a *Don Quixote.* He has certainly used a great many other and gentler devices when they were called for. The particular effect of this one is double: first it shocks one's stuffiness, then it delights one's sense of truth.

People shocked and puzzled by *Opus 34* have taken to the comfortable cliché that its devices and ideas are "the old-fashioned ones of the German twenties." This is nonsense for anyone who knows those twenties. Their characteristic was the protest, the resentful whine, the morbid self-dramatization. The ideas of *Opus* are consistently and clearly the opposite ones. It looks destiny in the face; it accepts catastrophe as a test of courage.

But what makes the ideas in the ballet appear with such expressive power is the way the stage action at every moment seems to fulfill the intense dramatic potency of the music. When the ballet is over you are convinced that you "understood" the score, you have felt its grandeur and theatre. The music is Schoenberg's *Opus 34*—Movie Music. Balanchine has set it twice: the first time he makes you see the forces of its tight logical form, the second the wide stream of its expressive rhetoric. In the first part of the ballet you watch the compressed phrases, the reversals, the intricate developments; wonderful how the dance reveals the hidden majesty of rhythm, reveals the intense spring of action left in the interlocking structure. In the second part, the music floods out like a soundtrack, weird as a spell of science fiction, inexorable in the timing of its dreadful stream. The sounds of it, the whirrs, squeals, reverberations, hums and thuds, have frozen the first time on strictly limited dance movements, as if crystal by crystal their logic immured the dancers; then the second time, the same sounds have liquidly lifted up a few solid gobs of nightmare, like the whisper of ghosts in a river that foretell what has happened already. Even if you don't look for the consistent narrative meaning *Opus* has, but follow it merely moment by moment as movements set to a particular score, the ballet makes its grand effect. That it offers two stage versions of the same very difficult music, each musically right and dramatically right, is a fantastic feat of choreographic virtuosity; but the expressive power, not the virtuosity, is what you feel as you watch.

In the pantomime the episodes become frightening because their exact timing projects them so forcefully. Note for instance the scarey effect of the waits between when nothing at all happens. The gestures themselves are not those psychological pantomime, nor are they stylized; they are the large simple factual actions that classic ballet has preserved from earlier theatre. Note how real the effect is when the surgeon backs away from the tables, turns once, and then backs further away into the wings; or when legs wiggle without bodies out of the clasp of the waves; or the scare you feel when the sister picks up the piece of silk, though there is nothing special about the prop, and only a change of pace in her movement. The simple costumes and props by Esteban Francés, the complex lighting by Jean Rosenthal are to be sure marvels of theatrical imagination, so beautifully they suit every shade of the action.

The tense consistency of the pantomime's dramatic atmosphere might have been shattered at the point where the two dancers make a few startling dance movements; it isn't broken because these steps are in key with pantomime, they have the specific pantomime quality of movement. Similarly in the dance part of *Opus* the gestures derived from pantomime or modern dance do not jar with classic steps because they have been purposely given the specific quality of classic movement. They are made from a classic center, in classic balance, and in the classic rhythm of musical meter. They do not have a narrative continuity, but become—like classic steps—momentary shapes whose only urgency is that of musical rhythm and dance action. Such a shape will look oppressive not because the dancer dances it oppressedly, but because of its

94

own visual and rhythmic nature. Whatever the look of the shape, a classic dancer can dance it clearly and securely; she keeps her swiftness, her elegance, her ease of bearing. And so the ballet allows for a steady confident brilliance in performance, and whatever it says, is said nobly.

Brilliant the company looks as it performs, both girls and boys. No other company could duplicate the quickness of ear of these dancers; that they learned the piece in two weeks is an achievement unique in ballet history. Happily, the score is also played very handsomely and it is because the management provided for enough orchestra rehearsal—another admirable feat.

Opus 34 is a great ballet, and fans—even if they get angry—shouldn't miss it. It is in every way an exception among ballets, but it is legitimately classic wherever you test it. Such an exception is an honor to the company. It is worth a fight. It affirms the company's stand as the most adventurous anywhere, and it offers an adventure to the public.

My one objection is to the light that (if you sit in the orchestra center) shines in your eyes at the very end of the piece. It shines for nine seconds; the effect of the first four I like very much and wouldn't miss; during the last five seconds nothing more happens on stage, and I close my eyes and listen to the last grandiose whirrs of the music. If the light hurts your eyes too, you can try this solution. But just now a fan who has come into the room tells me he likes the whole nine seconds very much. *(1954)*

Western Symphony and *Ivesiana*

THE TWO NEW PIECES presented by the New York City Ballet during its fall season—*Western Symphony* and *Ivesiana,* both by George Balanchine—are as far apart as possible from one another in the kind of theatre appeal they offer. *Western* is likeable and lively, with good-natured jokes and fireworks, and it develops a dance momentum that for stamina, speed and climax is irresistible. *Ivesiana* develops no speed of momentum at all, no beat; it is carried onward as if way below the surface by a force more like that of a tide, and the sharp and quickly shifting rhythms that appear have no firm ground to hold against an uncanny, supernatural drift. *Ivesiana* is a somber suite, not of dances, but of dense and curious theatre images. Its expression is as subjective as that of *Western* is objective. But both ballets take as their subject matter familiar aspects of American life. And both are set to scores by native composers.

Ivesiana is set to six orchestral pieces by Charles Ives. They represent themselves as impressionist music, and the six titles specify what each is about. The material is noises of nature and scraps of everyday music treated as of equal musical value. The stream and pulse of the sonority, the extraordinary harmony, the eddies of conflicting rhythms sound unlike European music and fantastically apt to their local subject matter. The dimensions are compressed, rather than intimate. The wonder of the score lies in the nobility of expression in relation to its subject matter that it achieves. It does so with the utmost succinctness but with no meagerness—quite on the contrary, with a kind of eerie grandeur as true and sure as that of an Emily Dickinson lyric.

This queerly magnificent music is not in our regular concert repertory, and it is worth going to the ballet just to hear it. Watching the ballet, however, one hears it as if with a heightened distinctness, hears its characteristic nuances and its grand expressive coherence as the theatre images on stage shockingly confront one.

Such a theatre image is the action on stage to the music entitled "The Unanswered Question." Out of the darkness a beautiful young girl in white appears aloft, carried by a team of four men, and a shadowy fifth precedes the cluster, turning, crawling, reaching toward her. Carefully, as in a ritual or a circus act, the girl is lowered and lifted, revolved in fantastic and horrifying fashions. In all the shapes her body takes, she is never any less beautiful or less placid. At moments her hair brushes the questioner's face. There is no awareness of his question or of his humiliation on anyone's part but his own. And the cortege moves forward again and disappears—like a great ponderous knot floating about in a shoreless obscurity. This scene, with its casual ghastly incident when the girl falls backward headfirst into space, is the central one of the ballet.

The ballet begins with "Central Park in the Dark." A close wedge of girls appears way upstage in the dark and oozes forward spreading, covering the stage, kneeling, swaying. A girl runs in searching among them, a boy enters, they meet, and the stage looks like an agitated woods that surges around them—oddly bushy like the Park itself—as they struggle together, lose and catch one another in the monstrous dark. She drops; instantly with a frantic gesture he rushes off. Slowly the woods shrinks to the far away clump it first was; much more slowly the girl feels her way with her hands across the deserted forestage. Next comes "Hallowe'en." It is a rushing whirl and whirr, a flurry as brittle and spooky as that of leaves at the end of New England October; and leaves too, or with the leaves, a boy and girl whirl and leap forward and away together and are struck down.

After the hymn-like "Unanswered Question" comes a noisy city scene, "Over the Pavements." Five boys and a girl jump, crawl, inter-twine, innocently brutal, while several bands glare at once—a sightless massive energy like that of city streets—then the girl drops her head on a boy's shoulder, he runs off after the others, she skips unpreoccupied in another direction. Next, to a jazz that is small, sour, meticulously insane comes "At the Inn." It is the elegant summer "inn" of New England, and a young couple side by side—with an intoxicated abandon and a miraculous rhythmic edge—invent a dizzy fluctuation of tango, maxixe, charleston and mambo steps, wander into a horrid combination and out of it, and approach a rough climax, but stop, shake hands, leave each other. After that comes a brief concluding section called "In the Night," in which, in a phosphorescent dark light never seen before, a great number of erect figures move on their knees very slowly onward in unconnected directions, and over the nocturnal murmur of the orchestra, as if across invisible meadows, float the smallest and purest notes of bells. Listening for them, it is as if the stage, as if the whole company, had sunk half out of sight into another and slower world.

It all happens in twenty minutes, and it makes a great deal to see as it piles up. Painful situations, strokes of wit, local allusions, kinds of movement, shifts of impulse, intertwined rhythms, hallucinating contradictions. There is nothing comfortable to rest on. Details are as cozy as gravel. Events happen unexpectedly quick or distressingly slow, very odd or very obvious. The point of view contracts and expands: at one moment a part of a body grows over-visible, at another the sides of the stage overempty. The scale telescopes and so does the rhetoric: suddenness of expositions, brevity of climaxes, conclusions that open instead of shutting down. One can find it very irritating.

But the piece in its appalling shifts is steadily expressive. The theatricality is sanguine and decisive. It

98

doesn't waste a note or a motion. There is no vagueness for eye. *Ivesiana* juxtaposes anguish with innocent fact. It compresses a conflict and drops it into a reach of eternity. The tone is keen and positive. The ballet as one listens and watches moves very rapidly through an enormous range of fancy without a disproportion or a discontinuity. The speed kind of turns your stomach, but no harm.

There are many jokes at lightning speed. For instance, the innocence with which the boy and girl separate at the end of "Pavements" comes as a quick joke. But it makes the characters much more actual. The unexpected handshake in "At the Inn" looks like a gag. But the way it fits the musical conclusion that immediately follows, gives it a second expression, a scary realness. At the climax of "Central Park," when the boy tosses and grabs the drooping girl in an awkward position, the flash is comic; but the shock of the humor is that it suits the tragic situation so realistically. In "The Unanswered Question" the views of the revolving girl which are ludicrous only make her body the more personal and the poignancy of heartbreak the weirder, the more intimate. Jokes such as these show you a concise flash of fact at the moment you expect a flow of sentiment. They take the place of a tragic pathos, which would need a great deal more time and repetition to develop. Such queer fun is typical of New England. Both Ives and Balanchine theatricalize in it a large-scale tragic glee.

And so for the general audience, the meaning of the piece is not elusive. The meaning is the same in the music and on stage. It offers a view of our local life, not from the point of view whether it is good or bad, whether it is pleasant or unpleasant, but seen as a vivid fact wide open to tragedy. The view is Ives'. Balanchine has inserted no different meaning of his own. He has taken that of the score, its condensed amplitude, the characteristic structural devices, the particular evocations of feeling, and has found steps, qualities of movement, situations, theatre effects that correspond.

For the more special dance fan, Balanchine has found fresh developments, fresh values in familiar steps and in figurations he himself has already used. The startling weights, reversals, sequences in multiple rhythm flow with a miraculous easy vigor. To experienced classicists "Hallowe'en" and "Over the Pavements" will be a delight; a pity they were blurred on opening night by an unsteadiness in the pit. Classicists will find that the surprises (of action as of sound) are created by an imaginative tension of classic syntax. On stage the surprises develop by a tightening of the gesture value of classic elements. The tenseness of continuity gives to such a surprise the appearance of a normal event—the look not of a stop but of a flowering. I want to see it all again. "It's a dictionary of movement," a painter exclaimed after the opening; and a teenager kept repeating "It's fantastic movement, that's what he does, it's fantastic movement." Intermission talk had a look of concentration I remember seeing last at the premiere of *Deaths and Entrances*. The gallery had booed and cheered the ballet loudly. And one young man up there, just as the boy on stage rushed off at the climax of the first section, had cried out as if at pistol point, "Svengali!"

Ivesiana for a critic is as remarkable a novelty as *Four Temperaments* was. At first sight it is more phenomenal, less appealing. The older piece fuses weighty dance contrasts in the driving sweep of a strong beat; the newer one, with nearly no beat, condenses contrasting elements of gesture into solid theatre images and floats their weight fantastically on a sustained acuity of harmony. In ballet theory this cannot be done successfully. But neither could the other. Ballets such as both of these are an active part of intellectual life in the United States; they are, it seems to me, among its triumphs. In any case, they are a fight. That is why the spirit, the vitality of the New York City company depend on dancing them. The way the company undertakes the incredible difficulties of *Ivesiana*—no other company in the world would be equal to them—shows it enjoys the battle. It danced *Four Temperaments* several years before it won that one. *Ivesiana* is still a draw.

The ballet is wonderfully lit by Jean Rosenthal. It is

performed in practice clothes as an economy: the score was so difficult to play that extra orchestra rehearsals were expensive. I wish there were costumes, but the money could not have been spent better. And the New York City Ballet orchestra won a musical distinction our symphony orchestras can envy.

The other new ballet of the season, *Western Symphony,* was also danced in practice clothes. Costumes had been designed and are promised next season. I heard by chance what they were like: cowboy clothes for the boys, and for the girls dance-hall dresses of the Golden Eighties. There is a subtle and pervasive something in the dances of *Western,* a situation between the girls and boys, that these costumes would make charming and clear. Without them, one may unconsciously question what sort of American girls these dancing partners are, and why the score by Hershy Kay so insistently evokes a honky tonk or dance hall glamor.

Actually no one questions anything, the piece is so much fun to watch. Clear in any case is the healthy, normal Western American quality of movement it has. And Walter Terry in a brilliant first night review in the *Herald Tribune* stated at once the historic aspect of the ballet: that the Americanness of the boys and girls is expressed in terms of strictly classic steps. He pointed out that the expression they have does not come from "Westernizing" a familiar step. The step is left intact but the sequence gives it a novel speed, metric accent and visual emphasis which create an over-all Western look—a Western strength in physical impulse and rhythm, in playfulness or sentiment. He showed how different this procedure is from that used in other Western ballets—*Rodeo* or *Billy the Kid*—and other Americana. It is like the difference of writing in dialect or in straight English, one might say. Mr Terry's point will become more and more interesting and will be long remembered.

In *Western*—the action is like a big dance party, nothing but dancing—the dancers do everything possible with a four bar and an eight bar phrase. In the first section they fill it neatly full; in the third, they leap over the bar marks in a long rolling motion like an easy canter; in the fourth—I get so excited by the syncopation I can't tell you what they did, but it was wonderful. The fourth section is all climax and goes on and on getting more so—at least it does if the orchestra keeps to tempo. I liked especially the manly mixture of false dreams and true in the sentimental second part—a part that is like a cowboy's vision of a pure ballerina. At a rehearsal I saw Balanchine miming this cowboy; it was so real, one would have thought he had never been anything else.

Something about the dancing gives an illusion of the clear desert air. "It clears your eyes," a young poet remarked to me as we came out after the performance. The company never looked so easy and fresh, though the piece isn't easy at all to dance. Tanaquil LeClercq and Jacques d'Amboise were the special heroes of the first night. But Patricia Wilde and Herbert Bliss had danced beautifully, and Janet Reed and Nicholas Magallanes couldn't have been more touching and true in their delicate comedy. Miss LeClercq and Miss Reed were brilliant too—quite differently brilliant—at the opening of *Ivesiana,* together that time with Allegra Kent, Todd Bolender and Francisco Moncion.

The two ballets, one sociable, the other singular, are Balanchine's first direct treatment of American subject matter. He seems to know all about it, and have a great deal more to show us. *(1954)*

Roma

Roma, Balanchine's new ballet, is delightfully buoyant
and firmly formal. The feeling of buoyancy it has is like a
sense of many fountains splashing and purling deep in the
quiet of a Baroque garden. The formality of it is that of
classic ballet—of the strictest French Petipa tradition. As
one watches it, hearing the clear music, what one feels in
the lightness is the graceful intimate impulse of the dancing. The grace of it seems modest as it takes place; but
the sense of happiness it gives remains fresh in one's
memory in a quite magical way.

Balanchine has set *Roma* to three movements of Bizet's
Roma Suite—an extended pas de deux to the adagio, and
lively dances for a large cast to the two faster movements
that frame the slow one. The classicism is as correct as
that of *Symphony in C,* but the spaces of *Roma* are more
enclosed, more sheltered, more unspectacular. Within its
closer world, the dancing of the new ballet skims and
sparkles, it eddies and rushes. The fun, light-footed and
happy natured, is a crisscross of accent between the boys
and girls, a mutual grace of behavior. And even the
"folk-dance" romp at the end, with its elegant fireworks
of leaps, flutter of steps and rustle of tarantella tambour-
ines, creates the unpresuming dazzle of a sophisticated
friendliness.

One can see *Roma,* too, as Italian in character. The
dancers do not pretend to be Italians, and very likely they
would look foolish if they did. They dance as American

dancers do with a clear accuracy. But the figurations give them a particular lightness and quickness. It has in the very dance impulse of it a voluble vivacity, an easy politeness, a physical delicacy of contact. Not mimically, but in the quality of its impulse, it recalls the quick and sophisticated sociability of Italians.

From this point of view the three movements of *Roma* recall Italian qualities of gesture: the manners of young people promenading; a graceful sincerity in courtship; the candor, the crowded happy suddenness of a Neapolitan holiday. From this point of view *Roma* is a traveler's valentine to Italy, a happy and tender recollection of her daily life.

Her daily life, as a foreigner knows it passing through the streets. It was the same domestic charm of Italian streets that young Bizet wrote about in his *Roma Suite* a century ago. His score is intimate and lucid, spritely in rhythm and charmingly orchestrated. Very much the formal young Frenchman amused by Roman sensuousness. He loves the sweet weather, the light bubblings of speech, the rapid guitar tunes; he loves the cordiality around him. As for pomp and grandeurs, he isn't so interested—he enjoys the personal grace of everyday people. That is what his valentine is about, and very handsome it is.

The painter Berman, with Bizet and Balanchine the third of the travelers who have made *Roma,* has designed the set and costumes. The girls wear bright and softcut bodices, full-billowing skirts and underskirts from which the knee peeps demurely or boldly advances. The young men—a trifle military—have sleeves and short trousers of crushed-fruit colors with white tights up to mid-thigh (like boots). The white massive legs look particularly quick-footed. During the tarantella the caps everyone wears give the figures an extra succinctness. The costumes—period of Bizet in their allusions—are in the formal tradition of classic ballet dress. Within that tradition—in which Berman is a master—they recall how flavorsome a feeling for the figure Italian clothes naturally have.

The set—like a lofty ruin and like a slum square—evokes a Roman massiveness, russet golden and many-storied against a heavy green sky. An iron railing, the railing one finds on a height in ruins and slums, opens at the back on a vastness of air. One feels the unseen view lying beyond and is drawn to it. Particularly during the pas de deux, which is magically lit, the scene is noble in its sentiment. For the concluding tarantella, a wreath of bulbs lights up story over story, like at nocturnal illuminations of local southern saints. Laundry appears, too, strung up high from wall to wall—very natural looking—and gives the neighborhood a Neapolitan friendliness. The scene is one of Berman's finest. It has an intense Italian presence of the open air that accords with the sociable dances, and an ancient melancholy that contrasts with their liveliness.

Roma was not too much of a success at its opening. Its modesty turned out to be an extremely avant-garde effect. People went to see what new twist Balanchine had dreamed up and when they were shown the innocent art of dancing they were too bewildered to recognize it. But a bright-eyed lady beside me for her part was delighted. "So wonderfully buoyant," she said. "That's just what I wanted to see. No, I don't want to look at any more ballets, I want to go home and remember this one." She remarked too that though she had always enjoyed the manliness of Eglevsky's dancing, this time she enjoyed it much more—a more gentle considerateness for his partner gave it a grace of expression it often had lacked. She was delighted with Tanaquil LeClercq and spoke of the beautiful turns of her head—"like those of longnecked Italian Madonnas"—as improbable as the painted ones and as delicious. "She has become a classic ballerina," she said, and spoke of her beautiful feet. I was delighted that my friend, who had not been to the ballet for some time, had so readily seen the new fantastic beauty of motion LeClercq has shown a number of times this winter, and which has struck me as a major dance event of it. She has become a marvel.

The long adagio pas de deux for LeClercq and Eglevsky is a most unusual one. It has an equable current and a stillness that do not allow the dancers the relief of a big climax. One can feel the attention of the audience, but also how new the quiet is to them. On stage one notices an astonishing invention—a supported arabesque that slides over the two dancers' linked hands, and as it rests there and the ballerina is turned on point, it changes to a renversé extended in first, and the girl looks miraculously cradled as she is slowly spun. In the classic formality of the dancing one may sense the current of a more and more absorbed conversation—from a gentle pleasure in acquaintance, in tentative contact, to a playful ease in intimacy, and then to a sweetly earnest profession of faith. After that there is a mysterious courtesy between the two young people that spins to rest in a still pose swooping like a swallow's flight at dusk. Then the girl withdraws a little, smiling, and returns instinctively to a final pose of trust. It seemed to me a touchingly honorable and a very Italian and happy courtship. The lovers were interrupted by the explosive rush downstage—with their heads down —of two threesomes of tarantella dancers, a wild dash like that of Naples' children.

The charm of the pas de deux is a spontaneous delicacy of feeling between two young people alone. The novelty of it is a modesty in the accentuation of heroic dance feats. The quiet climaxes of the music give the dance its intimate stress. Beautiful for instance is that on a moment when the dancers pause separated upstage, each against the sky. Or that on a pose twice repeated—an arabesque grandly supported from the front (as if grandly sheltered), an arabesque felt rather than seen. The two dancers dissolve the pose before the musical climax is quite over, and the particular emphasis of it is like a poignant cadence of verse. To paraphrase such images in story terms does not convey the spontaneous pleasure of them or the transparency.

The way the pas de deux is set to the score gives the drama its sincerity of character. One responds to the inner impulse of the music as one sees that of the dance spring from a particular note or more amply lift from a phrase or a crescendo. Before and after the adagio, the faster dancing suits its steps to the measure, the phrase to the phrase. The dancers dance on the beat, as people naturally do; but being dancers they hardly touch the floor, or play with the beat several ways at once in counteraccents and syncopations.

The strictness of classicism in *Roma* and the strictness of the musical setting of the steps shows the nuance of dance impulse more clearly. Dancers classically trained find in classicism a theatrical spontaneity and transparency. The expression of their dance can look sincere. And their personal quality in classicism—unconsciously transparent—can become a view of what the stage character represented is like "really". So for instance LeClercq's delicacy of timing can give her characters a grace in courtesy, a quick awareness, that makes them exceptionally interesting. Fonteyn—a quite different dancer—has a similar courtesy.

It gives a wrong view of *Roma* to saddle its lightness with ideas. Interesting ones are present in it if one chooses to recognize them. One can enjoy so happy a grace and not notice the sophistication it also shows, or the theatre modesty. *Roma* is brilliantly danced by the company, which deserves every praise, or very nearly; particularly by Eglevsky, who at the last performance reached a new peak in his career. I hope the piece stays with us awhile. *(1955)*

Three Sides of *Agon*

Agon, a ballet composed by Igor Stravinsky in his personal twelve-tone style, choreographed by George Balanchine, and danced by the New York City Ballet, was given an enormous ovation last winter by the opening night audience. The balcony stood up shouting and whistling when the choreographer took his bow. Downstairs, people came out into the lobby, their eyes bright as if the piece had been champagne. Marcel Duchamp, the painter, said he felt the way he had after the opening of *Le Sacre.* At later performances, *Agon* continued to be vehemently applauded. Some people found the ballet set their teeth on edge. The dancers show nothing but coolness and brilliantly high spirits.

Agon is a suite of dances. The score lasts twenty minutes, and never becomes louder than chamber music. On stage the dancers are twelve at most, generally fewer. The ballet has the form of a small entertainment, and its subject—first, an assembling of contestants, then the contest itself, then a dispersal—corresponds to the three parts into which the score is divided.

The subject is shown in terms of a series of dances, not in terms of a mimed drama. It is shown by an amusing identity in the action, which is classic dancing shifted into a "character" style by a shift of accentuation. The shift appears, for example, in the timing of transitions between steps or within steps, the sweep of arm position, in the walk, in the funniness of feats of prowess. The general effect is an amusing deformation of classic shapes due to an unclassic drive or attack; and the drive itself looks like a basic way of moving one recognizes. The "basic gesture" of *Agon* has a frank, fast thrust like the action of Olympic athletes, and it also has a loosefingered goofy reach like the grace of our local teenagers.

The first part of the ballet shows the young champions warming up. The long middle part—a series of virtuoso numbers—shows them rivalizing in feats of wit and courage. There is nothing about winning or losing. The little athletic meet is festive—you watch young people competing for fun at the brief height of their power and form. And the flavor of time and place is tenderly here and now.

TWO

Agon shows that. Nobody notices because it shows so much else. While the ballet happens, the continuity one is delighted by is the free-association kind. The audience sees the sequence of action as screwball or abstract, and so do I.

The curtain rises on a stage bare and silent. Upstage four boys are seen with their backs to the public and motionless. They wear the company's dance uniform. Lightly they stand in an intent stillness. They whirl, four at once, to face you. The soundless whirl is a downbeat that starts the action.

On the upbeat, a fanfare begins, like cars honking a block away; the sound drops lower, changed into a pulse. Against it, and against a squiggle like a bit of wallpaper, you hear—as if by free association—a snatch of *Chinatown, my Chinatown* misremembered on an electric mandolin. The music sounds confident. Meanwhile the boys' steps have been exploding like pistol shots. The steps seem to come in tough, brief bursts. Dancing in canon, in unison, in and out of symmetry, the boys might be trying out their speed of waist, their strength of ankle; no lack of aggressiveness. But already two—no, eight—girls have replaced them. Rapidly they test toepower, stops on oblique lines, jetlike extensions. They hang in the air like a swarm of girl-size bees, while the music darts and eddies beneath them. It has become complex and abstract. But already the boys have re-entered, and the first crowding thrust of marching boys and leaping girls has a secret of scale that is frightening. The energy of it is like that of fifty dancers.

By now you have caught the pressure of the action. The phrases are compact and contrasted; they are lucid and short. Each phrase, as if with a burst, finds its new shape in a few steps, stops, and at once a different phrase explodes unexpectedly at a tangent. They fit like the stones of a mosaic, the many-colored stones of a mosaic seen close-by. Each is distinct, you see the cut between; and you see that the cut between them does not interrupt the dance impetus. The novel shapes before you change as buoyantly as the images of a dream. They tease. But like that of a brilliant dream, the power of scale is in earnest. No appeal from it.

While you have been dreaming, the same dance of the twelve dancers has been going on and on, very fast and very boring, like travel in outer space. Suddenly the music makes a two-beat cadence and stops. The dispersed dancers have unexpectedly turned toward you, stopped as in a posed photograph of athletes; they face you in silence, vanish, and instantly three of them stand in position to start a "number" like dancers in a ballet divertissement.

The music starts with a small circusy fanfare, as if it were tossing them a purple and red bouquet. They present themselves to the public as a dance-team (Barbara Milberg, Barbara Walczak, Todd Bolender). Then the boy, left alone, begins to walk a "Sarabande," elaborately coiled and circumspect. It recalls court dance as much as a cubist still life recalls a pipe or guitar. The boy's timing looks like that of a New York Latin in a leather jacket. And the cool lift of his wrong-way-round steps and rhythms gives the nonsense so apt a turn people begin to giggle. A moment later one is watching a girls' duet in the air, like flying twins *(haute danse)*. A trio begins. In triple canon the dancers do idiotic slenderizing

110

exercises, theoretically derived from court gesture, while the music foghorns in the fashion of *musique concrète*. Zanily pedantic, the dance has the bounce and exuberant solemnity of a clown act. The audience laughs, applauds, and a different threesome appears (Melissa Hayden, Roy Tobias, Jonathan Watts).

For the new team the orchestra begins as it did for the previous one—first, the pushy, go-ahead fanfare, then the other phrase of harmonies that keep sliding without advancing, like seaweed underwater. (The two motifs keep returning in the score.)

The new team begins a little differently and develops an obvious difference. The boys present the girl in feats of balance, on the ground and in the air, dangerous feats of lucid nonsense. Their courage is perfect. Miss Hayden's dead-pan humor and her distinctness are perfect too. At one point a quite unexpected flounce of little-girl primness as in silence she walks away from the boys endears her to the house. But her solo is a marvel of dancing at its most transparent. She seems merely to walk forward, to step back and skip, with now and then one arm held high, Spanish style, a gesture that draws attention to the sound of a castanet in the score. As she dances, she keeps calmly "on top of" two conflicting rhythms (or beats) that coincide once or twice and join on the last note. She stops and the house breaks into a roar of applause. In her calm, the audience has caught the acute edge of risk, the graceful freshness, the brilliance of buoyancy.

The New York audience may have been prepared for *Agon's* special brilliance of rhythm by that of *Opus 34* and *Ivesiana,* two ballets never shown on tour. All three have shown an acuteness of rhythmic risk never seen and never imagined outside the city limits. The dangerousness of *Agon* is as tense as the danger of a tightrope act on the high-wire. That is why the dancers look as possessed as acrobats. Not a split-second leeway. The thrill is, they move with an innocent dignity.

At this point of *Agon* about thirteen minutes of dancing have passed. A third specialty team is standing on stage ready to begin (Diana Adams, Arthur Mitchell).

111

The orchestra begins a third time with the two phrases one recognizes, and once again the dancers find in the same music a quite different rhythm and expression. As the introduction ends, the girl drops her head with an irrational gesture more caressing than anything one has seen so far.

They begin an acrobatic adagio. The sweetness is athletic. The absurdity of what they do startles by a grandeur of scale and of sensuousness. Turning pas de deux conventions upside down, the boy with a bold grace supports the girl and pivots her on point, lying on his back on the floor. At one moment classic movements turned inside out become intimate gestures. At another a pose forced way beyond its classic ending reveals a novel harmony. At still another, the mutual first tremor of an uncertain supported balance is so isolated musically it becomes a dance movement. So does the dangerous scoop out of balance and back into balance of the girl supported on point. The dance flows through stops, through scooping changes of pace, through differences of pace between the partners while they hold each other by the hand. They dance magnificently. From the start, both have shown a crescendo and decrescendo within the thrust of a move, an illusion of "breath"—though at the scary speed they move such a lovely modulation is inconceivable. The fact that Miss Adams is white and Mr. Mitchell Negro is neither stressed nor hidden; it adds to the interest.

The music for the pas de deux is in an expressive Viennese twelve-tone manner, much of it for strings. Earlier in the ballet, the sparse orchestration has made one aware of a faint echo, as if silence were pressing in at the edge of music and dancing. Now the silence interpenetrates the sound itself, as in a Beethoven quartet. During the climactic pas de deux of other ballets, you have watched the dancer stop still in the air, while the music surges ahead underneath; now, the other way around, you hear the music gasp and fail, while the two dancers move ahead confidently across the open void. After so many complex images, when the boy makes a simple joke, the effect is happy. Delighted by the dancers, the audience realizes it

112

"understands" everything, and it is more and more eager to give them an ovation.

There isn't time. The two dancers have become one of four couples who make fast, close variations on a figure from the pas de deux. The action has reverted to the anonymous energy you saw in the first part. Now all twelve dancers are on stage and everything is very condensed and goes very fast. Now only the four boys are left, you begin to recognize a return to the start of the ballet, you begin to be anxious, and on the same wrestler's gesture of "on guard" that closed their initial dance—a gesture now differently directed—the music stops, the boys freeze, and the silence of the beginning returns. Nothing moves.

During the stillness, the accumulated momentum of the piece leaps forward in one's imagination, suddenly enormous. The drive of it now seems not to have let up for a moment since the curtain rose. To the realization of its power, as the curtain drops, people respond with vehement applause in a large emotion that includes the brilliant dancers and the goofiness of the fun.

The dancers have been "cool" in the jazz sense—no buildup, inventions that did not try to get anywhere, right after a climax an inconsequence like the archness of high comedy. But the dramatic power has not been that of jokes; it has been that of unforeseeable momentum. The action has had no end in view—it did not look for security, nor did it make any pitiful appeal for that. At the end, the imaginary contestants froze, toughly confident. The company seems to have figured jointly as the off-beat hero, and the risk as the menacing antagonist. The subject of *Agon,* as the poet Frank O'Hara said, is pride. The graceful image it offers is a buoyance that mystifies and attracts.

THREE

A program note says that "the only subject" of the ballet is an interpretation of some French seventeenth-century society dances. The note tells you to disregard the classic Greek title (*Agon*) in favor of the French subtitles. It is a pity to. The title and the subtitles are words that refer to civilized rituals, the former to athletics, the latter to dancing. Athletic dancing is what *Agon* does. On the other hand, you won't catch anyone on stage looking either French or Greek. Or hear musically any reason they should. French Baroque manners and sentiments are not being interpreted; elements or energies of forms are.

The sleight-of-hand kind of wit in the dancing is a part of that "interpretation." You see a dancer rushing at top speed, stop sharp in a pose. The pose continues the sense of her rush. But the equilibrium of it is a trap, a dead end. To move ahead, she will have to retract and scrounge out. She doesn't, she holds the pose. And out of it, effortlessly, with a grace like Houdini's, she darts away. The trap has opened in an unforeseen direction, as music might by a surprising modulation. At times in *Agon* you see the dancer buoyantly spring such traps at almost every step. Or take the canonic imitations. At times a dancer begins a complex phrase bristling with accents and a second dancer leaping up and twisting back an eighth note later repeats it, then suddenly passes a quarter-note ahead. The dissonance between them doesn't blur; if you follow it, you feel the contradictory lift of the double image put in doubt where the floor is. Or else you see a phrase of dance rhythm include a brief representational gesture, and the gesture's alien impetus and weight—the "false note" of it—make the momentum of the rhythm more vividly exact. These classic dissonances (and others you see) *Agon* fantastically extends. The wit isn't the device, it is the surprise of the quick lift you feel at that point. It relates to the atonal harmonies of the score—atonal harmonies that make the rhythmic momentum of the music more vividly exact.

At times you catch a kind of dissonant harmony in the image of a step. The explosive thrust of a big classic step has been deepened, speeded up, forced out farther, but the mollifying motions of the same step have been pared down. In a big step in which the aggressive leg action is normally cushioned by mildly rounded elbows the cush-

114

ioning has been pared down to mildly rounded palms. The conciliatory transitions have been dropped. So have the transitional small steps. Small steps do not lead up to and down from big ones. They act in opposition to big ones, and often stress their opposition by a contrariness.

The patterns appear and vanish with an unpredictable suddenness. Like the steps, their forms would be traditional except for the odd shift of stress and compactness of energy. The steps and the patterns recall those of Baroque dancing much as the music recalls its Baroque antecedents—that is, as absurdly as a current Harvard student recalls a Baroque one. Of course, one recognizes the relation.

Agon shifts traditional actions to an off-balance balance on which they swiftly veer. But each move, large or small, is extended at top pitch. Nothing is retracted. The ardent exposure is that of a grace way out on a limb.

The first move the dancers make is a counteraccent to the score. Phrase by phrase, the dancers make a counter-rhythm to the rhythm of the music. Each rhythm is equally decisive and surprising, equally spontaneous. The unusualness of their resources is sumptuous, like a magnificent imaginative weight. One follows the sweep of both by a fantastic lift one feels. The Balanchinian buoyancy of impetus keeps one open to the vividly changeable Stravinskian pressure of pulse and to its momentum. The emotion is that of scale. Against an enormous background one sees detached for an instant, the hidden grace of the dancer's individual move, a chance event that passes with a small smile and a musical sound forever into nowhere. *(1957)*

In the Abstract

TAKE THE ASPECT of rhythm which is familiar to everybody when they first learn ballroom dances, the matter of stepping to the measure or beat of music. When you watch couples dancing on the dance floor, most of them step to the measure, but they seem to first hear and then step with a sort of tiny lag. That is the respectable or "square" way of dancing. Other couples, particularly to soft music, don't hold to the beat, they also step across it—now a bit too soon, now a bit too late—with a swooping flow that corresponds over several measures to a phrase of the music. They look gracefully sentimental, or as the children say, like creeps. These are two kinds of dance rhythm, the first with an even beat, the second with an uneven one, and neither of them builds up pressure in the long run.

The high school couples cultivate a third kind, a kind that builds up pressure. They dance with a rhythmic thrust that is quick and exact, but percussive, not staccato. Watching the beat both as a pulse and as a time unit, they can take the exact lift of the upbeat to dance on. So they dance on top of the beat. They seem to me to keep on the edge of the upbeat awhile, getting their double balance on it, and they explode in a counter-rhythmic break, like wire-walkers turning a somersault in the air and landing on the wire again. It isn't only the gift and the nerve I notice, it is also the strict discipline of ear nobody has imposed on them but they themselves. They are absorbed and dance all-out.

Quite a lot of Americans have danced "on top of the beat" in high school, or have recognized the thrill of it then, watching classmates; and some recognize it in the second generation watching their children and their children's friends. Locally, that type of rhythm has those associations.

If you take the three ways of ballroom dancing I described—behind the beat, across the beat and on top of the beat—as three types of rhythm, you can more or less recognize them in other kinds of dancing too. "On top of the beat" is a jazz expression. But with quite different music, with quite different steps, gestures and accents, what you recognize isn't any derivation from jazz, not at all. What you recognize is an on-top-of-the-beat type of dancing, the percussive kind of continuity and its special pressure of pulse. You see individual great dancers who have that rhythm, dancers black, yellow, red, white and greenish-pink. The Balinese little girls and grown men dancing in "noble styles" have that type of rhythm to perfection. And a strong tendency toward it distinguishes the New York City Ballet from the great classic companies abroad. You see it here and there in European troupes, but their main tendency goes in another direction.

Of the great European companies, the Paris Opera and the Moscow Bolshoi specialize in phrasing. You keep seeing the dancers not hit the beat; they prefer to hit it just now and then, and in between step a trifle ahead or a trifle behind, accelerating or retarding within the length of the phrase more obviously than the orchestra. Within the length of the phrase, they keep gaining and losing impetus. The art of this across-the-beat rhythm is that of a dramatic recitation. And when the dance phrase occurs at a dramatic story crisis, the across-the-beat rhythm can be very striking like—"is-this-a . . . DAGGER . . . that-I-see-before-me." But everybody who dances on stage isn't in a state of story crisis all evening long. Many of the dances add no more to a story than "tralala, tralalee, trala-loo." The company phrases these too. It gives to the rhythm a suggestion of local speech rhythm—the Parisians make it staccato, chattery and charming, the Moscovites make it legato, sing-songy and soulful. To appreciate their artistry, you need only watch it in the right language. So too in the old-fashioned Bournonville style of the Danes, when a dancer "swallows" part of a classic step now and then, she isn't being careless; she is echoing an adorable "glug-glug" of the local polite speech rhythm.

If the Royal British danced with an Oxford accent, what glorious swallowings we should see. But it doesn't do that. It phrases across the beat only where the story justifies it, and then discreetly. And the Royal Danish in contemporary choreographies does the same thing. Both of the Royals generally follow the beat, follow it with a tiny lag. Nothing reprehensible about that type of rhythm. It gives these excellent companies—as it does to dancers in a ballroom—a touching look of civic virtue. As companies, they dance with an air that is discreetly majestic.

Many people notice that the New York City dances more strictly to the measure than the Europeans. It holds as strict a beat, whether in rhythm or counter-rhythm, as the orchestra does. That gives to the dancers the lift of a steady upbeat pulse. To hold that pulse, that impetus, they do the step with a distinct and steady action—soberly. And the steady impetus allows—like in on-top-of-the-beat dancing, or like in driving a car—a quicker timing and a higher speed. Many people have noticed that the New York City is unique in the lucidity it keeps at high speed; none of the other companies is able to remain as distinct in complexities of beat and step continued so long at top speed. None has the high-tension stamina necessary. The strictness of the New York City has been called its Swiss-watch technique.

If the company is a watch, I never but once saw as pretty a one; that was the one I was given when I was nine, and that lasted three days.

Balanchine's Swiss-miracle watch, when he sets it to music and winds it, knows what it is doing. The dancers keep not only on top of the beat, but also on top of the mounting momentum. What does that mean? Well, the musical momentum of a score has a force of traction which begins to pull when it gets ahead of the dancers. That is a dance effect of 1910 which nobody goes all-out for today. So one doesn't see the New York City company dragged by a score's momentum, with opulent, swooning eyes and arms like a raped Europa. Instead, one sees the company's active impetus and hears that of the score. At moments one sees the dancers on the edge or brink of the surging momentum stepping out beyond it with their lovely impetus. And the music reaches out its edge of sound into the void ahead just as they need a place to land. Sometimes the dancers and the music compete till the curtain falls and the momentum catches up and hits full force with its accumulated images.

The impetus of the New York City seems to me more fierce and more fun than that of the companies abroad. The impetus makes some scores unexpectedly "listenable"—scores whose momentum is unforeseen by the public—the Schoenberg of *Opus 34*, the Ives of *Ivesiana*, the Stravinsky of *Agon*, the Webern music of *Episodes*. They become listenable because Balanchine's choreographic rhythm and the company's dance rhythm focus moment by moment on the concrete impetus of the music. Quite as extraordinary is to listen moment by moment to Mozart's *Divertimento 15* or the Gounod *Symphony* as if they were music with an unforeseen momentum. You come to appreciate the orchestra, the most intelligent ballet orchestra in the world.

While dance ballets like these are going on, you can recognize the pattern game that music and dance are playing. In the music you recognize the classic conventions—or at least the classic type of noise. In the dance—at least for the most part—you recognize steps and figurations, the classic harmony of motion and grace of behavior, the drama of solo, pas de deux and ensemble. Like in a familiar game, you catch the surprise of a fast play. You catch the sudden image the play leaves. And as you follow the nervy, personal impetus by which each of the dancers is individually creating the composite dance, you begin to sense between dance and music—as if it were a slower and larger image that took time to communicate—the image of a real quality of motion the vitality of which is a secret of art.

What does a quality of motion mean? A girl walking down the street looks wonderfully pretty at one moment and average-pretty at another. It is your luck if you can see her at the right moment. At the right moment she has for you her real life and all of that real life from beginning to end is wonderfully pretty. In art that luck is an image, but in art to really have that luck, a flash isn't enough, it takes some time.

In California Khrushchev asked, "Which is better, your ballet or ours?" The fact is, the Bolshoi choreographers couldn't have imagined dances like *Agon, Episodes,* or *Divertimento 15.* Bolshoi dancers couldn't have danced them, or the conductors played the scores so straight. It may be that the New York ballet public is the only one quick enough of eye and ear to enjoy these pleasures. Does that prove our ballet is better? It only proves it's different. No matter. I am willing to prophesy that forty years hence, a decrepit New York City fan, huddled one night around a launching pad far far from home with a bunch of youthful Uzbeks will suddenly be asked in awed tones, "And did you really see the New York City in 1959? Did you see *Square Dance?*" And a spark will flash in the aged eyes, "And did I? Pat's *gargouillades*—absolute heaven! You know, the music goes . . ." and so forth in the Uzbec tongue through all the legendary names till dawn. *(1959)*

The Bolshoi
at the Met

IN THE SPRING of 1959, The Great Moscow Bolshoi Ballet disappointed some ballet-goers. "We'd all expected so much, and they aren't superhuman after all," a bright young lady exclaimed as we met at the door after a performance of *Swan Lake*; she quickly added the warmest praise for Ulanova in *Romeo and Juliet*.

About Ulanova I quite agreed. At first sight her vividness of motion, unique among the dancers around her, reminded me of Martha Graham's. As for the company, the first half hour shows it is a great one—highly skilled, convinced, attentive, lively. In *Romeo* everybody did a great deal of pantomime. They didn't all prove striking actors—nor would that be possible. But the company doesn't make hasty or shrunk up or "unpurposeful" gestures. The movement of a gesture has that amplitude of strength, that full support from the waist, traditional among Russians, but which the Bolshoi has excellently trained. The large-scale easy power of movement, whether of mime or dance, I found a remarkable pleasure.

But let me describe the Bolshoi *Romeo and Juliet*. The score is Prokofiev's; the story, Shakespeare's. Costumes and sets look like stock nineteenth-century stage properties—Renaissance style. The action shows you, one after another, the familiar "big" scenes of Italian grand opera—the morning market, the street affray with drawn swords, the ballroom festivity, the carnival, the duel with a slow death followed by another with a quick one, the

121

clan oath of vengeance, the family row, the burial by night with torches and tapers. Regulation opera house humor is offered, the regulation populace of Italian opera turn up, wenches, pedlars, down to the ragged urchins played by girls *en travesti*. Every bit of it done in earnest, with complete conviction and, of course, total laryngitis. It goes on for nearly four hours. At first you wonder that despite the Italian opera model nobody on stage behaves with an Italian irony or elegance; then you realize that everybody is behaving like the brutal Boyars and dimwitted serfs in a conventional movie about Ivan the Terrible.

The pantomime points of the crowd scenes are made obvious and then made obvious again. Succinctness, surprise, leaps in logic—the fun of pantomime—is avoided. The crowd slowly prepares a mass climax, then it slowly milks it, then comes a lull in interest, a cover scene, carefully protracted. The pace is that of an army's indoctrination lecture.

When the crowd dances, the dancing is more stage business. Briefly the love scenes—the Balcony, Bedroom and Tomb duets—hint at a kind of dance that isn't stage business—on the Balcony, a few classic steps, in the Bedroom a few lifts, in the Tomb a single lift, a very fine one. But even alone together the lovers keep pantomiming: the ballet doesn't venture into the other world of metaphor a dance can develop. In Shakespeare the love scenes develop an expression wonderfully alien to the Verona scenes, and that radiant difference makes the drama. Pasternak says of the play, "And to the din of butchery and cooking, as to the brassy beat of a noisy band, the quiet tragedy of feeling develops, spoken for the most part in the soundless whispers of conspirators."

The company's opening bill in New York was *Romeo*. Ballet-goers here had seen many a pantomime piece more brilliant and beautiful. But what they had looked forward to seeing was the Bolshoi's fabulous dance power, and *Romeo* kept that under cover all evening.

Ulanova's vividness saved the first night. Bending her neck toward her partner in a lift of the Bedroom Scene, the gesture had the tragic quiet Pasternak speaks of. Or

122

take the opposite kind of moment. Faced with marriage to County Paris, Juliet, her mantle flung round her, desperately rushes along the apron to Friar Lawrence; armed by him with the sleeping potion, she flings the mantle round her again, and rushes desperately along the apron back home. The fling, the rush, the exact repeat are pure *Perils of Pauline*. But Ulanova's art at that moment is so brilliant the audience breaks into delighted applause.

You can find out something about Bolshoi's style by trying the gymnastics of Ulanova's fling and rush yourself. Standing in the middle of the room, fling an arm across your chest, and at the same time raise the breastbone as high as it will go, bending it over at the top so it pushes the neck back. Don't let go, keep forcing the breastbone further, but in addition push the neck forward as hard as you can, and lift your head until you feel "desperately resolved." (It may make you cough.) And now, keeping the stance you are in unchanged, rush about the room with an incredible lightness and rapidity. If your family is watching, they will pick you off the floor, and urge you to try harder.

The special stance of fling and rush you just tried (it involves a backbend between the shoulder-blades) is not classical. It has been called the pouter-pigeon silhouette by Walter Terry, and that is just how it looks. But when Ulanova does it, you feel it means, "Here is my heart."

But if you notice that, you also notice her feet. In light runs on toe (bourrée steps) they seem to touch the floor sensitively. You see how keen the pointed foot looks in the air, during attitudes, arabesques, and passés, how clearly the leg defines and differentiates the different classic shapes. Below the waist Ulanova is a strict classicist; above the waist she alters the shape of classic motions now slightly, now quite a lot, to specify a nuance of drama (for example, the pouter-pigeon silhouette). Neither element—the lightness below or the weight above—is weakened for the sake of the other; the combined motion keeps fluid. And often while one movement is ebbing to its end, another seems already welling up in the midriff.

The Bolshoi women share Ulanova's method, but not her

vividness. The pacing—the pulse—of their movement is less varied, more predictable. Ulanova shows the unguarded timing of a spontaneous gesture. And she keeps that "motivation" throughout a role. You watch the rhythm of a specific character, the irremediable individuality. The imaginary creature on stage is much more unforeseeing than anyone around her. That holds your eye and your sympathy. Ulanova uses no other charm. She does not take the audience into her confidence, she attends to the literal mimic meaning at every moment. Her manner is that of an heroic post-mistress. And yet in the pas de deux from *Sylphides* where the meaning lies in a particular buoyancy of dancing to music, she was also at her most poignant.

At the age of nearly fifty, Ulanova does not have the luscious ease of a young ballerina. Other women of the company are stronger, more acrobatically striking, or fresh and sweet. None of them can give to a stage heroine a convincing heroism.

Though not as vivid actresses as I had expected, the principal women of the Bolshoi are dancers with authority, handsome feet and charming figures. The impression of heaviness they give is due to effects of Bolshoi style. The pouter-pigeon stance for instance. The first time you see the *Swan Lake* Swans hit it full strength, stepping in slow straddles and uncoiling their arms Hindu-style, they look like women of great weight specially trained to move; they looked prepared for immolation. When several women go into the stance with men on stage, you wonder that the men pay little attention. Later you see why. The Bolshoi women go into pouter-pigeon in all kinds of situations, at several angles, with different steps and gestures, and out again. The stance is a regulation formula. For a formula, it is rather unattractive. It shortens the woman's neck, it makes the head look helpless, the figure dumpy. Other formulas are no less hard on the women. You keep seeing open mouths, hunched shoulders, jutted chins, arms turned inside out at the socket and avidly reaching; you keep seeing elbows bent stiff or stretched stiff, hands crooked at the wrist, impatient arms, agitated hands, bobbing heads. When the women go into this formula they

124

look fidgety. Another formula has them look so preoccupied with an inner trouble they can't be gracious to each other or to the men. The general idea seems to be that when a woman feels deeply, she looks a bit countrified.

The men of the Bolshoi haven't the women's light feet nor their heavy emotion. They are pleasant to each other and to the women, and four-square in their bearing. They don't try for a classic distinctness in low shoulders, upright neck, and level head, they don't much turn out at the thigh, or clearly stretch their feet, or define their descent from a leap. They are self-effacing, and reliable lifters; but given the chance, several become striking dramatic dancers and mimes.

The difference between the style for men and the style for women throws the sexes into relief. On the other hand, relations between the sexes keep to a Victorian propriety. This isn't so easy in some of the big lifts where the mutual holds and tosses are far from Victorian.

But in two folk-hero parts, Vasiliev, a very young man of nineteen, showed what the Bolshoi style for men is capable of. One or two other men leapt as high as he, but none as they leapt and danced had his power of sculptural contour in motion or his power of upbeat in rhythm. None as actors had his lion-hearted magnanimity toward the heroine, the entire company, and the whole world. In dance or mime Vasiliev's instinct for generosity and delight couldn't be bigger and truer. His style is plain; his poetic gift—no simple one—is as radiant as that of the fabulous Russian dancers of the past.

Three of the youngest women principals, Timofeyeva, Maximova, Kondratieva, are ravishingly pretty and only the least bit stuffy. A fourth, Bogomolova, according to the local experts, can meet both Bolshoi and Western standards of ballerina technique. Samokhvalova could too, very likely. Bolshoi technique stresses big jumps more than quick toes; it stresses mobility of shoulder and upper spine, and acrobatics like those of a vaudeville adagio-team. Western ballerina technique requires a sharply versatile, high-speed exactitude of step and of ear and a high-tension stamina—which are not Bolshoi characteristics.

But as one grows used to Bolshoi style, the gifts of a score or more of principals, men and women, become evident. The *Highlights* programs showed their dance power best, and on those, in good-natured acrobatic audacity, the ballerina Plisetzkaya outdid anybody in the world. I grew to like the individual dancers better and better.

The productions however did not gain by being seen twice. *Swan Lake,* a revised version, developed less momentum than the traditional one in London, and no poignancy. *Giselle* began well, but becoming longer and longer, lost its drive in each act. *Stone Flower,* a Moscow novelty, tried for dance momentum and fun, but like the other Bolshoi choreography, it kept losing the upbeat of the rhythm.

The Bolshoi's dance rhythm—choreographically speaking—is neither big like Fokine's nor clear like Moiseyev's. The dances are apt to go on without gathering momentum, without getting anywhere. They come down heavy on the downbeat and slur the upbeat. At a climax they pound the downbeat. They haven't the lilt of lifting off it, or the fun of matching a counter-rhythm to the musical rhythm. They miss the upbeat buoyancy of a musical momentum, the exhilaration of a rising sweep of impetus. The rhythm is weak on resilience.

The dancers are expected to perform it with rubato, ahead or behind the music. They "shape" each phrase, treating the time-values of the rhythm more elastically than the orchestra does. Each phrase has urgency, each phrase lacks repose.

You see the dancers do with devotion what they are asked to. During climaxes of emotion they are not asked for the calm and completely erect carriage of the classic ballerina and of her partner. They are not asked for the climactic suspense, the extreme responsibility of the lightest finish, the lightest musical phrasing. Since Diaghilev's time great Russian dancers have been showing us these extreme traditional resources of their art. At tragic and at happy climaxes they have shown us the

126

power of radiance ballet can achieve. The lovely young Bolshoi ballerinas do not spread that radiance. The young Soviet violinists and pianists who visit us are in command of all the traditional musical resources, not only of amplitude of strength but also of edge and elegance and quiet. No reason the dancers should not have them too.

The Bolshoi has formalized its style and it does what it does on principle. It covers up with care the brilliantly unreasonable resources of expression which are the glory of ballet dancing. It does so to stress instead an acted mime meaning. Four or five in the company can do this convincingly; the rest, though sincere and convinced, haven't a gift for vivid acting. Nor has the choreography a gift for narration. At a three hour stretch the company's mime of deep feeling and psychological motivation isn't absorbing. Where the Bolshoi convinces all evening is in the ample strength of a movement, and in the weight of one. And for these dance qualities, too rare in the West, it will always be welcome.

The Bolshoi means to uncover its dance power in the next few years. When it does, it will add to the literal meaning of pantomime the metaphorical meaning of dancing. As of now, Western ballet—and even our own part of it—offers more fun, a fiercer luster, more grace of irony, and much more imaginative excitement and poetic courage, though it isn't stronger and is ever so much less secure.

A Midsummer Night's Dream

BALANCHINE'S *A Midsummer Night's Dream* with a flock of children on stage and a well-known story is family entertainment. It opens, as the Mendelssohn music does, deep in the magic forest. The children on stage are charming—their steps clean, their music cues prompt, they glisten with responsibility. Against their light rhythm—like an insect hum—the adult elves brilliantly dart and soar. As for the story, when you see the tiny Indian Changeling over whom Oberon and Titania are quarreling, a parent remembers the earnestness of a quarrel at home about who the new kitten was to go to sleep with. And as the fairy royalties speak in Shakespeare—regal, delicate, with a child's heart—so they each dance beautifully among their separate elves in different clearings of the enchanted forest. It is a visible re-telling of the story, close to its poetry. You see Oberon show Puck the magic flower, and send him circling round the globe. The lovers' misadventures are told in rapid dances, too fast to put pressure on them; Titania and Bottom-turned-donkey too—the gentlest of donkeys and delightfully convincing. In the forest the pace of events slows down or speeds up unpredictably. The first act reaches its climax with a long, unreassuring mixup of funny reality and scarey dream, and at the last minute ends happily.

The second act brings Duke Theseus' Wedding Ball, where everybody dances extremely well. The first act has been remarkably interesting; the second somehow isn't, except during a brief virtuoso pas de deux and an epilogue back in the magic forest, a sudden sweetness and silence.

At home, after putting the family to bed, a parent reflects that the ballet gave both the children and the adults roles in which they could shine. Lithe, wonderfully live in unexpected pauses, sunny in action, the lead character, the Puck of Arthur Mitchell, is the truest Puck one is likely to see anywhere. Since Balanchine understood the play so well, the parent wonders why he avoided the Pyramus and Thisbe side of it, and its wide-open buffoonery. But though he did, what a pleasure to find in the ballet's many inventions the Shakespearean sweetness and lovely irony unfalsified. The aftertaste of the long evening is a very pleasant one.

This view by an imaginary parent seems to me reasonable, and I imagine that a choreography fan would agree. But while the parent drops innocently to sleep, the choreography fan wants first to identify the weakness of the second act Wedding Ball. Most of it had been taken up by a divertissement, a pas de quatorze, that packed so many steps so amazingly close, it changed at every moment, and as drama didn't budge. But where did he get that impression; no clear picture comes back to him.

The picture that comes back to him instead is the Wedding March with which the Ball had opened—the music's interminable repeats, the chorus walking their designs looking as stuffy as in church, the orchestra blaring the tight two-bar phrase pattern. Obligatory boredom. The fan began to count on the next number for relief, the divertissement, the evening's climax. But the music for it, a Mendelssohn symphony, right away set the same tight phrase pattern, and the dance did too. The prospect of a grand climax confined to a two-bar seesaw—no travel—exasperated him. He watched the confined phrase pattern continue through the long divertissement, including the pas de deux. It continued through a court dance that briefly concluded the Ball. Wedding March, divertissement, court dance, each had run to a modest ending, march and court dance keeping to the phrase pattern conventionally, the divertissement keeping to it, but not at all conventionally.

Not at all conventionally, though the steps of it were regulation school steps. Remarkably interesting to the fan, a brief men's pas de six. That moment of grandeur reminds him of more fugitive impressions. In the choral sections, delicate small steps, majestic open ones had flashed and vanished, finding room as if by magic. Oddly counted to the bar, a step found its buoyancy and time enough to open its classic shape and close it. The thicket of choral steps in a phrase seemed to turn on a dime, and hover an inch above the floor as they turned. Their momentum seemed to come from the melody—that was the music's energy, and none of it was lost to the ear. It sounded young, ingenuous, at moments heavenly.

It looked dense as a tapestry forest. Deep in the forest, a clearing—the brief pas de deux. (The variations for the stars had not been performed.) But brief as it was, the change from many dancers to just two gave a focus; suddenly the final dangerous supported falls made contact with the audience; a retard, an absorbing image.

The moment of image, ingenuously tender and noble, serious, had been for the fan the only absorbing one of the divertissement. The sweet Mendelssohn symphony develops very little drama, and so does its pas de quatorze. The number is more ornament than drama. The word "drama" taken in its pure dance sense—the kind of drama of which Balanchine's *Valses et Variations* with its happy summer morning dazzle is so full of. Had the pas de quatorze been so outgoing a climax as that, the fan and the public too would have been better satisfied. And yet, speaking for myself, I miss a regulation climax less than I miss before the number begins ten minutes of Pyramus and Thisbe buffoonery—that far-out timing and wildly off-balance gesture. It would make me ready for the divertissement's extremely far-in style, the vigor which keeps forming one unusual wholly positive classic phrase after another with the exact few steps there is room for inside the fatally predictable phrase length.

A fan, however, would point out that a contrast has already been made. The phrases of dance and mime in Act One are of constantly changing lengths. The whole first act has a pace livelier and more flexible than any full length ballet had before. Dance and mime events move or pause with what seems a spontaneous variety of musical momentum. The beauty of the pauses strikes a fan's eye. Time enough to see what happens and not a moment more. But "time enough" changes in ballet: mime communicates instantly; dramatic dance tells its meaning fairly fast; lyric dance, which tells its meaning by many unfoldings and foldings, echoes and disappearances and returns, takes a good deal of time to happen. Act One of *A Midsummer Night's Dream* keeps sharp these differences of pace and even stresses them.

The dancers make their mime points so clear at high speed, they look like accomplished actors. More unusual yet, the ease with which they shift between mime, dramatic dance and lyric dance. Such an ease is normally the secret of a few great classic stars. In *A Midsummer Night's Dream* mime and dramatic gesture do not try for a period style—Elizabethan or Greek—nor do they try for naturalistic theatre. In principle they keep to classic dance carriage and gesture, modified by situation and character; in practice, the vividness of action is that each gesture goes straight to its dramatic point, and that the "psychology" is perfectly clear by its timing. Timing is set to counts in the score.

The dramatic dances, based on familiar pas de deux figurations, can with as little as an unexpectedly averted head or a hastily extended hand make a story point without interrupting the dance. For instance, Titania dancing with Bottom in a supported figure when her back is turned to him makes clear by a slightly accentuated developpé that she is imagining him as a handsome partner; as the same figure an instant later turns her to face him and she sees he is actually a donkey, her next action is sweetly to find him some grass. The dance continuity gives its mime nuances lightness.

This kind of mime and dramatic dance has a pre-Fokinian precedent. Balanchine has long used it. A practical action—handling a prop dagger, or picking an invisible flower—is done literally; a gesture of emotion is done in the range of classic movement. A fan can compare the classic ballet mime of *A Midsummer Night's Dream* with the stylized ballet mime usually seen; the classic kind looks more direct and natural. It does when Balanchine invents it—no other choreographer has observed the gestural secrets of classic movement so lovingly.

Watching the cinematic cross-cutting between dance and mime at the climax of Act One, the rolling ground fog, the duels quick as Chinese theatre, the dogs turned horses, the people turned sacks, Hippolyta vertiginously spinning with no floor beneath her, Puck watchful at the last moment not to repeat his former mistake, the fan recognizes that the scarey omen of this prenuptial dream is one Hippocrates would have been delighted by. But the ominous tone of it is in the text—Oberon's "fog as black as Acheron" speech, and Puck's grisly answer.

But two other dreams, earlier in the act and deeper in the magic forest, delight a choreography fan even more: the weather-like shifts of pressure between serenity and menace at Titania's court when Puck tries to kidnap the Changeling; and the unmotivated serenity of Oberon's court, like nature's unmotivated beauty, dancing her Platonic ideas among her moths and dragonflies.

Some balletgoers tell me they would like Balanchine to make a full-length ballet as extraordinary as *Agon, Liebeslieder Walzer* or *Divertimento 15*. Such a ballet has never existed. Balanchine has mentioned a hope of setting the "Ninth." One can imagine for some world festival of peace two hundred of the world's best dancers putting themselves at his disposal for it. How I should like to see it and hear Beethoven shouting, "We enter, drunk with fire, heavenly joy, your sanctuary." An equivalent quote from *A Midsummer Night's Dream* is "Shall we their fond pageant see, Lord, what fools these mortals be." The voice in one's heart that says it is a lighter one. *(1963)*

For a Foreign Tour

THE NEW YORK CITY BALLET has often been called Balanchine's company. He has choreographed three fourths of its repertory and most of the dancers have grown up in the school on Broadway that he directs. He came to New York at the invitation of Lincoln Kirstein to open that school, to develop a company and choreograph for it. Six months later, for a school performance, he made *Serenade*, one of his loveliest. That was in 1934. Kirstein was twenty-seven, Balanchine, thirty. They knew as well as anybody that a similar project had taken the Romanoffs a century. But they were men of genius, and believed that the project was worthwhile.

And so in 1948 they founded the New York City Ballet. During the intervening years, Kirstein had presented seventeen new Balanchine ballets and twenty-two by young local choreographers; and at a time when Kirstein was in the army, Balanchine had shown five or six more of his. But despite their energy, and the devotion of a nucleus of dancers, it had proved impossible to found a permanent company. Now the New York City Center, a private cultural organization offered its theatre for some weeks yearly. From this home the troupe derives its name.

In those days Jerome Robbins joined the company as choreographer and dancer for five very successful years. Other choreographers of those early years were Tudor, Ashton, Christensen, Dollar, Cunningham, Bolender, Boris and Cranko. Much later Birgit Cullberg produced one of her ballets. On the occasion of an homage to Webern, Martha Graham choreographed the first half for herself and her company, Balanchine the second half for his, including in it a long solo for one of her dancers, Paul Taylor.

The New York City Ballet has from the first been very active. Since 1948 Balanchine has made fifty-five ballets for it, three of them "full length" ones, and has revived for it eight or nine he had made previously. They all have shown the highest standard of craftsmanship, they have shown the dancers to advantage, and been made during the hours permitted by union rules. About half have remained in repertory. Some have been kept because they proved popular, some because they are extraordinary and belong to the great works of art of our time. Though the fans recognized these, several have been difficult to save, because they became popular so slowly. Even *Raymonda Variations* took a year to become popular; *Four Temperaments* and *Divertimento* took ten, and it was the dancers who fought to save them. The glorious *Figure in the Carpet* has not been given for some time; *Opus 34,* alas, has been lost.

His "full length" ballets and several others have situated their dances in a clearly told story; the rest have been dance ballets. They are in the tradition of the dance entertainment. They do not dance to a story, they dance to a score. They are often called abstract; perhaps they are, in the sense that the movements of a waltz are abstract, or those of a frug or a minuet. But these ballets dance classic steps to concert music. Their gift is the buoyancy they keep, whether the music is simple or complicated. As dance entertainments, their adroitness is delightful. In a number of them at first view, the brilliant impetus of the dancing, the lucid large-scale audacity of its grace look cool and smooth. Here and there a gleam of irony shows. Just as dancing, one enjoys them very much; but each of them has also a character, a dance range different from the rest.

The difference is startling between one like *Symphony*

in C which exhibits the traditional steps, and one like *Four Temperaments* which offers a stream of fantastic forms. However rapid, these forms are instantly defined. They have an abrupt weight, an off-center thrust; precarious though they look, they move with a thrilling momentum. Their action looks classic and counter-classic both at once. Hindemith, the composer of the score, had chosen as subject the "four humors of the blood" of medieval medicine. The dance, which includes jokes, also reflects eccentric inner powers and the mysterious grandeur of their joint energy.

The condensed energy of such a counter-classic classicism in other ballets takes quite different shapes. In the Stravinsky *Movements,* fantastically concise, it looks, of all things, Olympian. In his *Agon* it looks ebullient. In the Webern *Episodes* (except for the last part) the lucid abnormality has a wit like Beckett's. *Bugaku* on the other hand looks deeply medieval Japanese. These ballets are usually called advanced. Their individualities assert themselves explosively.

The ballets choreographed in traditional steps open their individualities more mildly. They seem each gradually to gather their particular lyric resonance. The sprightliness and mounting spirits of *Symphony in C* leave behind a very different impression from the autumnal richness of *Gounod Symphony,* hovering over a stately score, its steady fourbar phrases punctuated in thirty thousand ways, all correct. *Donizetti Variations* has an Italian good humor in balletic virtuosity, a few broad jokes and many for the quick-sighted. *Serenade* in its dreamlike speed and poignance uses the ensemble less to corroborate the principles than to weave their fragments of adolescent romance into the unwearied rush of immortal space. *Divertimento* distills in virtuoso steps the graceful wit, the quick presence of an eighteenth century amiability; its andante movement, a pas de deux in which the partners change but the tender intensity continues, is Mozartian in its spell. The intimacy of *Liebeslieder Walzer* is even more complex. Set to two cycles of Brahms Lieder, it begins with four charming couples and the spontaneous

135

variety of implications as they play waltz games; later, in a moonlit change, it seems in an impalpable way to be revealing wonderful secrets of mutual love, each with a beautiful ending. It has a perfume of roses. On the other hand, Balanchine's version of *Swan Lake* is like recognizing the face of a long celebrated beauty on a photograph taken when she was fifteen. He tells the Act Two story in a sequence of dances, some entirely new and deliciously fresh; the steps are Ivanov style, the impetus is Balanchine style, and leads to a long finale of outright dramatic power. Far from that is the sunny nonsense of *Harlequinade* which, like an improvisation, bursts with an equal vividness now into foolery, now into the loveliest grace. *Raymonda, Tarantella, Stars and Stripes,* these are all happy pieces, each one quite different from all those mentioned.

One of New York's best critics, after mentioning the implications of *Liebeslieder Walzer,* added that her interpretation of them was pure fantasy; and that, in any case, watching for implications was much less pleasure than watching the dance as dancing. This is excellent advice. When a Balanchine ballet becomes perplexing, I listen more attentively to the music. Not that what the music does, the dance mirrors; it doesn't. They are more like different people in a friendly dialogue which is simultaneous and in different kinds of language. The music is saying something or other beautifully, and the beautiful dancers are responding in their own language. I begin to follow the mutual momentum of both, and to be carried by it. In the movement of a step, some element of unintentional gesture deploys and folds and vanishes. It called no attention to itself. It is as if a magic presence in the air had smiled and said, "See." Much later, remembering the image, it is your own recognition of what happened, that opens.

But the image you keep remains that of the dancer you saw, a particular dancer creating an image as she moves. A choreography is remembered in the way it was danced. I have spoken of Balanchine's, but when I have seen it, I have been watching the dancers. One does not see his imagination without seeing theirs. Ballet is that kind of a pleasure and that kind of an art. It is not one of the solitary ones.

For him and his dancers—those now and also those before them—the repertory, the dance style have evolved year by year as a mutual discovery. The classicism of their style is an American one. It looks for a rubato and nuance that will not blur the shape of a step or shift its musical accent; it wants everywhere a steady momentum. These characteristics were not those of the Paris Russian dancers for whom Balanchine made his early masterpieces. Their gift was a different one. He did not create the American gift, any more than Petipa did the Russian, or Lulli, the French. For the past thirty years he and his dancers have been working together to heighten the gift into a style. The style and the many particular dancers who advanced it are those of his choreography. It could not be his without being theirs. Their individualities, their imagination, their good faith invent each night the living illusion. The fun of showing interesting dancing, the delight of showing beautiful dancing, is the true motive for what you see.

About *Don Quixote*

BALANCHINE'S THREE-ACT *Don Quixote* tells the famous history of the Don's madness related to its social background—the Spain of Philip II. It is also a sumptuous spectacle, the handsomest in international repertory. It offers an enormous amount to look at—sets, indoors and outdoors, hundreds of costumes, props, beards, small children, a 30-foot giant, animals, a penitential procession, a travelling marionette show, a village festival, a court ball, a divertissement, a masque, a long classic *pas d'action,* lots of pantomime—the way to watch shifts unpredictably. Rich and strange, bitter, delicate and tragic, the piece gathers in one's imagination. When it is finished, it seems to have become a somber story of alienation. Its dramatic force has been an increasing pathos.

As the curtain falls, pathos has become the dramatic force, but the spectacle element has never been so unrepetitive in any large-scale ballet. As usual with full-length ballets nowadays, the scenic style is old-fashioned opera house. Unprecedented in that style, is the subtlety with which the scale of the set to the dancers is varied, both in respect to size and to weight; and the variations of weight in the costumes. Effects of drawing and color in the set, which in a representational style on so large a stage often tend to harden and to dwarf the dancers, are not emphasized. The imagination and the sincerity with which Esteban Francés, the painter, has put himself at the service of the complex drama cannot be valued highly enough.

Nor can the same qualities be valued highly enough in Karinska's execution of the costumes, or in that of the artists who made the props.

Imagination and sincerity are everywhere present among the performers, ranging from stars to children. Dulcinea, the heroine—pensive young Suzanne Farrell—is ravishing in the lucid grace of her mime and of her miraculous dancing. Joining her in the pas d'action climax, Mimi Paul and Marnee Morris dance too beyond belief. Before that, Gloria Govrin, Patricia McBride, and particularly Suki Schorer (in a duet with John Prinz) have been extraordinary. All the dancing is remarkable in strict dance numbers, and acceptable in the character dance ensembles. But since the ballet tells a realistic story it depends on the distinctness of its mime gesture, and the conviction of its timing.

Don Quixote, a quiet part with a very large range, is acted by Richard Rapp with a beautiful honesty—even after Balanchine's marvelous performance, Rapp's was admirable. Lamont's Sancho too is a beautiful achievement. At Don Quixote's death bed, the housekeeper (von Aroldingen) and the curate (Arshansky) together with Dulcinea and Sancho doing almost nothing, shocked the audience out of its wits. Arshansky is very funny in another part. Nobody overplays. Each detail of mime in the ballet, if you look for it, counts.

The ballet starts with mime. It starts as the novel does with Don Quixote among his books of chivalry. He falls asleep. A great monster swoops down. A tiny blonde girl perched on a book implores his help; tiny knights in armor and tiny armed monsters attack. He rescues her, she escapes. He is sound asleep in his chair when a young servant girl enters, quietly goes across the room to raise a curtain and let in the sunrise light. Her quietness tells she has often done this before. He wakes and sees her waiting by his chair. Now she washes his feet and with a quick gesture loosens her hair to dry them. She gives him his shoes and he kisses her forehead. He walks forward, thinking about chivalry. She runs after him, drops on her knees, and with a swift movement offers him his sword,

139

pretending to be the page of an imaginary knight. Then she rises and goes out to her work without looking back. With the sword held high he is watching her. The room disappears and he is standing sword in hand facing an immense arid plain. On a cart the image of the Virgin appears. It is the same dancer who a moment before was the servant. To the Virgin Don Quixote, as if entranced, dedicates his sword. Sancho runs in, the armor and spear in his hand clattering, and takes a pratfall.

So one discovers at the start who Dulcinea is—the Virgin, a shy country girl growing up in his house, and a tiny blonde princess in a nightmare. The gesture of drying his feet with her hair suggests the Magdalene; more than that it is an ancient gesture that belongs to washing a child. These clear pictures, one right after the other, add up to a complex emotion. Dulcinea is both very close and very far off. From then on, one is ready to see her through his eyes. In the novel, Dulcinea, heroine and motive of the story, is never seen, though she is a real country girl as well as an ideal empress of beauty. The Cervantes fan sees that these mime pictures recombine widely scattered details of the book, as well as adding visual metaphors of their own.

To follow the action of the ballet does not require more than a hearsay acquaintance with the novel. Here is an outline of the action.

After Don Quixote has made Sancho knight him they don't find adventures right away. Then grisly projections appear in the sky; on stage two incidents from the novel, briefly mimed, leave the Knight and Sancho badly beaten up but beginning to recover as they so often are in the book. The scene changes to the ancient plaza of a remote small town with loungers and three village girls dancing. More girls and boys join in. Neither the scene nor the dance quite pattern. The dancing has something random in its shifts of activity. One friend of mine found no focus; another said it was the best village festival he had ever seen in ballet. I too had seen in a remote Spanish town, a couple of hours before High Mass, just such impromptu dancing as this suggested. (The steps on stage were ballet steps with a few Spanish arm positions.)

Sancho runs in hugging a stolen fish and dodging the fish wives. Two Guardia Civil grab him and turn him over to the loungers who enjoy manhandling him. Arriving on horseback, Don Quixote rescues him. A further comic scene is interrupted by a man who drags in a shepherdess—Marcela. He points to a dead man on a bier; the villagers threaten to kill her. She is the same dancer who takes the part of Dulcinea, now in pastoral ballet costume. The Knight rescues her, and she dances a classic variation. The program book quotes her beautiful speech to him from the novel; her dance is amazing, so transparent, so distinct, so unforeseeable in its invention. It is about virginal freedom. A painter friend exclaimed, "It's marvelous. There she is on toe, and everybody else is on their flat feet. What a theatre idea."

A curtained cart appears. Its small curtain rises on a puppet show, adorable in action and in decor—a perfect pleasure. The tiny blonde heroine of it is captured by the Moors. With drawn sword Don Quixote madly rushes to her rescue, the puppet theatre collapses on his head and knocks him out. The local duke and duchess with some friends come onto the plaza, find the Don, and invite him to their palace at once. (They know him from the novel.) Barely conscious, he is lifted on Rozinante, Sancho follows on Dapple, the villagers are delighted, and the first act is over.

The curtain rises on a vast black and gold throne room in the Duke's palace. The noble guests in black and gold court dress appear followed by the Don, festive in scrubbed armor, and humble Sancho. The Duke and Duchess seat our friends near the throne; the aristocratic guests welcome the knight with exaggerated deference. He and Sancho watch a court dance which the Duke and Duchess soon join. Unexpected spurts of speed and individual timings make it look "real," as they did the unaristocratic village dance before. The Spanish arm gestures are amusingly elaborate. A divertissement of five numbers follows, performed by hired entertainers. Their garish bits of costume are as alien to Spanish hauteur as those of gypsies. (I remembered in Madrid at three a.m. deliciously haughty debutantes wearing family diamonds with young escorts in dinner jackets watching a gypsy entertainment such as I had never dreamt of.) Some demi-character steps of the divertissement, extremely virtuoso, are based on the frug in the sense that the Fairy Variations of Petipa are based on the can-can. Several brilliant girls make the wit sharper by playing it to their partner or to a world of their own rather than to the public.

Suddenly one, then more masked aristocrats point to Don Quixote; and the Duchess invites him to dance. In a swirl of ironic masked figures she whispers to the Duke, and then returns to the courteous Don. It is a prearranged hazing. Sancho tries to lead his master away, but the Duchess prevents him. Master and man are blindfolded, are made sport of, Sancho escapes, thoroughly scared, brave Don Quixote is crowned Emperor and whipped and left exhausted.

A vision of Dulcinea appears, he stumbles after her, he recovers, he is about to follow her. A masked lady taps him on the shoulder, he turns to her, another taps him, you hear a soft thud and see his face blinded by whipped cream. He pauses, then turns blindly toward the disappearing vision of Dulcinea. The curtain falls.

The curtain rises on the third act. An immensely high gate fences in a moonlit forest in the foreground—the most mysteriously beautiful setting of the evening. Sancho is leading his exhausted master, and leaves him asleep by the trunk of a tree. Masked courtiers sneak up at once and cover him with a net. A moment later filmy girls appear—a dream, waving Elysian arms. Never has a moonlit dream begun more consolingly—this is the classic pas d'action. Dulcinea and her two friends are supported by three bold knights. Though Dulcinea's dazzling pas de deux ends on a hint of threat, miraculous variations follow, one girl boldly striding and turning, another at top speed resting utterly still for an eighth note, then dancing at top speed again. Like a dream, these dances remind you of something recent. Is it perhaps the divertissement,

142

perhaps the shepherdess? The man's powerful variation (Anthony Blum) has arm gestures from the court dance. Dulcinea's variation—marvelous in the feet, in the novel and unorthodox epaulements—carries the hidden secret to its climax. Dancing faster and faster, more and more desperate, opposed by a woman in black like the Duchess, tortured by the enchanter Merlin, Dulcinea at last appeals to the sleeping Knight—he starts up—the horror has vanished, faithful Sancho takes off the encumbering net. But the garden has turned into a landscape of windmills. He is challenged by a giant who grows as big as a windmill. Unappalled, the Don charges him, his lance caught in the windmill fan he rises high in the air, drops, crawls still alive toward Sancho. Sancho binds his bleeding head. A charging herd of swine stampede him. Masked courtiers of the Duke carry on a cage and open the cage door. The Knight on all fours feebly crawls away. They move the cage to catch him. Sadly Sancho heads him into it, and they shut it. Like a beast, he is carried to his own home. There Sancho helps him out, the old housekeeper, the old curate undress him and put him to bed in a fever. They leave. In a fever he sees the Inquisition approach. He sees the burning of his books. He is humble but does not recant. A vision of the Virgin on a cart appears—the image with which the ballet began—after a long pause she raises her head and looks at him. He is lifted in ecstasy, as mystics are by levitation. She vanishes, he collapses sobbing (at this point the machinery creaks) to his bed. His friends return with the shy servant girl. He dies and they mourn him. The servant girl picks up two small sticks, she goes very slowly to the corpse and lays them on his chest to form a cross. The curtain falls.

At the first performance the Don recognized his friends and died sane as he does in the novel. At a later one he was dead when they returned, a simpler effect.

The tragic pathos of the ballet is simpler than the enormous comic buoyancy of the novel. But the novel no less than *Romeo* or *The Tempest* has long been material for imaginative reinterpretation. Auden's brilliant reinterpretation of the novel from which the program quotes, is quite as "free" as Balanchine's very different and equally brilliant one.

Balanchine has reinterpreted comic details of the book in a wider tragic sense—the hooded penitents transporting a statue of the Virgin become the Inquisition; the burning of books by his best friends becomes an *auto da fe;* ordinary pigs become half-human, their gleeful stampede morally swinish; the Don's cage, a kindly stratagem leading to broad jokes, becomes an image of horror; a buxom country girl becomes a delicate ballerina. Similarly the masked hazing of Don Quixote at the Duke's, gracefully as it moves, by the shock of its pauses—particularly the last pause, the face blinded by whipped cream, turned immobile to the public—becomes a bitter denunciation of society's meanness. The ballet is not only gloomily lit, but also somber in ideas it suggests. Even if the Inquisition is shown as an hallucination, one recognizes the social fact it represents in a contemporary sense; and remembers the Inquisitor in Dostoevski.

Man's inhumanity to man is one of the two forces at conflict in the ballet. The other is man's good will to man. It is shown by the touching pictures of Don Quixote's domestic friends, particularly humble cheerful Sancho, a stout man light on his feet. It is shown by the Don's cool and lovely Dulcinea, by the marvelous vision of his third act dream—though even that ends in menace; by his innocent courage and his deeper idea of grace. Even in its strongest form this force does not triumph. At the end, after looking at him, it vanishes and leaves him sobbing.

The Establishment at all its levels pressuring the imaginative individual into alienation, into failure, that is what you watch. The ballet's images, like those of poetry, are fluid and contradictory. But they are not conciliatory. They are aggressive. The cruel ones get worse. On the other hand, though his ballet is about failure, Balanchine has never made dances more glorious in their novel beauty than that of Marcela and all those of the long pas d'action, or sweeter than the Mauresque duet; nor has he ever invented so many striking mime images, often extravagantly speeded up or slowed down without recourse to stylization.

A few times scenes are protracted beyond their active effect—the projection scene of Act I, the masked scene of Act II, the vision of the Virgin in Act III. I do not press the point. A full-length ballet so rich in imagination and with so complex a theatre form, presented without dress rehearsal, can be allowed several uncertainties, even if they prove, like some of Shakespeare's, incurable.

Seeing Balanchine act Don Quixote a number of fans got the idea that the ballet portrayed the choreographer. This ballet contradicts many others of his; but if this portrays him, all the others do equally.

As for the score by Nicholas Nabokov, it is descriptive, a bit of everything, well educated, rhythmically weak, with a tendency to fall back from a two bar climax. A great composer remarked in conversation, "It's Louis Phillipe. *Pièces de genre. Pièces de style,* everybody is bored with that, nowadays one can't keep that up more than five minutes. *Pièces de genre,* one can go on with that longer." As for me, I am grateful to the score for serving so interesting a ballet. I have heard many fans say the ballet isn't interesting. I find it is, and have said why, both from the point of view of a fan and a theatre-goer.

Part Two

Theory and Practice

Forms in Motion
and in Thought

IN DANCING one keeps taking a step and recovering one's balance. The risk is a part of the rhythm. One steps out of and into balance; one keeps on doing it, and step by step the mass of the body moves about. But the action is more fun and the risk increases when the dancers step to a rhythmic beat of music. Then the pulse of the downbeat can lift the dancer as he takes a step; it can carry him through the air for a moment, and the next downbeat can do it again. Such a steady beat to dance on is what a dancer dreams of and lives for. The lightness that music gives is an imaginary or an imaginative lightness. You know it is an illusion, but you see it happen; you feel it happen, you enjoy believing it. There is a bit of insanity in dancing that does everybody a great deal of good.

It has been doing people good for a long time. Looking at Paleolithic cave paintings, one can recognize the powerfully developed dance sense our ancestors had fifteen thousand years ago. What are all those bison of theirs floating on, if not on a steady beat? A Brooklyn teen-ager would feel at home among the Magdalenian cave painters once the dancing started and he heard that beat. And a late Paleolithic youth who dropped in on a gym or a ballroom going wild at two in the morning to the blasts of a name band, would see right away that it was a bison ritual. And if he broke into a bison step, the kids near enough to see him would only say, "Wow," or "Dig that rustic shag."

And an educated late Paleolithic magician, if he dropped in on a performance of classic ballet in an air-conditioned theatre would find a good deal he was familiar with—the immense, awesome drafty cavern, the watching tribe huddled in the dark, and in a special enclosure the powerful rhythmic spectacle which it is taboo to join in. As a magic man he would find it proper that the dancers are not allowed to speak, not allowed to make any everyday movements, to show any signs of effort, or even of natural breathing; and equally correct that the musicians are kept hidden in a ritual pit. The orchestra conductor would strike him as a first-class wizard. This singular character stands up in the pit waving a wand and is respectfully treated by the audience as invisible. Though it is hard for him, he does his best not to look at the dancers; when his eyes stray to the stage, he pulls them down at once, visibly upset. He keeps in constant agitation, without ever doing a dance step or touching an instrument, and his costume consists of a pair of long black tails. The Magdalenian visitor, familiar with demented clowns who represent pre-male types of fertilization, would recognize the ironic function of this indispensable figure. And as the curtain fell, he would clap with the rest, delighted by a ceremony so clever in its nonsense and so sweeping in its faith.

If a New Yorker were to tell him, "But you're missing the point, ballet is an art, it isn't a ritual," he might answer, "You no like that word 'ritual.' You say it about our ballet, so I think maybe nice word." And his Paleolithic girl friend might add, "Please, are you a critic? We hear critics will roast fat dancer tonight, just like we do at home. Yum, yum."

Students of culture have suggested that an art of dance preceded that of Paleolithic painting. One can see it might well be so. One can see hints of dance at stages of living one thinks of as extremely remote. The stage of culture at which our species showed the first hints of dancing need not have been beyond that of several species of contemporary wild animals. Some of them that can be greedy and fierce have sexual maneuvers that are harmless and take time. On the one hand such a ceremony can be interrupted, it doesn't necessarily lead into the sexual act; on the other hand the act may occur with a minimum of ceremony. The animals seem to be aware of a ritual that is imaginative and that is fairly impractical. Their ceremonies aren't all sexual ones either. Wolves and fishes have special fighting ones. And the birds that swoop low and soar up sharply at dusk over a town square or in a clearing of the woods, are very likely catching an insect in their open bills, but they seem to be ritualizing the action in a way they don't ritualize their feeding during the day. It is a special bedtime one. Standing among the ruins of the Palatine toward sunset late in October, I saw a flock of migrant birds keeping close like a swarm, beating their small wings almost in unison, forming—the swarm of them—a single revolving vibrating shape which kept changing in the air—a shape that distended, that dived like an hour-glass, that streamed out like a spiral nebula, and then condensed again into a close sphere, a series of choreographic figures which rose and fell above the city as the flock drifted upstream and out of sight. A social celebration and a prehistoric pleasure.

Birds seem to have made a number of dance inventions that strikingly resemble our own. They have sociable group numbers, intimate duets and perhaps trios, and private solos. You see the performers assume a submissively graceful or a show-off air. They seem to be enjoying a formal limitation as they move in relation to a center, and even as they move in relation to a lapse of time. Much as we do, they compose their piece out of contrasted energetic and gliding motions, out of reiterated gestures, out of circular paths and straight lines. Bees even use path patterns for a sign language. A returned honeybee performs for her hivemates a varying number of circles which she keeps cutting with a straight line always in one direction, and her audience understands from her choreography in what direction and how far off are the flowers she has newly discovered. After that she passes around samples of the honey, as if she were giving her dance a

150

title. Such an action does not seem like a ritual to us, but the bees find it very practical.

A formal path involves electing a base from which to move, it involves giving a spot an arbitrary imaginative value. It is a feat of imagination essential to dancing. Birds understand the feat. Cats are very good at it when they play games. One can see their cat eyes brightening with an imaginative light as they establish their base. Kittens begin to play with no sense of a base and gradually learn to imagine. It would be fun to see lions playing from a base the same way, pretending to hunt a bright rag on the end of a rope, pouncing, prancing, darting, tumbling head over heels. I imagine they do it in a wild state and would enjoy doing it in the circus if a lion tamer could be found to play with them.

Animals tame or wild do not seem to mimic anybody but themselves. One notices that their dance-like inventions are formal in principle. One may infer from it, how far back in our history or how deep in our nature the formal aspect of dancing is.

But one notices too that the wild animals don't enjoy watching our performances as much as we do theirs. Rattlesnakes are glad to escape from a bunch of fertility-celebrating Indians. Hungry wolves and lions have never been known to venture on a group of enthusiastically stepping Russians or Africans. Our primitive social celebrations intimidate them. It may be they find the energy of them overpowering, or else that they are appalled by the excessive regularity of them, that is foreign to their habits. None of them time their movements to a regular beat of artificial noise as we do. Dancing to a beat is as peculiarly human a habit as is the habit of artificially making a fire.

Stepping to a man-made beat is a dance invention of a formal nature that we alone have made. Presumably we first danced without a beat the way animals and small children do. Even trained animals don't catch the formality of a beat. Seals and monkeys like to clap, they can learn to play tunes, but they can't keep time either way. Riders can direct horses to keep time, and I remember a circus orchestra taking its beat from an old she-elephant

151

who danced the conga, but it was her rhythm, not the orchestra's. How could our species ever have been bright enough to invent the beat; nowadays we aren't even bright enough to explain it.

There used to be an opinion that the beat was invented by externalizing or objectifying our heart beat, that it was first beaten and then stepped to. The prevalent opinion now seems to be that both the regular acoustic beat and the regularly timed step were invented simultaneously, as a single invention. One tries to imagine unknown races of men—tens of thousands of years before the elegant Magdalenians—as they hopped in the glacial snow for fun, laughing and yelling, and first heard a kind of count, an oscillating one two in their ritual action. They may have heard it in the grunt of their own shout, broken as they landed full weight from a leap, over and over. Or else heard it when an older woman out of pleasure at the tumultuous stepping of the young men, clapped sedately, and one of the boys found himself keeping time with her, and both she and he got more and more excited by the mutual communication. Or else they might have heard a beat when a word shouted over and over as they were stepping turned into a unison metric chant that they stepped to. Perhaps as they stepped and exaggerated a hoarse panting noise of breathing, they heard each other's breath and their own coming simultaneously and were thrilled by the simultaneous step action.

However people began to keep time, one imagines the eerie thrill they felt as they found themselves aware of hearing a beat from the outside and of taking a step from the inside, both of them at once. One can still feel a far echo of that thrill as one first finds one's self hitting the beat; or later in life, as one finds one's self stepping securely to a complex rhythm one isn't able to follow consciously. It is a glorious sensation inside and outside of one. For our ancestors the experience, subjective and objective at the same instant, must have been a wonderful intensification of identity. So peculiar a thrill could have been discovered and then forgotten and rediscovered by exceptional geniuses along successive races and successive climatic epochs. The invention ended by becoming an immensely popular one. But we cannot say that it has been entirely successful. Even now after fifty or a hundred thousand years of practice, a number of us still can't keep time, and shuffle about a ballroom floor missing the measure.

Keeping time isn't the same thing as grace of movement. Animals, small children and even adults moving without a beat but with the grace of dancing enjoy what they do and look beautiful to people who like to watch them. But doing it in strict rhythm as much for those who watch as for those who do it has a cumulative excitement and an extra power. The extra power is like a sense of transport. People are so to speak their better selves. They fly by magic.

People who dance till dawn in a ballroom or who are performers on stage can cheerfully pour out as much extra energy as they otherwise would be able to do only grimly in a matter of life and death. The wild animals cannot waste so much energy on fun. To our species the invention of stepping to a regular beat of man-made noise offers an occasion for the extravagant expense of powers which is the special achievement of our human civilization. And when there is grace in the extravagance and beauty in the excess, we are delighted with ourselves.

Looking back then, one can see that animals invented for their ceremonies a formal limitation of movement. They do not move in every possible way, they move in a few particular ways. For us the added formal invention of the beat increased the artificiality much further. What had once been only instinctive animal patterns, became human objective rhythms as well. They gained an objective measure. The subjective-objective or double awareness of stepping which the beat awakened gave an extra exuberance of power to the dancers. It also sharpened a sense of representation, the sense that a step action can also be a magic emblem. So dancing became exhilarating not only to do, but also to watch, to remember and to think about. From being an instinctively formal pleasure, it became the kind of beautiful communication we call an art. In this way our ancestors invented an art—and perhaps all of art—when they regularized their dancing to a timed beat and a timed step.

The rhythmic stress of stepping is a habit of communication or expression which reaches into the present from unrecognizable races, from epochs and festivals when individuals of genius first made fires, first spoke in sentences. They grin and glare at us, and sit down beside us, these astonishing geniuses, and we feel their powerful wonder as they watch our young people dance, as they watch the bright ballet danced on stage at the same time as we do. They wonder at it, but they know how to watch it, they can see that it is some special kind of dancing.

I seem to be prowling about the subject like a nature photographer prowling about the countryside. The subject is expression in ballet. And I think you see what I am concerned with. I am bringing up some very general features of expression, and am trying to catch the expression of ballet from various points of view. Unless you can catch it in motion, you don't catch it at all. What I have caught of it, seems to be as unspecific as a blur on the edge of the camerafield. But you will notice something or other about it, I believe, and recognize something about the expression, and see it independently of what I say, as a fact of nature, I mean as a fact of human nature. That is what I am concerned with.

We were discussing the beat of the step in general terms. As you step to a beat, you feel the rhythmic pressure of your foot against the floor. You have the rhythm in your feet, so people say, and your feet start to dance. The rhythm of steps is beaten by the floor contact. It is stamped, or tapped or heel-struck, or shuffled. The onlookers catch the rhythm and they instinctively participate in the dancing as long as they stay with the step rhythm.

As the dancer steps he can hear the beat elsewhere than in the feet. And he often makes gestures that are visible rhythmic accents. In the Sahara there is a beautiful solo dance in which the girl moves only on her knees and beats the rhythm with sharp elbow, wrist and finger positions. But in any dance the shape of the body is just as evident when it isn't hitting the beat as when it is. Between beats it keeps moving rhythmically, it keeps making contrasting motions. And as it does, it makes visual shapes the rhythm of which is a sculptural one. Watching the dancers, one sees this other rhythm of shape that their bodies make. Sometimes the dancers and onlookers are so obsessed with the acoustic beat of the step rhythm that they take very little interest in the visual shape rhythm; on the other hand, they sometimes take a great deal of interest in the action of the shapes.

Watching the shape of a movement is something we all do a great deal of in everyday life. You may recognize your friends at a distance by the shape of their walk, even unconsciously. One can often recognize foreigners in America or Americans abroad by a characteristic national shape of walking, that one has never particularly thought about. As for average citizens passing down a city street, plenty of them have oddities in the shape of walking one notices right away—a turned-out forearm that dangles across the back, or a head that pecks, a torso that jiggles up and down, a chest that heaves from side to side. Men and women walking on the street keep making personal shapes with their legs—they snap their heels at the sidewalk, they drawl one thigh past the other, they bounce at each step or trip or stalk or lope, or they waddle, they shuffle or bombinate. Sometimes an oddity looks adorable, but one recognizes it perfectly well as an oddity.

Battalions of parading soldiers manage to avoid the oddities of civilian walking. They show very clearly the basic shape of a walking step—the swinging arm following the opposite leg, the twist at the waist, the dip in the figure's height and the roll. Marching West Pointers can give it a massive containment, and marching parachutists can give it an undulant grace. Young women marching don't seem to give it anything pleasantly collective. They don't seem to take an innocent pride in the achievement of a step the way young men do—a pride as innocent as that of a trained dog. A collective step becomes depersonalized or homogenized only after considerable training.

155

And then it is a monotonous shape, of interest only in multiplication.

In a parade the body looks more two-footed than usual. Two feet traveling from place to place haven't mathematically much choice in the order they can go in. Soldiers at Forward March go from two feet to one foot, then they keep going from one foot to the other foot, and they go from one foot to both feet at Halt. That makes three kinds of step and two more exist: a hop on the same foot, a broadjump from both feet to both feet. These five kinds are all there are. Soldiers could be trained to do all five instead of only three, and you can see right away that once they were trained, the five would look hardly less monotonous than the three.

Dancers have no more feet than other people, and so they live with the same limitation. One could try to watch a ballet from the point of view of the five kinds of step, and see how it keeps scurrying about from one kind to another inside the narrow limits of a two-footed fate. One could try, but one doesn't. As you watch a ballet, the dancers do plenty of different steps and often some new ones you hadn't seen before. One doesn't keep watching the feet to see the sequence in which they are contacting the floor. You keep watching the whole shape of the body before and after the floor-contact.

Between a ballet and a parade, take watching a ballroom dance, especially one where the partners break, like a Lindy or a Mambo or a Virginia Reel. You see the steps exhibiting the dancer's figure, the boy's or the girl's, in a series of contrasting shapes. You see it advancing toward a partner, or turning on itself; it lightly bends and stretches; the thighs close and separate, the knees open and shut, the arms swing guardedly in counteraction to the legs, or they lift both at once. The feet, the hands, the head may refuse a direction the body inclines to or they may accept it. When the waist undulates Cuban-style, the extremities delay following it with an air of detachment. As you watch a good dancer, it all looks very cute, the figure and its movable parts, and you get to know them very pleasantly.

156

The contrasting shapes you see the figure making are as depersonalized as those of a military step—they are sometimes close to a marching step, and the difference is no more than a slight containment, a slight glide of the foot. But the next moment they are quite unmilitary. The dancers move backwards and sideways as much as forward, they kick and spin, they interweave and sway and clap, and the boys and girls keep making mutual shapes. One can see that the dance shapes add particular motions to the basic kind of step they relate to. But one also sees that if you take basic steps to be walking steps then dance steps don't originate in them. Dance steps belong to a different species, so to speak. They don't give the body that useful patient look that walking does. They were invented for mutual fun and for the lively display of sculptural shapes. In Basque folk dancing and in ballet it is normal for a dancer to leap up and make a rapid quivering back-and-forth shape with his feet that is as far from common sense as a bird's brief trill. An entrechat suits the kind of common sense dancing has, but not any other kind.

The action of ballet exhibits the dancer's figure much further and more distinctly than that of a ballroom dance. The shapes are more exact and more extreme. The large reach of all the limbs, the easy erectness of the body regardless, the sharpness of pointed feet, the length of neck, the mildness of wrists, the keen angle of kneebends, the swiftness of sweeping arms, the full visibility of stretched legs turned out from thigh to toe, spreading and shutting; the figure in leaps, spins, stops in balance, slow motion deployments, the feet fluttering and rushing and completely still. Passing through such a dazzling series of transformations, you see the powerfully erect figure, effortless and friendly. It appears larger than life, like in an illusion of intimacy. And you are astonished when a performer who on stage looked so big, at a party turns out to be a wisp of a girl or a quite slender-looking boy.

A ballet dancer has been carefully trained to make the shapes of classic dancing, and one can readily see that they have specific limits. Classic steps limit the action of the joints to a few readily visible differences; so the trajectory of the body as it makes the shape is defined. A classic dancer has a habit of many years' standing of rotating, bending and stretching the several joints of legs and arms, of the neck and spine, in movements of which the start, the trajectory and the finish have become second nature. How such a movement draws after it the rest of the body, or how it joins a movement before it or one after it, have become for him instinctive. The whole of the shape is second nature to him, and so are its component parts. He can alter a specific detail without becoming confused in the main shape. He is familiar with the impetus he must give that will mould it very clearly in each of its dimensions. And in all these shapes, whether large or small, the dancer has come to judge his momentum and his balance at varying speeds by instinct. So they appear effortless and unconfused and in harmony.

A classic dancer's legs seem to move not from the hip joint but from further up, from the waist and the small of the back; and the arms not from the shoulder, but from lower down, from the same part of the back as the legs; it lengthens both extremities and harmonizes them. The head moves at the end of a neck like a giraffe's that seems to begin below the shoulderblades. The head can also move without the neck, just from the joint where head and spine meet, tilting against a motionless neck. Then you see its small motion enlarged by the unexpected contrast to so very long and separate a neck. In the same way a flick of ankle or of wrist can be magnified by the long-looking immobile leg or arm it is at the far end of. So aspects of scale appear.

Classic action exhibits the dancer's body very clearly but it steadily exhibits aspects of it that everyday life shows only at rare moments. Classic arms, for instance, keep to a few large trajectories and positions, they keep distinct from the torso, and the quality they exhibit in arms is the long lightness of them. They minimize the activity of elbow and wrists. In everyday life arms and hands do all the chattering, and the legs growl now and then. On the contrary in classic dancing the legs seem to carry the tune, and the arms add to it a milder second voice.

Classic legs turned out from the hip joint down look unusually exposed. One sees the inside surface of them, though the dancer is facing you. One sees the modeling of their parts, the differentiated action of·the joints flexing or rotating—the lively bend of the knee especially. One watches the torque and powerful spread of the thighs at their base. The ballerina holds the bone turned in its socket rigid, and the leg extends itself to its complete stretch in the air, sideways, to the back or to the front. The visually exposed action of the legs, fully turned out, fully bending and stretching, can look wonderfully generous.

No matter how large the action of legs and of arms, the classic back does not have to yield, and its stretched erectness is extremely long. It bends in or out when it chooses. The low-held shoulders open the breast or chest. But classicism doesn't feature the chest as a separate attraction the way advertising does; a slight, momentary and beautiful lift of the rib-cage is a movement of the upper back. At the back of the torso or at the front, it is the waist that one keeps looking at. Looking at it you see the figure's changing silhouette at a glance. The waist is the center of the dance shape, or the implied center. You seem to sense in its quickness a lightning anticipation of the next motion. The power of the·waist is that of an athlete's, but the quickness of it is a child's.

Among the ways classicism exhibits the body that are different from those of everyday life, the most different is that of toesteps which look like tiny stilts the girl is treading on. She can step onto them, or she can rise into them, rising with a soft flick of both feet. She can step about on them with a fanatic delicacy and a penetrating precision. She can spin on them like a bat out of hell. When she jumps or runs on them one hears a muffled tapping that sometimes sounds fleshy. From the side you see the sole curving like a bending knifeblade with at the back the queer handle of the heel. From the front they over-elongate the leg and alter the body's proportions; and the extreme erectness of the foot seems in keeping with the extremely pulled-up waist and the stretched lightness of the slender ballerina. Sometimes a figure on a single toe-point, as its shape deploys from so narrow a balance, looks intently alone by itself, and even if a partner supports it, intently individual. At other times one feels the contrast between the large pliancy of the knees, the lesser one of the ankles, and the scarcely perceptible give of the bones of the arch.

Toesteps sharpen one's eye to the figure's contact with the floor. The action of rhythm and the action of shape meet and keep meeting at the moment of floor contact. Classic dancing can make that moment keen to the eye so the rhythm it sees has an edge. Take for instance the moment on the ground between two leaps. You see the feet arriving stretched through the air, the ankles flex in a flash, you see the feet on the floor, motionless in their small position, catch the flying body's momentum, and instantly the ankles flash again as the legs stretch off into the air in the new leap. The feet have tossed the dancer's momentum forward, without a wobble or a blur. The eye has caught their moment of stillness the more sharply because the position they held is a familiar one that keeps returning. And that almost imperceptible stillness of theirs cuts the first shape from the second, and makes the rhythm of motion carry.

In these peculiar appearances and the recurrent complete stillness of the classic body, the eye recognizes or the imagination recognizes the sensual meaning of the exhibited parts, and the dramatic implication of their motions. It sees these implications and meanings appear and disappear. They are exhibited without the continuity or the stress that could present them as if in states of greed or of anxiety. Their moment by moment sensual innocence allows the imagination the more unembarrassed play.

The steps keep unfolding the body in large or small ways, and reassembling it in vertical balance like a butterfly. The peculiarity of its grace in motion is consistent and is shared by all the figures on stage. The expressive meaning is divided between recognizable details and the visual grace, the very light alternation of weight of an over-all unrecognizable consistency. The consistency is as if the most usual and easy of ballet steps set a pitch for the eye —a pitch of carriage and balance in action—to which everything that is done on stage keeps a clear relation by its quality of impulse and of carriage. The over-all effect is that of a spontaneous harmony of action. But its common sense remains that of a dance.

The peculiar values of classic style we have been considering are an invention extending from nowadays back into a collective past. They are in that sense traditional values. Ballet began as the kind of dancing current at village festivals around the Mediterranean from the times of King Minos and Daedalus to those of da Vinci. Young Boccaccio and young Dante before him danced these local steps; and Homer had danced them locally as a boy. The village dances changed so slowly that they were always traditional. At the edge of the holiday crowd, when the piper played, the tots tried to do the steps before they could keep time. Everyone had grown up knowing the sequences and the tunes that went with them, and knowing from having watched it the harmony that the dance could show. People always liked to watch the boys and girls do it, and liked giving a prize to the sweetest dancer. The steps were a part of the brightness of the recurrent holiday, and they brought back other bright faces and festivals that the little region had known in the past. The sense of such holidays was strong at the center of civilization for a long time, and one finds echoes of it reaching back from verses of the *Divine Comedy* to a carved Minoan cylinder three thousand years earlier depicting harvesters marching home with a band, singing and joking. In classic Greek representations of a dance step the harmony is sometimes so rich it implies contrary steps and extended phrases. Scholars have traced a number of ballet movements to classic Greek prototypes. No reason to suppose that the ancient dances were simple.

When, around the middle of the millennium before Christ, urban prosperity spread to Europe from the East,

161

the country steps were theatricalized first for Greek theatres, and later for the elaborate and ornate theatres of the Roman Empire. Then prosperity retreated eastward again, and for another thousand years dancing was again that of lively young people doing their local steps at balls or church festivals, with here and there some hired mimes or an anxious acrobat passing the hat. These hard-bitten comics were tramps and outsiders.

When prosperity and a pleasure in grace of behavior spread again—this time from Renaissance Italy—the country dances were theatricalized once more. Like the earlier Greek professionals, the new Italian ones rearranged the steps to new tunes, they turned them out a bit to face the public, and gave them a thread of story. They saw that the pleasure of the dances was their harmony. The pantomime they took over was that of the original holiday occasion, that of pleasant social behavior. Professionals developed indoors a sense of lyric expression in dancing. But the outdoor mimes, thanks to the same prosperity, had developed their capers and their insistent explosive pantomime into a rowdy Italian buffoonery. These two opposite kinds of expression had existed in the ancient theatres as well, and existed time out of mind, sometimes blending, sometimes not. By the seventeenth century, when theatre dancing became organized, the ballet dancers were likely to sustain the sentiment, but the comics were likely to steal the show.

And here we are watching ballet in the prosperous mid-twentieth century. In a number of professional terms and steps dancers can recognize three hundred years of continuity behind them. Ballet-goers can recognize two hundred years in a number of documents that evoke an artistic excitement related to their own. Though the comics still steal the show, the element which holds a ballet together and which creates the big climaxes is the one we call classic dancing. Classicism has stretched the ancient country steps and all the others it has added to them—it has stretched them vertically and horizontally to heighten the drama of dance momentum. But in its extended range of large-scale theatre steps and their spectacular momentum, ballet has kept the gift of harmony it began with. Today's professionals of ballet are artists, they are virtuosos, craftsmen specialized for life. But as one watches them, just when they are at their best, history seems to vanish. The quality of character that makes a dancer seems the same as three or four thousand years ago. The nature of the pleasure they give by their genius as dancers does not seem to have changed much since Minoan times.

One July noon, in an Aegean village on the Greek island of Mykonos, two friends and I, after visiting a monastery, were waiting in the sun for the single daily bus. The torrent of heat and light was so intense that we went into a cafe for shelter. Inside the radio was playing folk tunes and a young farmer was dancing solo to it, while two stood around watching him and waiting for their turn. But when the second young man began, the miracle happened. The traditional steps produced an effect entirely different. The rapidity of decision, the brilliance of impetus, the grace were unforeseeable, as if on another scale. He was a dancer in the class of the classic stars one sees on stage. It was an extraordinary delight to watch him. He finished his turn. But while the next young farmer was dancing, the bus honked outside, and we foreigners ran out to catch it.

An extraordinary delight such as this is the standard of theatre performance. It is the standard that nature sets. A genius for dancing keeps turning up in a particular boy or girl who are doing the regulation steps they grew up with. Outside the theatre or inside it, the gift creates an immediate communication. For some people watching such great moments at a ballet performance, the steps themselves disappear in a blaze of glory. For others the steps remain distinctly visible, but they make as much sense as if one could do them one's self. One understands them. It is like the sensation of understanding a foreign language because a girl has looked so ravishing speaking it.

But for professionals as they watched ballet dancers of genius at such great moments, and knew each step they were doing from long experience, it was the revelation of the large-scale effect possible in the familiar steps that

163

fascinated them. Being professionals they tried to catch the technical method. And what they caught of it during several hundred years has become classic style.

Style in its professional aspect is a question of good habits in the way steps are done. And so ballet has gradually settled on several habits it prefers. It has decided on the turned-out thighs, on the pulled-up waist that joins them to the erect spine, on the low-held shoulder line. It has decided on a few main movements of the head, of the arms, of the torso, of the several leg joints. And on fifty or so main steps. These main steps and the main movements that can modify them are the habitual exercises with which good habits of balance and carriage, with which habits of harmony and rhythm can be trained in apprentices to reach a large-scale theatre effect. They form a common basis of action for professionals. And the history of them is that they have always been specifically dance steps or elements of dance steps, enlarged in scale by constant use in the theatre.

In ancient Italian towns the narrow main street at dusk becomes a kind of theatre. The community strolls affably and looks itself over. The girls and the young men, from fifteen to twenty-two, display their charm to one another with a lively sociability. The more grace they show the better the community likes them. In Florence or in Naples, in the ancient city slums the young people are virtuoso performers, and they do a bit of promenading any time they are not busy. A foreigner in Rome, who loses his way among the fifteenth and sixteenth century alleys and squares, hunting in those neighborhoods for the Sybils of Raphael or the birthplace of Metastasio, discovers how bright about their grace the local young Romans can be. They appreciate it in themselves and in each other equally. Their stroll is as responsive as if it were a physical conversation. Chunkily built though they are, they place their feet, they articulate the arms and legs, the boys stress the opening, and the girls the closing of the limbs. Their necks and waists have an insinuating harmony. They move from the waist turning to look, or stepping back in effacé to let a girl pass, or advancing a sheltering arm (like in croisé). They present their person and they put an arm around each other's waist or shoulder with a graceful intimacy. Their liveliness makes these courteous formalities—that recall ballet—a mutual game of skill. The foreign ballet fan as he goes home through the purple Roman dusk, charmed by the physical caress of it, confuses the shapes of Raphael with those of the performance. But he realizes what it means that ballet was originally an Italian dance, and he becomes aware of the lively sociability of its spirit and of its forms.

The general question I have been considering is harmony in classic dancing. But I hope the reference to Italy has not been misleading. Classic dancing doesn't look Italian when Americans do it, or when English dancers do it, or Russian, or French or Danish dancers; it doesn't, and can't and needn't. But it has harmony when any of them do it. It has a visual harmony of shapes due to the specific action of the body that we were considering earlier. Let us go back to the single step, and make sure where we are, close enough to the Atlantic seaboard.

As one lies with closed eyes in bed or on a beach far from town trying to recall what a single step looks like, one sees several steps and dancers combined in a phrase, and sees the shape of a phrase as if it were an extended step, many-legged and many-armed, with a particular departure, trajectory and arrival. And, as phrases succeed one another, one sees them take direction on stage, and one sees the visual momentum their paths can have with relation to a center of action, or to several centers, coming down stage, retiring back, escaping to the sides, appearing from the wings. The momentum of phrases accentuates the angle at which a figure is presented, or at which it acts, the directions it takes or only aspires to take. The momentum disengages a leading quality of motion, hopping, fluttering, soaring, stopping dead. It carries along a single figure, or several mutually or a group. It draws the figures deeper into dramatic situations, serious or comic ones.

But the action of a step determines the ramifications, the rise and fall of the continuous momentum. You begin to see the active impetus of the dancers creating the impetus moment by moment. They step out of one shape and into another, they change direction or speed, they erect and dissolve a configuration, and their secure and steady impetus keeps coming. The situations that dissolve as one watches are created and swept along by the ease and the fun and the positive lightness of it. They dance and as they do, create in their wake an architectural momentum of imaginary weights and transported presences. Their activity does not leave behind any material object, only an imaginary one.

The stage by its stationary center and its fixed proportions accumulates the imaginative reality. Stage area and stage height appear to be permanent actualities. Within them the brief shape that a dancer's body makes can look small and lost, or it can spread securely and for an instant appear on their scale. One can respond to the visual significance—the visual spaciousness—of such a moment of dance motion without being able to explain it reasonably in other terms.

The shape the dancer makes at such a moment has no specific representational aspect. You have seen the same shape before with different feelings. And yet often the whole house responds to such a moment of classic climax. It seems not to insist on being understood rationally. It presents no problem, it presents a climax of dancing. One can leave the ambiguity of it at that and enjoy at once both the climactic beauty of it and the nonsense.

Or else as one responds in the moment to the effortless sense of completion and of freedom that its spaciousness gives one, one may feel that the expression of the motion one is watching has been seen throughout the piece without being fulfilled until now. It is the expression the piece is about. One feels the cumulative drama it rises on. Then its visual spaciousness offers to one's imagination a large or a tragic image to recognize. It is not frightening, the lucidity of the moment is as sweet as happiness. Like a word you have often heard that spoken without pressure at a certain moment is a final one, as large as your life, so the classic shape is an effortless motion that replies.

To the Symbolist poet Mallarmé, it appeared as an emblematic reply—as of blossom or dagger or cup—a climactic perception of mutual identity. Like in a lucidity of perception there is in the motion no sense of intention or pressure. The significance of it appears in the present moment, as the climactic significance of a savage ritual appeared at the moment it occurred in our racial past.

As you lie on the hot deserted beach far from town and with closed eyes recall the visual moment of climax, and scarcely hear the hoarse breathing of the small surf, a memory of the music it rose on returns, and you remember the prolonged melodious momentum of the score as if the musical phrase the step rose on had arrived from so far. So deep in the piece it appears to have been.

The power of projection that music has strikes me as mysterious but it is a fact of nature. I have heard people who considered themselves unmusical modestly make acute remarks on the music of a ballet; and I once sat next to a deaf mute who followed the performance with delight and enrolled in a ballet school afterwards. However one is conscious of it, without music classic dancing is no more real than swimming is real without water around it. The more ballet turns to pantomime, the less intimate its relation to the music becomes; but the more it turns to dancing, the more it enjoys the music's presence, bar by bar. Even when the steps stand aside and let the music alone, they are intimately aware of it.

We spoke of the beat at the beginning and here we are back to it. Take a specific ballet step. An assemblé looks different if it lands on one of the measure or if it lands on four; an entrechat looks different if the push from the floor comes on the downbeat, or if on the downbeat the legs beat in the air. A promenade en arabesque done at the same speed looks different if it is done in three-four time or in four-four. The stress of the measure supports a different phase of the step; it gives the motion a different lift and visual accent and expression. And as the stress of the beat can give a different look to the step, so can the stresses of the other kinds of musical emphasis—the stresses of dynamics, of melody, of harmony, of timbre, of pathos.

All these stresses offer their various support to the steps. They are like a floor with various degrees of resilience to dance on. The steps step in some places and not in others. They make a choice of stresses.

But as you hear the piece the stresses merge into a musical momentum that varies and into a musical expression that changes; and they build into large coherent sections and finally into a completed structure of musical sound with a coherent identity. We are used to sensing the coherence of music sometimes in one way, sometimes in another. And while we sense a coherence it has, we can believe in the coherence of long sequences of dancing we are watching. We see their coherence from the point of reference of the musical meaning. A long dance gathers power by coherence.

But the relation of eye and ear is a mutual one. The visual action also makes particular stresses in the music more perceptible, and continuities more clearly coherent. Watching the sweep of the dance momentum, you feel more keenly the musical one, and the visual drama can give you an insight to the force of character of the score. A dance happily married to its score likes to make jokes without raising its small voice, and the thundering score likes it too.

But the steps of classic dancing have always enjoyed being timed to the notes of music, and their rhythm has always responded to musical rhythm. Inside the labyrinth of complex musical structures, you see ballet following the clue of the rhythm, you see it hearing the other musical forces as they affect the current of the rhythm, as they leave or don't leave the rhythm a danceable one. You see the dance listening and choosing its own rhythmic response. A dance ballet gets its power of projection by the choice of its response to the larger structures of musical rhythm. So its power of character reveals itself in a more complexly happy marriage. Timed as classic dancing is to strict measures of time, confined to a limited range of motion, lighter in the stress it communicates than everyday motion, the power of character, the power of insight it develops and sustains in reference to its chosen score is a power of its own creation. Mutually to the music, you watch the dance take shape and make sense and show the dazzling grace of an imaginative freedom. It is worth watching for.

What we have been considering is what is usually called the form of classic dancing. I am not suggesting that a ballet has no content, and I am not suggesting either that its form is its content. I have heard these statements but they make no sense to me. I think the meaning of the two words is approximately clear, and that they describe different ways of approaching an event, or of discussing it. I have been avoiding the distinction because I have been discussing what classic dancing looks like regardless of the subject matter of the ballet, what one is aware of at the moment one sees the dancer move, what one is aware of before one makes the distinction between content and form. It is a fairly confused awareness, but it is real enough. One doesn't, as far as I can see, make any sharp distinction between content and form in the case of pleasant events while one is enjoying them, or of people one is in love with; one instinctively doesn't.

The forms of classic dancing are one may say no less instinctive for being formal. The way a cat comes up to you at night in a deserted city street to be patted, and when you crouch to pat her, the way she will enjoy a stroke or two and then pass out of reach, stop there facing away into the night, and return for another stroke or two, and then pass behind you and return on your other side—all this has a form that you meet again on stage when the ballerina is doing a Petipa adagio. And while cats one meets on different nights all like to follow the same adagio form, one cat will vary it by hunching her back or rolling seductively just out of reach, another another night by standing high on her toes as you pat her, and making little sous-sus on her front paws; a third by grand Petersburg-style tail wavings; a fourth, if you are down close enough, by rising on her hind paws, resting her front ones weightlessly on you, raising her wide ballerina eyes to yours, and then—delicate as a single finger pirouette—giving the tip of your nose a tender nip. When a cat has had enough adagio, she sits down apart; or else, changing to mime, she scampers artificially away, pretending to be scared by the passing of a solitary nocturnal truck. Dogs—dogs you take on daytime country walks are virtuosos of allegro. They invent heroic dashes, sharp zig-zags running low ending in grand jetés that slow down; or else in the midst of a demi-manege at cannonball speed they stop dead. They mean you to get the joke, and they make it dead-pan like troupers. Then they come up to you at an untheatrical dogtrot, smiling, breathing hard, with shining eyes; they enjoy your applause, but they distinguish between the performance when they were pretending and the bow they take after it is finished when they are honest dogs again.

One watches ballet just as one would the animals, but since there is more to be seen, there is more to watch. More to be seen and also more to recognize. Not only the formal shapes but also the pantomime shapes with their specific allusions. And everybody likes to see pantomime in the course of a ballet evening. It gives the feeling of being back in a more familiar rational world, back safe from the flight through the intuitive rhythmic world of irrational symbols and of the charming animals.

We have been considering ballet from its aspect as dancing. Its aspect as pantomime is equally interesting; so is its aspect as an art of the choreographer and as an art of the dancer. They are all part of ballet just as much as what I have been discussing—and I love them just as much, and they don't lose any of their beauty merely by being unmentioned.

Dancers, Buildings
and People in the Street

ON THE SUBJECT of dance criticism, I should like to make clear a distinction that I believe is very valuable, to keep the question from getting confused. And that is that there are two quite different aspects to it. One part of dance criticism is seeing what is happening on stage. The other is describing clearly what it is you saw. Seeing something happen is always fun for everybody, until they get exhausted. It is very exhausting to keep looking, of course, just as it is to keep doing anything else; and from an instinct of self-preservation many people look only a little. One can get along in life perfectly well without looking much. You all know how very little one is likely to see happening on the street—a familiar street at a familiar time of day while one is using the street to get somewhere. So much is happening inside one, one's private excitements and responsibilities, one can't find the energy to watch the strangers passing by, or the architecture or the weather around; one feels there is a use in getting to the place one is headed for and doing something or other there, getting a book or succeeding in a job or discussing a situation with a friend, all that has a use, but what use is there in looking at the momentary look of the street, of 106th and Broadway. No use at all. Looking at a dance performance has some use, presumably. And certainly it is a great deal less exhausting than looking at the disjointed fragments of impression that one can see in traffic. Not only that the performance is arranged so that it is convenient to look at, easy to pay continuous attention to, and attractive, but also that the excitement in it seems to have points of contact with the excitement of one's own personal life, with the curiosity that makes one want to go get a special book, or the exciting self-importance that makes one want to succeed, or even the absorbing drama of talking and listening to someone of one's own age with whom one is on the verge of being in love. When you feel that the emotion that is coming toward you from the performance is like a part of your own at some moment when you were very excited, it is easy to be interested. And of course if you feel the audience thrilled all around you just when you are thrilled too, that is very peculiar and agreeable. Instead of those people and houses on the street that are only vaguely related to you in the sense that they are Americans and contemporary, here in the theatre, you are almost like in some imaginary family, where everybody is talking about something that concerns you intimately and everybody is interested and to a certain extent understands your own viewpoint and the irrational convictions you have that are even more urgent than your viewpoint. The amplitude that you feel you see with at your most intelligent moments, this amplitude seems in the theatre to be naturally understood on stage and in the audience, in a way it isn't often appreciated while you are with the people you know outside the theatre. At a show you can tell perfectly well when it is happening to you, this experience of an enlarged view of what is really so and true, or when it isn't happening to you. When you talk to your friends about it after the curtain goes down, they sometimes agree, and sometimes they don't. And it is strange how whether they do or don't, it is very hard usually to specify what the excitement was about, or the precise point at which it gave you the feeling of being really beautiful. Brilliant, magnificent, stupendous, no doubt all these things are true of the performance, but even if you and your friends agree that it was all those things, it is likely that there was some particular moment that made a special impression which you are not talking about. Maybe you are afraid that that particular moment wasn't really the most important, that it didn't express the idea or that it didn't get special applause or wasn't the climax. You were really excited by the performance and now you are afraid you can't show you understand it. Meanwhile while you hesitate to talk about it, a friend in the crowd who talks more readily is delivering a brilliant criticism specifying technical dance details, moral implications, musicological or iconographic finesses; or else maybe he is sailing off into a wild nonsensical camp that has nothing to do with the piece but which is fun to listen to, even though it's a familiar trick of his. So the evening slips out of your awareness like many others. Did you really see anything? Did you see any more than you saw in the morning on the street? Was it a real excitement you felt? What is left over of the wonderful moment you had, or didn't you really have any wonderful moment at all, where you actually saw on stage a real person moving and you felt the relation to your real private life with a sudden poignancy as if for that second you were drunk. Dance criticism has two different aspects: one is being made drunk for a second by seeing something happen; the other is expressing lucidly what you saw when you were drunk. I suppose I should add quite stuffily that it is the performance you should get drunk on, not anything else. But I am sure you have understood me anyway.

Now the second part of criticism, that of expressing lucidly what happened, is of course what makes criticism criticism. If you are going in for criticism you must have the gift in the first place, and in the second place you must cultivate it, you must practice and try. Writing criticism is a subject of interest to those who do it, but it is a separate process from that of seeing what happens. And seeing what happens is of course of much more general interest. This is what you presumably have a gift for, since you have chosen dancing as a subject of special study, and no doubt you have already cultivated this gift. I am sure you would all of you have something interesting and personal to say about what one can see and perhaps too about what one can't see.

Seeing is at any rate the subject I would like to talk

173

about today, I can well imagine that for some of you this is not a subject of prime interest. Some of you are much more occupied with creating or inventing dances, than with seeing them; when you look at them you look at them from the point of view of an artist who is concerned with his own, with her own, creating. Creating, of course, is very exciting, and it is very exciting whether you are good at it or not; you must have noticed that already in watching other people create, whose work looks silly to you, but whose excitement, even if you think it ought not to be, is just as serious to them as that of a creator whose creating isn't silly. But creating dancing and seeing dancing are not the same excitement. And it is not about creating that I mean to speak; I am telling you this, so you won't sit here unless you can spare the time for considering in a disinterested way what seeing is like; please don't feel embarrassed about leaving now, though I agree it would be rude of you to leave later. And it is not very likely either that I shall tell you any facts that you had better write down. I rather think you know all the same facts I do about dancing, and certainly you know some I don't; I have forgotten some I used to know. About facts, too, what interests me just now is how differently they can look, one sees them one way and one sees them another way another time, and yet one is still seeing the same fact. Facts have a way of dancing about, now performing a solo then reappearing in the chorus, linking themselves now with facts of one kind, now with facts of another, and quite changing their style as they do. Of course you have to know the facts so you can recognize them, or you can't appreciate how they move, how they keep dancing. We are supposed to discuss dance history sometime in this seminar and I hope we will. But not today.

At the beginning of what I said today I talked about one sort of seeing, namely a kind that leads to recognizing on stage and inside yourself an echo of some personal, original excitement you already know. I call it an echo because I am supposing that the event which originally caused the excitement in one's self is not literally the same as the event you see happen on stage. I myself, for instance, have never been a Prince or fallen in love with a creature that was half girl and half swan, nor have I myself been an enchanted Swan Princess, but I have been really moved, and transported by some performances of *Swan Lake,* and by both sides of that story. In fact, it is much more exciting if I can feel both sides happening to me, and not just one. But I am sure you have already jumped ahead of me to the next step of the argument, and you can see that not only have I never been such people or been in their situation, but besides that I don't look like either of them, nor could I, even if I were inspired, dance the steps the way they do. Nor even the steps of the other dancers, the soloists or the chorus.

You don't seem to have taken these remarks of mine as a joke. But I hope you realized that I was pointing out that the kind of identification one feels at a dance performance with the performers is not a literal kind. On the other hand, it is very probable that you yourselves watch a dance performance with a certain professional awareness of what is going on.

A professional sees quite clearly "I could do that better, I couldn't do that nearly so well." A professional sees the finesse or the awkwardness of a performer very distinctly, at least in a field of dance execution he or she is accustomed to working in; and a choreographer sees similarly how a piece is put together, or as the phrase is, how the material has been handled. But this is evidently a very special way of looking at a performance. One may go further and say that a theatre performance is not intended to be seen from this special viewpoint. Craftsmanship is a matter of professional ethics; a surgeon is not bound to explain to you what he is doing while he is operating on you, and similarly no art form, no theatre form is meant to succeed in creating its magic with the professionals scattered in the audience. Other doctors seeing a cure, may say, your doctor was a quack but he was lucky; and similarly professionals may say after a performance, Yes, the ballerina was stupendous, she didn't fake a thing—or else say, she may not have thrilled you, but there aren't four girls in the world who can do a something or other

175

the way she did—and this is all to the good, it is honorable and it is real seeing. But I am interested just now to bring to your attention or recall to your experience not that professional way of seeing, but a more general way. I am interested at the moment in recalling to you how it looks when one sees dancing as non-professionals do, in the way you yourselves I suppose look at pictures, at buildings, at political history or at landscapes or at strangers you pass on the street. Or as you read poetry.

In other words the way you look at daily life or at art for the mere pleasure of seeing, without trying to put yourself actively in it, without meaning to do anything about it. I am talking about seeing what happens when people are dancing, seeing how they look. Watching them and appreciating the beauty they show. Appreciating the ugliness they show if that's what you see. Seeing this is beautiful, this ugly, this is nothing as far as I can see. As long as you pay attention there is always something going on, either attractive or unattractive, but nobody can always pay attention, so sometimes there is nothing as far as you can see, because you have really had enough of seeing; and quite often there is very little, but anyway you are looking at people dancing, and you are seeing them while they dance.

Speaking personally, I think there is quite a difference between seeing people dance as part of daily life, and seeing them dance in a theatre performance. Seeing them dance as part of daily life is seeing people dance in a living room or a ballroom or a nightclub, or seeing them dance folk dances either naturally or artificially in a folk dance group. For that matter classroom dancing and even rehearsal dancing seems to me a part of daily life, though it is as special as seeing a surgeon operate, or hearing the boss blow up in his office. Dancing in daily life is also seeing the pretty movements and gestures people make. In the Caribbean, for instance, the walk of Negroes is often, well, miraculous. Both the feminine stroll and the masculine one, each entirely different. In Italy you see another beautiful way of strolling, that of shorter muscles, more complex in their plasticity, with girls deliciously turning

176

their breast very slightly, deliciously pointing their feet. You should see how harmoniously the young men can loll. American young men loll quite differently, resting on a peripheral point, Italians loll resting on a more central one. Italians on the street, boys and girls, both have an extraordinary sense of the space they really occupy, and of filling that space harmoniously as they rest or move; Americans occupy a much larger space than their actual bodies do; I mean, to follow the harmony of their movement or of their lolling you have to include a much larger area in space than they are actually occupying. This annoys many Europeans; it annoys their instinct of modesty. But it has a beauty of its own, that a few of them appreciate. It has so to speak an intellectual appeal; it has because it refers to an imaginary space, an imaginary volume, not to a real and visible one. Europeans sense the intellectual volume but they fail to see how it is filled by intellectual concepts—so they suppose that the American they see lolling and assuming to himself too much space, more space than he actually needs, is a kind of a conqueror, is a kind of non-intellectual or merely material occupying power. In Italy I have watched American sailors, soldiers and tourists, all with the same expansive instinct in their movements and their repose, looking like people from another planet among Italians with their self-contained and traditionally centered movements. To me these Americans looked quite uncomfortable, and embarrassed, quite willing to look smaller if they only knew how. Here in New York where everybody expects them to look the way they do, Americans look unselfconscious and modest despite their traditional expansivity of movement. There is room enough. Not because there is actually more—there isn't in New York—but because people expect it, they like it if people move that way. Europeans who arrive here look peculiarly circumspect and tight to us. Foreign sailors in Times Square look completely swamped in the big imaginary masses surging around and over them.

Well, this is what I mean by dancing in daily life. For myself I think the walk of New Yorkers is amazingly beautiful, so large and clear. But when I go inland, or out

West, it is much sweeter. On the other hand, it has very little either of Caribbean lusciousness or of Italian *contraposto*. It hasn't much savor, to roll on your tongue, that it hasn't. Or at least you have to be quite subtle, or very much in love to distinguish so delicate a perfume.

That, of course, is supposed to be another joke, but naturally you would rather travel yourself than hear about it. I can't expect you to see my point without having been to countries where the way of walking is quite different from what ours is here. However, if you were observant, and you ought to be as dance majors, you would have long ago enjoyed the many kinds of walking you can see right in this city, boys and girls, Negro and white, Puerto Rican and Western American and Eastern, foreigners, professors and dancers, mechanics and businessmen, ladies entering a theatre with half a drink too much, and shoppers at Macy's. You can see everything in the world here in isolated examples at least, peculiar characters or people who are for the moment you see them peculiar. And everybody is quite peculiar now and then. Not to mention how peculiar anybody can be at home.

Daily life is wonderfully full of things to see. Not only people's movements, but the objects around them, the shape of the rooms they live in, the ornaments architects make around windows and doors, the peculiar ways buildings end in the air, the watertanks, the fantastic differences in their street façades on the first floor. A French composer who was here said to me, "I had expected the streets of New York to be monotonous, after looking at a map of all those rectangles; but now I see the differences in height between buildings, I find I have never seen streets so diverse one from another." But if you start looking at New York architecture, you will notice not only the sometimes extraordinary delicacy of the window framings, but also the standpipes, the grandiose plaques of granite and marble on ground floors of office buildings, the windowless side walls, the careful, though senseless, marble ornaments. And then the masses, the way the office and factory buildings pile up together in perspective. And under them the drive of traffic, those brilliantly

178

colored trucks with their fanciful lettering, the violent paint on cars, signs, houses, as well as lips. Sunsets turn the red-painted houses in the cross-streets to the flush of live rose petals. And the summer sky of New York for that matter is as magnificent as the sky of Venice. Do you see all this? Do you see what a forty or sixty-story building looks like from straight below? And do you see how it comes up from the sidewalk as if it intended to go up no more than five stories? Do you see the bluish haze on the city as if you were in a forest? As for myself, I wouldn't have seen such things if I hadn't seen them first in the photographs of Rudolph Burckhardt. But after seeing them in his photographs, I went out to look if it were true. And it was. There is no excuse for you as dance majors not to discover them for yourselves. Go and see them. There is no point in living here, if you don't see the city you are living in. And after you have seen Manhattan, you can discover other grandeurs out in Queens, in Brooklyn, and in those stinking marshes of Jersey.

All that is here. And it is worth seeing. When you get to Rome, or to Fez in Morocco, or to Paris, or to Constantinople, or to Peking, I hope you will get there, I have always wanted to, you will see other things beautiful in another way, but meanwhile since you are dance majors and are interested and gifted in seeing, look around here. If you cut my talks and bring me instead a report of what you saw in the city, I will certainly mark you present, and if you can report something interesting, I will give you a good mark. It is absurd to sit here in four walls while all that extraordinary interest is going on around us. But then education is a lazy, a dull way of learning, and you seem to have chosen it; forget it.

However, if you will insist on listening to me instead of going out and looking for yourselves, I will have to go on with this nonsense. Since you are here I have to go on talking and you listening, instead of you and me walking around and seeing things. And I have to go on logically, which we both realize is nonsense. Logically having talked about what you can see in daily life, I have to go on that very different way of seeing, which you use in seeing art.

For myself, I make a distinction between seeing daily life and seeing art. Not that seeing is different. Seeing is the same. But seeing art is seeing an ordered and imaginary world, subjective, and concentrated. Seeing in the theatre is seeing what you don't see quite that way in life. In fact, it's nothing like that way. You sit all evening in one place and look at an illuminated stage, and music is going on, and people are performing who have been trained in some peculiar way for years, and since we are talking about a dance performance, nobody is expected to say a word, either on stage or in the house. It is all very peculiar. But there are quite a lot of people, ordinary enough citizens watching the stage along with you. All these people in the audience are used to having information conveyed to them by words spoken or written, but here they are just looking at young people dancing to music. And they expect to have something interesting conveyed to them. It is certainly peculiar.

But then, art is peculiar. I won't speak of concert music, which is obviously peculiar, and which thousands every evening listen to, and evidently get satisfaction out of. But even painting is a strange thing. That people will look at some dirt on a canvas, just a little rectangle on a wall, and get all sorts of exalted feelings and ideas from it is not at all natural, it is not at all obvious. Why do they prefer one picture so much to another one? They will tell you and get very eloquent, but it does seem unreasonable. It seems unreasonable if you don't see it. And for all the other arts it's the same. The difference between the "Ode on a Grecian Urn" and a letter on the editorial page of the *Daily News* isn't so great if you look at both of them without reading them. Art is certainly even more mysterious and nonsensical than daily life. But what a pleasure it can be. A pleasure much more extraordinary than a hydrogen bomb is extraordinary.

There is nothing everyday about art. There is nothing everyday about dancing as an art. And that is the extraordinary pleasure of seeing it. I think that is enough for today.

Balanchine Choreographing

WHEN GEORGE BALANCHINE was about to choreograph *Variants* to a new score by Gunther Schuller, I was asked to report the process as clearly as I should be able to; Rudolph Burckhardt was to take photographs. Mr. Balanchine very generously gave us permission to attend rehearsals.

The wall-clock in a large classroom at the School of American Ballet marked five minutes before the hour. Two dancers, Melissa Hayden and Arthur Mitchell, were doing a few final stretches at the barre; they paused and began to wipe their faces and necks. Balanchine stood beside the piano intently reading his copy of the score. He turned to the pianist and asked a question; the pianist played several dissonances and they discussed the point for a moment. Balanchine went back to reading. The dancers had come to the center of the room, where they stood gossiping in subdued voices, glancing toward the piano and then into the mirror which faced them the whole length of the wall. Still absorbed, the choreographer put down his score, looked pleasantly at the dancers, and went over to join them. He signaled to the pianist. The music began with a single note, then a pause, then a chromatic tinkle of rapid notes; the tinkle stopped, started off willfully in another direction; dissonant chords accompanied unpredictably. Balanchine clapped his hands and the pianist broke off. The pianist then repeated from the beginning and broke off at the same point.

Balanchine took his dancers to a far corner of the room—equivalent to the upstage wings, stage left. He placed the boy in front of the girl. At the single first note, they were to run to the center of the room and stop at the beginning of the tinkle. They did this to music. Then without music he showed the boy how to step aside, turn toward the girl, take a step sideways upstage, and offer her his right hand. Taking the girl's part, he showed her how to take the boy's right hand in her left, at the same time turning to face him and stepping boldly back, so that she ended clasping his hand at arm's length, standing with bent knee on one foot, leaning toward him, her other leg extended horizontally behind her in a ballet pose called arabesque. The moves for both dancers were very fast, the final pose was held for a moment. All this the dancers did at once with no difficulty, and repeated it to music. Then Balanchine, substituting for the boy, showed him how to step back, raising the hand by which he held the girl; the action pulled her forward; she caught her balance on both feet, her knees bent a bit like the boy's. Still clasping each other's hand, but with rounded backs pulling away from one another, the two bodies seen in profile made a kind of "O" figure, which held them poised. The dancers did this at once and repeated everything from the beginning, to music. "Tha-at's right," said Balanchine in an absorbed way, looking at the final pose. "Then maybe we do this."

Taking the girl's part, he showed her how to raise the hand which joined her to the boy, bending her arm at the elbow, and at the same time turning away, so she pulled him after her in profile for a few rapid steps on toe toward the side of the room. That they did easily. Next, as she stood, one foot before the other on toe (in fourth position), the boy, pulling back from the waist, and bracing himself one foot against the other, stopped her. At this stop their bodies made a second and different "O" figure. But the dancers could barely manage it. The boy couldn't, in this fast move, brace himself very firmly. Balanchine, who had first done it, now did it again. He showed the boy the foot position—the left on the ground, the right turned out, pressed on the instep of the left and pointed down. The dancer tried again, the choreographer showed once more. When Balanchine did it, the pull back from the waist looked quicker and sharper; when he braced his feet, the toe of the raised one seemed to cling to the floor. But when at the third try the dancers did this figure no differently from at first, he said, "Tha-at's right," and went on. Taking the girl's part, he showed her how to turn the wrist of the hand by which she held the boy, then turn that arm at the shoulder, and extend it, so without letting go she now had room to step ahead. She took two steps, swung out in a deep lunge, and ended poised on one foot, with bent knee; her free arm had swung ahead, the free leg back in arabesque again. She had pulled the boy a step or two after her. With this move the dancers had no trouble.

Now Balanchine asked them to go back to the beginning and set the whole sequence to counts. They went back to the far corner; but as they stood ready, he stopped them. He now put the boy behind the girl instead of in front of her. This required a change at the end of the first run to center, because now when they stopped, the boy had to step aside and down stage to give her his hand, instead of aside and upstage. No difficulty. They were about to start when he stopped them again. He told them not to run in on the first note as before, but to wait a moment and run in on the silence; he explained that the single first note would be played on the vibraphone, and would reverberate; there wouldn't be a silence on stage as there was now with the piano. They now began again.

The run looked different. Before, the boy running ahead seemed to be blocking the girl's escape. Now she stopped of her own free will and gave him the opportunity to invite her to dance. It was less tense; but with less time, the run became faster and fresher.

At the first note of the tinkle they started to count. They counted aloud by eighth notes to a bar or half-bar, doing the motions and rests at the same speed, or within a hairsbreadth, as they had been doing them before; but with more edge. They were delighted to find when they reached the last lunge, that everything fitted. "Tha-at's right," the choreographer said. The second "O" figure, the bothersome one, had lost a half count's rest in the process, but he went ahead. Taking the girl's final lunging pose, he found after a few tries that she could easily step back erect, and then whirl toward the boy, still holding his hand. Whirling around twice, she wrapped herself first in her arm and then in his. As she whirled, her unattached arm was wrapped in with her. She now stood facing front, close to the boy, imprisoned so to speak, and he could step closer yet, and put his free arm lightly around her waist. But no further initiative was left her. Balanchine took the imprisoned girl's part; then he took the boy's part; he seemed to consider various directions but he found none he liked. The dance had run itself into a blind alley. He asked the dancers to repeat the last moves, and watched them twice. They looked as if their hearts were bravely sinking. Then as they stood in the final pose, he went up to the girl, took her by the shoulders and started pushing her toward the floor. After a moment, she understood and tried sinking out of the arms wrapped around her. Balanchine took her place and did it easily. She tried again, and struggled hard, but something or other was in her way. It couldn't be done. Watching her closely, as she struggled, he went up to her and started pulling on the unattached arm that was wrapped in front of her, her right arm. With a happy smile, she caught on; she went back to the previous lunge, and the whirl that followed, wrapping herself up, then extricating the extra arm, she found room easily to sink down out of her imprisonment, duck under the arm she held the boy's hand by, and come up outside, free to move anywhere, but still holding his hand. For the dancers this move was a Houdini-style joke, and they were delighted. Setting the move to counts was easy.

The girl now stood facing center-stage, and in a few steps she led the boy there; now they both stood center, facing front, they let go of each other's hand, and began to a 5/8 count a stylized Lindy kick figure, in counter-rhythm to each other, just as the music burst into a 5/4 bar of jitterbug derivation.

By that time three quarters of an hour had passed since the rehearsal began; everybody had worked cheerfully and fast. But beginning with the 5/8 Lindy-type figure everybody's concentration seemed to double. Balanchine invented one novel figure after another. They began and ended within what seemed to be a bar or two. The figures kept the dancers within hand's reach of each other, and now more, now less, kept the flavor of a Lindy-type couple dance. Very rapid, unexpectedly complex, quite confined, the figures, sharply contrasted, kept changing direction. But in sequence the momentum carried through. When the entire ballet was finished, this turned out to be a general characteristic it had.

At that first rehearsal, the choreographer did not mention that he intended it, or what he intended. Nor did the dancers ask. They concentrated on the moves he was making. They hurried to learn each figure as it was invented, to repeat it by counts, and memorize the sequence by counts to the score. At the end of two and a half hours about one minute of the ballet had been made. On stage this turned out to be the first half of the fourth of the ballet's seven sections—a section for solo vibraphone and a chamber-sized orchestral group.

As for the part described in detail—the ten second introduction—on stage it turned out that the composer wanted for it a tempo radically different from the one it had been choreographed at; the steps were changed, and passed unnoticed.

Making a ballet takes an unbounded patience from everybody concerned. An outsider is fascinated to be let in on the minuteness of the workmanship. But then he finds no way out of that minuteness. Listening to the same few bars pounded again and again on the piano, watching the same movements started at top speed and broken off, again and again, the fascinated outsider after two hours and a half of that finds himself going stir crazy. Seeing a ballet in the theatre the momentum of action and music carries the audience into a world of zest and grandeur. In performance the dancers look ravishing. In rehearsal they look like exhausted champions attempting Mt. Everest, knowing how limited the time is, step by step, hold by hold, roped together by the music, with the peak nowhere in sight.

In the second half of the Hayden-Mitchell pas de deux, Balanchine invented a figure in which the girl, facing front, poised with bent knee on one toe, performed a little "turned in" adagio-exercise, as she reached back for support to her partner, who was doing a sideways shuffle behind her in 5/8. The dancers caught on after a few tries. Even after they had, the choreographer calling the counts sharply, made them repeat it—quite unlike his usual procedure. He did it again at a much later rehearsal when—though he wasn't aware of it—Miss Hayden had pulled a calf muscle the night before on stage. As she repeated the figure again and again—so she told me—the injury became painful. But as she kept repeating it, angry though she was, and trying to give the rhythm a keener edge, she found the key she had been looking for—the key to the character of her role.

At the third rehearsal, Balanchine began a pas de deux for Diana Adams and John Jones. From the start it was a violently explosive dance. Within a few minutes, Miss Adams stopped with a slightly pained look and turned away, but a moment later she was back at work. She didn't mention that her right arm had been badly wrenched. For the rest of the rehearsal, many of the very fast moves she memorized required her partner to give her sudden pulls to her arm, now to one, now to the other, often while the arm was suddenly being turned inside out. Rehearsal the next day was even more strenuous. After two hours of it, at a move the unsteady execution of which puzzled the choreographer, she apologized, saying she was sure she could do it right at a later rehearsal when her arm was better. He at once changed the next move to her good arm, saying, "We need that arm tonight." And work went on. That evening she was to dance the ballerina part in the full-length *Nutcracker*, the season's first performance, and all the reviewers would be watching her. She danced it beautifully.

Variants was rehearsed during the ballet season, when the dancers, in addition to performance and class, have repertory rehearsals as well; union rules specified the hours available. Besides inventing his ballet at such hours, Balanchine also had every morning and evening decisive responsibilities in running the company and planning its future.

Between September and November, he had made four new pieces. The first, to the most recent Stravinsky score, was followed by a ballet to Donizetti music; then he presented an hour-long ballet set to two song cycles by Brahms, and called *Liebeslieder Walzer*. *Liebeslieder Walzer*—with a cast of eight—turned out to be a masterpiece, glorious and magical. No other choreographer, no other company could have done it, but one isn't aware of that, the poetry of it—the secret image—is so absorbing. Two weeks after *Liebeslieder* he presented *Ragtime*, a duet witty and deceptively elementary in a way the Stravinsky score is. Six days after *Ragtime*, he began *Variants*.

Balanchine usually prepares a ballet far in advance. He has said that he prepares for a long time by playing and studying the score—"I listen, listen, listen, listen." On the other hand, he does not look for steps until the actual performers are with him in the rehearsal studio.

Variants had been commissioned at his request. Like some of Schuller's previous music, it was to be in Third Stream style, scored for the Modern Jazz Quartet and symphonic orchestra. The choice implied a Third-Stream-type ballet, a non-existent species. Balanchine prepared for it by listening to jazz albums. He didn't study the score during the summer lay-off while he was growing roses, because until September Schuller was too busy to begin writing it. The last installment of the piano version was delivered in November.

The composer's plan—a suite—featured the Jazz Quartet artists singly and jointly accompanied by small orchestral groups; the introduction was for full orchestra, the conclusion for full orchestra plus Quartet. The choreographer's plan was a dance suite. He wanted half the cast—two solo boys and eight ensemble girls—to be Negroes; but the girls weren't found. He picked his dancers, cast each of the dance numbers, decided which numbers to make first. At that point the first rehearsal sheet was posted; the date for opening night confirmed.

At the start of the first rehearsal he chose a way of working which he kept until the whole piece had been created. At every point he took each role. The process looked like this. Standing near the dancer, he signaled the pianist to play ahead, and clapped his hands when he wanted him to break off. The pianist repeated the fragment once or twice while Balanchine listened intently. Then without music, he took the position in which the dancer would have to start, and stood absorbed, sometimes turning his head very slightly in this direction or that, sometimes slightly moving on his feet. He was inventing the next figure. He seemed to test the feel of it, and decided. That done, he glanced at the dancer, stressed the starting position, and without music showed the move. The first time he showed it, he did it from start to finish at full performance force and speed.

The dancers reproduced it, adding to it at once—in ballet style—the full extension of the body, the turn-out of legs and feet, the toe-step or leap he had merely implied. A non-dancer might have wondered how they could guess so much; but they seemed to guess right almost always. As expert dancers they were following out the logical balletic consequences of the main move he had shown. Sometimes they asked about a detail left in doubt, and he specified the answer in ballet terminology.

Moving at the speed and force he had shown, the fully extended bodies of the dancers sometimes developed a sudden momentum that was scarey. But the jet of it took the dancer to the right spot at the right instant. The impetus came from eccentric swings from the shoulder or waist, the support from handholds. When the choreographer first showed such a move, he literally threw himself into it, and let his feet take care of themselves. When the

188

dancers couldn't manage the move, he repeated it. Between them they tracked down the trouble to a change of hand, a specific angle or stance, or an extra step which he had taken instinctively, and which the dancers had overlooked.

Soon, when he made such a move the first time, he repeated it at once, stressing how the feet stepped and the hands reached for support. At the second rehearsal, he spent more than a half hour on a fantastic sequence lasting a few bars that wouldn't work to counts; after that whatever took too long to learn he discarded before it was set by counts to the music. (Had he been making a piece in regulation ballet steps to music easy to remember by ear, the process would have been far less cumbersome.)

Balanchine's care was for the mechanics of momentum. He did not mention expression. Watching him do a move full force, an outsider might often have been struck by his expression in it—a quality of gesture which was directly to the point. It was beautiful. The dancers did not imitate that. Their expression when it appeared was their own, and he did not criticize it. Expression seemed to be treated as a Jeffersonian inalienable right. And perhaps it is.

Later rehearsals were moved to the theatre building, to a gloomy echoing room upstairs modeled on a chapter-room in a castle of the Knights Templar. Here Balanchine took the dancers by shifts and choreographed from ten thirty to six. "I work like a dentist," he remarked. He sometimes looked exhausted, but a joke revived him. When dancers lost the count, he did not nag or look depressed. The phrases he made for the chorus were easy motions, but their peculiar timing required exact counts. He kept checking the counts in the score. During ten minute or half hour breaks, he stayed alone in the rehearsal room, rereading the score, playing it, checking on the metronome speed. The composer who was to conduct the ballet watched a rehearsal, and Balanchine brought up the metronome speed; he referred to the metronome speed given in the score; Schuller, experienced with orchestras but not with Balanchine choreography, evaded his insistence. Solo rehearsals, chorus rehearsals, stage rehearsals, orchestra rehearsals, dress rehearsals, lighting rehearsals.

The first orchestra rehearsal for the dancers came the day before opening. The dancers had become used to recognizing landmarks or cues in the piano score. The colorful orchestration obliterated these. But they had expected as much. Since they had memorized the score by counts, they could perform to the measure whatever unforeseen noises the orchestra made. Disaster threatened nevertheless. Finding the music difficult, the instrumentalists slowed down; but the dancers rushing headlong couldn't slow down without toppling. The momentum of their off-balance rushes worked at a specific speed that had been agreed on between composer and choreographer and fixed by metronome. The dancers had to rely on it and now it turned unreliable. The choreographer's well-known coolness adjusted what was possible. And suddenly the first night's performance was over. There was polite applause.

Having seen as I had how the ballet grew and the adorably unselfish work that went into it, my view of the first night was not that of a theatre-goer or of a critic. But the first night flop did not deter later audiences. They came at least to hear the Modern Jazz Quartet and the new Schuller score. The concentration of the dancers, the virtuosity of the ballerinas were watched by these music fans with close attention; they appreciated the range of resource by which the dancing matched the twelve-tone logic of the score.

The dance fans agreed about all the virtuosity, but they found the twelve-tone "Third Stream" angle more strain than fun. In addition, the piece had been announced as "New Jazz," and it wasn't contemporary jazz in its dancing. They objected to the Thirties-type jive steps, to the show-biz type gesture, to the sour night-club look of the staging. As for the dancing, the partners couldn't let each other alone for a moment, the dances couldn't leave out a beat, nobody could dance except on top of the beat. Current jazz dancing separates partners, omits beats; lets the beat pull away, anticipates it, and that elasticity of attack characterizes the gesture, and varies it. The source of style isn't professional, but year by year in the private dancing of a few high school students; the measure of style is its "go." The dance fans had seen the athletic overtones of *Agon*, which in some unliteral way came closer to the image of jazz than any jazz ballet yet has. They hoped that *Variants* would do for jazz what *Liebeslieder* does for the waltz.

In performance on stage, *Variants* keeps reminding one of conventional Broadway—that sort of jazz plus modern plus ballet. The numbers suggest corny types of stage jazz—the hot number, the ritual-magic one, the snake-hips, the arty, the pert one; the long finale quotes from the show, and ends with a decorative modernistic collapse for the entire cast, capped by a Brigitte Bardot "beat" pose for the two leading ladies. The dancers suggest that hard-shell type of dance very handsomely. But the rhythm they dance to isn't show dance rhythm, it isn't quite jazz either. One recognizes jazz-like steps but one doesn't feel at home. The action of a step keeps being pointed up differently, retimed, rerouted, tightened, enlarged by ballet logic. At a retard several short numbers end with, one seems to watch a powerful momentum sink quickly from the dancers into the floor (like water into sand) leaving their last moves massive. The emotion is one of the grandeur, the gesture is show-biz. Becoming interested, one sees a massive dance momentum started, developed, ended within two minutes, a drive different from one number to the next. By the time one has found out how to "see" the piece, the finale comes and ruins it. The finale, four times as long as the previous numbers, and crowded, has no momentum; nor has it any in the score.

Schuller's score features the shy, extremely musical sonorities of Lewis's Modern Jazz Quartet surrounded by orchestral sonorities, original in color or jazz implication. Such a texture takes more rehearsal than a ballet company can afford. The Quartet, progressive style, implies a jazz beat while playing a variable nuance behind. Not the orchestra. It plays by measure.

The progressive style "delayed" beat, when featured, troubled the dancers who were dancing to the measure. But the jazz beat does not take over the score. The structural drive of the score is twelve-tone, not by beat, but by phrase. To the specific twelve-tone phrase, to its momentum and shape, Balanchine had set the dance—first by ear, then checking and re-checking the count of the measure by the written notes.

Unlike Balanchine's twelve-tone part of *Episodes*—particularly the section danced by Paul Taylor, in which the shape of a "step" became equivalent to the shape of a musical phrase—*Variants* did not keep surprising the onlooker by the dramatic fantasy of its gesture. But it did have extraordinary moments—during the Adams-Jones duet, for instance, when, at the speed of fury, the complexity and the force of momentum disassociate the gesture from its Broadway connotations, and burst open its hard shell. At such moments *Variants* became a jazz ballet more powerful and grandly integrated than any yet.

Between two rehearsals Balanchine, after answering a question of mine about jazz, added, "In any case, we don't do jazz here; we do ballet; we try to make it as interesting as possible." Before rehearsals began, Schuller brought up the matter of jazz nuances of rhythm; the choreographer listened and then said that the way he made dances, the dancers were "inside the nuance."

Watching Balanchine at work, one could see he was thinking in terms of ballet action flavored by jazz action. One did not see him worry where the flavor might take him, or worry about the over-all shape of a dance before he had made it. He seemed to be eating his way through the score, finding his way move by move. After he had found a move one could see that it took its point from the pressure of drama and, if one may say so, the pressure of visibility which at that moment of the dance were at stake. (The previous move might be topped by a contradiction or an unexpected evasion, as in dramatic dialogue.) But watching him look for a new move, he seemed to find it by following an instinctive dance impulse of his body. Nearly always he trusted to his body's first response, while he was concentrating on the exact force of momentum the music offered for the next move.

The force of dance momentum derived from the score is a resource of ballet that he has developed further than anyone anywhere. He keeps enlarging its powers of speed, agility, intelligence and fun. With twelve dancers he finds a momentum that feels like forty dancers; with forty, it feels like a hundred. His company dances three times as much per minute as any other.

Momentum and gesture are the dramatic resources of dancing, which ballet combines in several ways. One way is that of the nineteenth century prolonged dance climax, a grand pas de deux with related choral and soloist numbers. The climax may be a tragic or a festive event but—like in opera—the scale of it is expressed by lyric meditations on it. In principle the shining virtuoso dance feat is also a gesture-metaphor derived from the dramatic situation, and an echo of the feat reverberates in the other numbers before and after which prolong the momentum.

Balanchine's so-called abstract ballets extend this traditional merging of gesture and dance momentum. The specific gesture is implicit in the actions of the step. It appears in the formal momentum in shape and rhythm so organically fused that one responds to both of these poles of dramatic meaning jointly, and follows the highly active meditation with delighted astonishment. The individual's absorbed gesture, carried by a powerfully developed momentum which reverberates its secret, reveals a grander and more innocent meaning than one expects to see. Remembered, it grows on the scale of the momentum. This power of poetry has long been the glory of ballet, and Balanchine's is that he succeeds in it so often. But the question of how he does it is not answered by watching him at work. (*1960*)

Part Three

Reports

Obituary for *Ballet*

THE LONDON MAGAZINE *Ballet* closed suddenly after the October issue and went into voluntary bankruptcy. Founded just before the war, it had been resumed in '46 and in a short time became a publication unique in the dance world. "Ignorant," "irresponsible," "snobbish," "effete," "unpatriotic"—a string of adjectives by which one comes to recognize the presence of a critic of value—were hurled at its editor, Richard Buckle, more often and more vehemently than at any dance critic in English. A more honest word for his way of writing and of editing would have been "aristocratic."

Ballet had become the most attractive looking of dance magazines. Pleasing in its small size, handsome in its typefaces, appetizing in the transparent blacks of its reproductions, it presented itself with a specifically English elegance. It seemed to promise that inside the covers one would be addressed not as a harried fellow-professional, but—for once—as a guest at a pretty supper party. Pretty but not entirely safe. As one looked inside, a line drawing or a photograph among the rest met one suddenly like a quick disconcerting glance.

Buckle let everyone else in his magazine talk more than he and louder. But his own piece—commentary or a book review—was the first that one read in each new issue. His criticism was vivid, malicious, and wellbred; never niggardly. It had the mark of a born stylist. Written simply, it often took the dry tone of gentlemanly understatement that is a virtue more of the old England than of the new. To a New Yorker, it sounded unassertive. In London, as I found, it was the most feared, the most infuriating and valued. Despite its low pitched voice and air of frivolous luxury, *Ballet* became the most powerful dance magazine in Europe.

Rereading them now, one finds in Buckle's opinions nothing freakish; they are reasonable and bright, they reveal a man of educated taste but also a man of character and constancy. He has faith enough in England to look at foreigners with interest. And he often reminds the British dance world of the stodginess that a complacent insularity leads to. Such a reminder is valuable in any ballet-producing city—New York as much as London. So, for instance, when the sweetly extravagant young Champs Elysées company at its brightest first arrived from Paris in '46, though many Londoners loved it, the prevalent insular view condemned it as undignified. Buckle pointed to the value of such vivacity of imagination in dancing and such a grace of decor. It was only years later, when the Champs Elysées itself had dimmed, that Sadler's Wells nodded its great head in assent to Buckle. Similarly when the authoritative opinion was that the Americans lacked French vivacity and English dignity, he noticed virtues; when the average London critic, educated on story ballets, complained that Balanchine's were undramatic and all alike, Buckle countered that whoever cares to look at the dancing in them will see how various, how noble, how powerfully dramatic they become. Last summer—so a local fan whose work makes him follow the English press told me—the reviews of the New York City Company sounded, in general, even intentionally obtuse. (For my part, after sampling a few I had to stop; I felt an acute attack of chauvinism coming on.) Buckle took the situation as an English as well as an artistic impropriety. And besides pillorying the august London *Times,* he brought out a sheaf of really enlightening articles, the most original of which were his own and one by a young painter, Ronald Wilson.

Buckle influenced British taste by expressing his own

more adventurous one. He kept looking. In a profusion of pictures, in special articles (many by Beaumont), and in the editor's commentary, *Ballet* offers the record of new ballets as they appeared in London and of English dancers. But it includes, richly illustrated as well, news from abroad; a special appreciation of the Royal Danish Ballet; accounts of all·kinds of exotic dance styles seen by travellers or presented in London; vivid reminiscences by people of note; line drawings that the editor enjoyed looking at for a change; antiquarian iconography and texts in lively presentation. The energy of the editing is striking as one sees it expressed through the course of years. Buckle also took ballet lessons. He watched the development of young dancers. So, for instance, when David Blair was still a minor member of the Sadler's Wells Junior company, it was he who took Dolin to see him dance; it turned out to be the decisive event in the career of this young man who at present is the only one of his generation who shows the gifts of a danseur noble of the very first quality. Buckle's guess then was wild, but it was lucky for England. And though so great and so unique an artist as Margot Fonteyn is showered on all sides with praise, Buckle's tributes, particularly the one when she was first to appear in New York, evoke her image with a delicacy of respect that is touching and poetic.

Naturally an English critic's chief concern is Sadler's Wells. In a sharp review of a new ballet, Buckle, touching on general questions it seemed to raise, spoke of the three directors, de Valois, Lambert and Ashton, as the "three blind mice" of the nursery rhyme. It got him into real trouble. He found himself accused in the press of having caused the death of Lambert by his review. The accusation (by Sir Osbert Sitwell), though in vague words, seemed definite enough to people in the dance world, and Buckle would have been marked for life, if he had left it unchallenged. To future gossip it would not matter that Constant Lambert, superbly gifted, proud and combative, had died a month after the notice on his new ballet. He had died of diabetes. But bad as it could become for Buckle, the charge was also ignominious to the memory of Lambert. It is a pity that Ninette de Valois did not at once contradict it—for the sake of her dead friend and in view of Buckle's value to British ballet. Instead the accusation was repeated with emphasis. Buckle, abandoned by those who should most have defended him, was forced to clear up the shameful muddle in *Ballet*, and he did it in a brilliant polemical piece. He emerged from this sordid and dangerous episode with honor, and everyone shook hands all around.

Buckle is at his driest in danger. In his *Adventures of a Ballet Critic*—his own reminiscences occasionally printed in his magazine, there are passages as dangerous as snapshots of well-known persons caught in absurd situations; they are not unkind at all, but very lifelike and very funny. He does not diminish the good qualities of his subjects when he makes one laugh at them. But the fact that the humor lies in the literally reported actions and words of his victims, leaves them no escape but to laugh at themselves. There are moments in an active life when this is difficult. Dame Ninette once exclaimed one was afraid to speak to him because one couldn't tell what he would print. "Aren't you afraid?" she asked me with indignation. "Of course," I answered timidly. "So you see!" she cried. But what I saw was that this dauntless woman was resenting his independence, resenting it volcanically like the Empire builder she is. And I realized how much personal courage goes into Dickie Buckle's aristocratic sense of humor.

Ballet had behind it the personal courage necessary for elegance. A colleague, Miss Manchester, when she was told that the magazine had folded, exclaimed, "He had to have it beautiful." It is the highest of professional tributes. The magazine tried for the distinction of appearance and of character that ballet itself demands, and it maintained that effort under every conceivable difficulty. To do so was Buckle's personal responsibility toward the art he loves, his act of loyal homage. This aristocratic attitude was the unexplained source of the fascination *Ballet* exercised. Buckle is not the only educated and intelligent Englishman who writes about ballet, not at all. The other

British dance magazines are sound and earnest, but I find I rarely read them. Their character lacks romance. Odd that in London, a city so proud of its culture, so proud of being the capital of Western ballet, the one monthly that reflected this pride gracefully for an international audience should have been allowed to close. Now it will no longer sting with momentary shame and it will no longer inspire with faith either. (*1953*)

Books on Dance

THE KABUKI

If you go to Tokyo, it isn't easy to see a performance of the Kabuki theater. The place is always sold out. The price of a ticket is comparable to that for a musical hit. It seems that 250 years ago the price of a Kabuki ticket would have fed two people for a year. But if you do get in, the confusion and hubbub in the audience is as outlandish as the intensely formalized action on stage. The audience is free to chat, to come and go as it likes. There are no curtain calls. On the other hand, as an actor approaches a well-known climax, the whole house begins clapping to encourage him and the men egg him on with shouts: "You're the greatest actor in Japan!" "You're the greatest actor in the world!" "You're MacArthur!" (that was during the Occupation).

If you want to understand as much as possible about Kabuki, *The Kabuki Theater* by Earle Ernst is an authoritative guide. The book explains everything lucidly and painstakingly—the background, the facts, the emotions, both from a Japanese and a Western point of view. If you can keep paying attention you will find at the end that you seem to have been living in Japan for quite a while. A reader who expects to be amused will start skipping and miss the point. But a student will be astonished by how much Prof. Ernst manages to elucidate.

Prof. Ernst defines the Kabuki as a presentational and not a representational theatre—the actor does not behave as if he were "living" his role, he behaves as if he were

201

acting it. The set is not meant to look "real"; the stage picture is meant to thrust the actor visually forward toward the audience. The actors act as much as possible at the audience, they act as much as possible one after the other, and keep as much as possible visually separated from each other. When an actor needs a particular prop, it is brought to him by an assistant (who isn't an actor) at the moment he needs it, and it is taken off stage again as soon as it is used. If the actor tires, an assistant brings him tea, and he turns upstage to drink it. If he forgets, an assistant crouches behind him and prompts; if he has to make a quick costume change on stage, an assistant helps him.

Dance movement and music as the Kabuki theatre uses them are descriptive. They stylize gestures suited to the situation, but there is no formal element in them that can lead to extended forms, like the extended forms of our music and ballet. The acting, whether as dance-like motion or as chanted speech, does not tend to a continuous flow, but tends to a succession of climactic silent poses that are complete stops. So the character is presented in a series of detached moments. A continuous unity of character in which nuances appear—the larger emotional coherence of a character or of a play—is not attempted. The plays are episodic melodramas (or farcical acts) with no literary pretensions; and the emotion the audience most enjoys is a vague and delicate melancholy. The large emotion in the Kabuki which can take on tragic value is that of loyalty to the feudal order of the state, and loyalty also, in a less serious form, to the order of family, or even to that of a group of outcasts and thieves. But the kind of tragic inner conflict the Kabuki audience feels the depth of is that of a man who, to save his lord from being captured, disguises him as his servant, speaks to him as to a servant, and finally hits him. The captors are deceived, and he has saved his feudal lord's life but he has at the same time destroyed his own ethical sanity.

To a Westerner, the Kabuki seems to create the spell of a fabulously esthetic comic-strip. The sense of inbreeding that its minute traditionalism gives is incomparably more intense than that of our traditional ballet or opera. The Kabuki's imaginative elegance of gesture, and the brilliant imagination it displays in the colors and materials of the staging, are a Westerner's easiest approach to it.

Prof. Ernst remarks that the real Kabuki is not the same thing as the Azuma Kabuki that recently toured the U.S. And according to Alan Priest, who reviewed this book in the *N.Y. Herald-Tribune,* the Azuma Kabuki stands to the real Kabuki in a relation like that of the charming Russian Chauve-Souris company to the Moscow Art Theater—when they both appeared here in the twenties. (*1953*)

A NOTE ON PERFORMANCE

In 1960 an ensemble from the Tokyo Kabuki, headed by three great actors, Kanzaburo XVII, Utaemon VI, and Shoroku II, came to the New York City Center, invited by Lincoln Kirstein. The company brought with it a new idea, the running translation of the dialogue via transistor. It opened with a famous play, *The Subscription List.*

After twenty minutes of attention to everything on stage, helped by the transistor—and by having read Professor Ernst's book—the Kabuki stylization did not seem mysterious. But the great actor who took the second lead was so uninsistent that I began watching him. He acted his part when the drama required it; when it didn't, he marked it—and that was most of the time. He was very old. The voice had lost the lower register, which the Kabuki falsetto "breaks" into and out of to stress a syllable. But his diction was exceptionally distinct and melodious. His stylized movements too were beautifully clear in shape. Though the old man tended to lag in the middle of a long phrase, as it finished he somehow delivered the final accent unhurried in the nick of time. He sat erect and motionless during the hero's interminable tirades; gradually his gaze would blur; but when his cue came, the freshness of his reply was instantaneous. I recognized these professional traits from having seen them in very old, very fine Western actors. At one point his young attendants preceded him single file in a quick march to the "hurry door," a narrow exit about three feet high. Approaching it, the young men took two rapid steps in a deep kneebend and on the third passed through. I was distressed for the aristocratic old actor, who must have been in his late seventies and who was wearing a tall hat besides. In fast tempo, thin and erect, he took the first kneebend step, then the second, then even deeper, the third, and was safely through.

The soldier hero of the play, disguised as a monk, at the climax pretends to have achieved illumination. The more he speaks of it, the more one realizes that the silent old man with his mysterious moments of freshness must really be an illuminated sage or a Rishi who knows all the truth; and the play's ambiguities beautifully deepen. It was not by the stylized forms that the actor had achieved this, but by his actual age which had modified the forms very slightly at any moment, but over an hour's time unmistakably.

At the end of the same evening the same actor (Kanzaburo XVII) reappeared as the plump young husband in a farce, his black eyes snapping, his stylized speech and gestures vivid with physical charm, his foolishness delightfully comic.

On the next program the company performed several highly dramatic scenes from another famous play, *The Forty-Seven Ronin*. The three stars were each extraordinary; so was the rest of the cast and the entire production. I will describe some of the climax. The hero, a spirited young nobleman (acted by Kanzaburo XVII), has been condemned to commit suicide by an unscrupulous provincial governor. Immediately after his death, his estates will be seized, his noble young wife and his many retainers will be destitute. In a room of his mansion, the ritual preparations have been completed. The hero sits Japanese fashion on the floor, forward of stage center, his eyes straight at the audience, the honed short disembowelling knife laid at his side. He is alone except for two government witnesses, expressionless on chairs against a side wall. The young man's eyes are half-closed, sharp, motionless. He is steeling himself. No one moves. A pause. His face unchanged, he flicks one shoulder and his kimono slips from it. A pause. He flicks the other shoulder, the silk kimono drops, a swift gesture of his hands tucks it back. His position has not changed, his eyes have not moved. A pause. He is wearing a second kimono. Again he flicks a shoulder, and pauses; flicks the other, tucks the fallen silk back, and pauses. You see he has tucked the garments away from the abdomen he will pierce. Now he is wearing a third thinner snow white kimono and you sense that he will not shed it; he will stab the broad knife through it. Horrifying though the heroism of the ritual was, I noticed by this time that the recurrent pauses had each been a trifle too long. I was sorry that so great an actor should overplay so great a scene, even with the uncertainty of playing to a foreign audience. In any case his gleaming halfclosed eyes held us. Without moving them, he picked up the disembowelling knife, plunged it to the hilt, deep into the far left side of his belly; and screwing up his face pulled it slowly with both hands in a straight line toward the right. As he reached his middle, a commotion occurred at the back of the audience. Keeping his face screwed tight, he stopped, and held the knife firmly where it was. A retainer ran toward him across the hanamichi and prostrated himself, wailing and sucking in his breath. The hero in a thin clear voice asked him a commonplace question. The terrified retainer answered yes, and again prostrated himself whining. The hero was past hearing him. Both hands gripping the hilt, he steadily pulled the knife to the far right of his belly, eased it out, raised it to slit his jugular, and dropped awkwardly forward. As the knife clattered to the floor, away from the dead man, I was surprised to see no blood on it. So convincing had the scene been.

But the next day, recalling the actor's marvelous miming of the scene, the slightly overlong pauses came back to me, and with them the gleam of the steady halfclosed eyes. They were not those of a man steeling himself. I had seen that specific expression somewhere else, under quite different circumstances. Then I remembered. I had seen it

205

in the eyes of a composer friend, at the orchestra rehearsal of a manuscript work of his; he had been intently listening in the web of sound for wrong notes, due either to a copyist's mistake or to an instrumentalist's. The hero on stage had had exactly that look. Then I remembered the rest of the drama. He had in fact been listening for the approach of his chief retainer. He meant to pledge him to vengeance. It must have been to gain time that he prolonged the ritual pauses; but since the government witnesses were watching, he could prolong them only a trifle. He had fooled the witnesses and me too. And when the retainer had at last run in, the hero fooled us again. His commonplace remark (like a dying man's absurdity) had actually been his demand for vengeance. So the listening look in his eyes, and the slightly overlong pauses, which spoiled the perfection of form, were decisive to understanding the scene and the character of the hero. They were not stylized effects, they were realistic ones.

The Kabuki's great stylized effects are famous in the West; decisive realistic effects, such as those I have described, are also worth calling attention to. The Kabuki style plays in and out of its stressed stylized forms in a number of unstressed ways which a theatre fan will enjoy discovering for himself. Its elasticity in this respect makes for surprises, it distributes the tense moments, and the evening as a whole gathers a genial warmth of play-acting.

As dance the Kabuki stylization has less range than that of Chinese classic theatre, or than that of the two Balinese aristocratic styles. Its logic is less boldly non-verbal or acrobatic; it stays closer to the text. Dance logic as such appears to be farthest developed by Western ballet; the stylized Far Eastern theatres appear to have developed the art of mime the farthest.

They have also developed farthest the pictorial intelligence of stage decoration. The Kabuki which elects (like our own scenic tradition) a middle-brow or nineteenth-century Pop style, exhibits within that style an acuteness of pictorial intelligence that puts an observant Westerner in the best of humor. For its New York visit, the Kabuki had brought with it sets built to the measurements of the City Center stage—less than half as wide as its own. A Japanese warship had brought them to New York.

PRODIGIOUS DIAGHILEV

In Search of Diaghilev is a ballet book with a text that reads like a *New Yorker* profile. As you glance through its illustrations, you find unfamiliar stage sets, unfamiliar watercolors, costumes, caricatures, odd photographs from the Diaghilev epoch. Much of the material is new and all of it is shown in a lively way. The dancer Massine drawn by Matisse, by Bakst, by Derain, twice by Picasso—the five portraits facing each other—give a sense of the energy that surrounded the company. A Picasso drawing of Lopokova, eight set and costume sketches by Juan Gris are all wonderfully beautiful. But the pictures do not fix a limit of taste—they are not systematic or official. They seem more like personal mementos. They recall in a ballet the moment before it became a masterpiece, the moment when it was still a risk and a surprise. Something unpredictably personal that they have keeps the magic of stage performance.

Richard Buckle, who wrote and assembled the book, seems to have looked for proof that such a magic existed. He is too young to have known Diaghilev. He is an Englishman in his thirties who, for seven or eight years, ran the magazine *Ballet,* which he made the most remarkable in its field. For the 1954 Edinburgh Festival, he organized a Diaghilev exhibition that attracted 165,000 people first in Edinburgh, later in London. The astonishing wealth of material heaped in a fantastically theatrical setting (designed by the painter Rosoman) gave visitors a sensation of Diaghilev's zest. As if the show had been a dance, photographs of it miss the illusion and only capture a sort of backstage tackiness.

This volume is a truer souvenir of the show. The illustrations reproduce some of the best items collected or newly discovered for it. The search for material, the building of the show are told in the text. But as Buckle describes amusing incidents, his imagination keeps turning to the magnetic figure of the great Russian.

The incidents take one into several interesting English houses and several French ones. One looks about, one meets a number of well-known people and one hears them speak. Like in an English novel of manners they are completely different from each other in character and habits of living, but the meeting is completely real each time. The glimpses of Picasso at a bullfight, looking at paintings, as a fellow-guest at dinner with a former wife, are particularly brilliant. At another point, Sokolova recalls a one-night stand in Spain—the dancers find themselves doing *Shéhérazade* in the set for *Carnaval* and in mixed costumes from *Sylphides,* from *Daphnis* and *Cléopatre.* "Nobody knew who anybody was, or who to make for. . . . There were no swords, so they had to strangle us. My *dear,* we put *everything* into it. We never had such an ovation, before or since." The more Diaghilev survivors one comes to meet, the more one becomes aware of the unrecoverable past so enigmatically alive within them. But just when Buckle might turn profound, he is whirled away into the racket and the rush of putting on his show, and in the backstage excitement one hears Karsavina's happy laughter, reminded of her first Paris rehearsal in 1909. At the end Buckle imagines Diaghilev himself slowly lurching through the successful exhibition, a bit bored. The show is running, and he has lost interest. It is a natural anticlimax.

What is completed is the full-length portrait of him that has been building up all along. Buckle started as if he were writing a Diaghilev profile. Bit by bit the scope of the subject widens the range of style, of wit and of feeling. To catch the actuality of his hero Buckle uses whatever comes to hand, from scholarship to superstition. Through official and unofficial biography, through business letters, through chance events that occurred during his search, his penetrating sense of humor evokes the prodigious individual. It is the prodigious individual to whom we owe twentieth-century ballet. This book is not his official portrait, but it is the most vividly actual one that there is. There is an imaginative passion in it.

THE ART OF DANCE CRITICISM IN FRENCH LITERATURE

Miss Deirdre Pridden offers us through the ideas on dancing of a series of remarkable writers materials for a dance esthetic. Where her book is at its best—as in the thirty pages on the poet Mallarmé—it is not easy reading. But a few serious dance fans who do not know Mallarmé's criticism, if they begin slowly browsing in this chapter a page at a time, will I am sure be delighted by the gradual discovery of a ballet critic of unsurpassed penetration. Except for one single article (in G. Woolley's *Stéphane Mallarmé*) he cannot be read in English. Miss Pridden's book is invaluable because it gives for the first time in English a comprehensive though laborious account of all he wrote on dancing—perceptions phenomenally imaginative and phenomenally acute.

Mallarmé wrote little, he wrote in a tone of conversation, and he attempted only the most difficult side of his subject. He was intensely susceptible to what we now call the "abstract" values of classic ballet—an expressive force which seems to operate on a different region of sensibility than do the dancer's charms or the story's dramatics. Thousands respond to this peculiar theatre power, but the excitement of it is so illogical and so euphoric that the day after people are embarrassed to think about it or quite believe it so transported them.

It is this illogical, ambiguous, euphoric excitement that Mallarmé evokes in the motion of his words, a movement "of reciprocal reflections like a virtual trail of light across jewels." Mallarmé not only presents the magic illumination of such a moment of dance, he further suggests the sweeping imaginative power it is a token of. He makes one aware of the kind of meaning ballet has when it is most purely ballet and the grandeur of its flights of meanings—"of wings, of departures into for-forever"; he is,

209

one might say, the critic Balanchine deserved. His vividness, his scope, and the associative (or symbolic) logic of his criticism make him for people with an interest in dance esthetics the most dynamic of animators.

But I see that in the pleasure of speaking of him I have neglected to describe the general plan of Miss Pridden's book. It selects a series of notable French literary men who have written on ballet, a series that touches in turn the ballet of the 1840's (Gautier), that of the Eighties (Mallarmé, Lemaître), the Diaghilev epoch, and recent classicism (Valéry and Bergson). Each author is condensed, organized, and evaluated in the scholarly fashion of an academic thesis. It is odd how from this digestive processing the Diaghilev poets emerge as sweet but rather more banal than one would have expected.

Gautier too—the most graceful of ballet critics—does not appear to advantage. Miss Pridden's abstract is long and full, but it gives no impression of his particular genius, the sense of a dancer's physical presence as she dances across the stage which he can project so brilliantly in writing. His willfully unintellectual and sensual train of images, his foppish malice confuse her and she rather scolds him for misbehaving. His French theatre manners jar on her English ones. She is at her best again in the chapter on Valéry.

It is a pity Miss Pridden has not made a more readable book out of such excellent material—practically the best in its field. Looking more sharply at her work, one sees that she is herself a devoted ballet fan; her mind is sharp applied to complex and subtle texts; but in the creation of a framework of general ideas it is timid and uncertain. An introductory chapter which deals with general ideas is badly muddled and full of muddlesome commonplaces either of dance history or dance criticism. It is a chapter to be avoided. But in her abstracts, even where her evaluations are inexperienced or unenlightening, the scholarship is reliable. And the value of having the points of view of these variously brilliant critics convenient for reference or study is obvious.

A VERY PRETTY RAT

The spells of solitary Paris, of children's ballet class, of the Paris Opéra House, backstage and onstage—Odette Joyeux's *Child of the Ballet: Memoirs of an Opera "Rat"* evokes them vividly; for Paris fans and dance fans this little book is absorbing. But it is also a story the general reader can read with pleasure. "One of the rare classics of ballet," Arnold Haskell calls it in his preface; a readable book about ballet is in any case a rare find.

Child of the Ballet is the true story of Odette Joyeux, a small girl whose kind mother entered her in the ballet school of the Paris Opéra. "In the midst of the city . . . there was an island; on this island there was a fortress, a city." As a pupil, a "rat," Odette lives in the eerie and terrifying warren of backstage; she takes part, aged ten, in the supernatural performance. She "appears" in *Istar, Sylvia, Faust, Lohengrin.* Wondrous grownups appear too. In the dressing rooms, other games. In class looking at a foreign child she realizes the beauty of dancing; the child dies. A hounded teacher awakens in her the will to dance; the teacher disappears. Two years pass.

A smart ballet is given at the house of a rich patroness, and the child has a solo. An ovation, happiness. Suddenly the Opéra dismisses her. It is a catastrophe. A few friends stand by her, but she realizes she must vindicate herself; for two years she studies with a sweet ballerina she adores. The chance for reinstatement comes, and she discovers that the ballerina is an enemy. She dances once more at the Opéra, she has her moment of triumph, but it brings no joy. She is fifteen, no longer a child, and the book ends.

Child of the Ballet is autobiographical. Odette Joyeux did not become a dancer, she became a young actress, and is now a film star, with a "perverse" Parisian Alice in Wonderland radiance. The film *La Ronde,* in which she has a major part, has been an international success. She has written two plays and this is her second book.

Child of the Ballet is told like a contemporary Paris fairytale, the kind of graceful and ominous fairy-tale of which Jean Cocteau is the master. In the background monstrous shadows, poignant mystifications, abstract virtues gleaming now and then remote as stars. In the foreground, fantastic fragments of real scenes, flashes of persons. For instance, a majestic Venus in *Tannhauser* whose shell crashes from above stage back into the basement just before her aria; and who—down there among the dust, the screams of cupids and machinists, with the cataract of the Wagnerian orchestra pouring through the open trapdoor—disheveled, barebreasted, frantically bellows out her proper notes on cue.

The book is a montage of such fragments. It evokes Paris from a unique aspect, the environment, the career of a dancer. The author speaks lucidly of what classic dancing is about, and of the character that makes a classic dancer. But dancing is not her central interest. People she has seen, their destiny, the fantastic unconscious gestures they really make—these are her subject. Her scale is a small one, a Parisian intimacy of expression. Behind her story lies a feminine sense of the reality of art.

Arnold Haskell, the British ballet authority and director of the Sadler's Wells School, has translated it, and brilliantly illustrated his translation with the realistic etchings of small girls of the Paris ballet by Legrand. And drooly fans of etiquette will enjoy learning from Haskell that the word "tutu" is never used at the Opéra; only "juponages."

Romeo and Juliet

A Film Review

THE RUSSIAN feature-length ballet film, *Romeo and Juliet,* is more fun to watch if you don't like classic dancing than if you do. The whole cast keeps behaving like the operatic *boyars* and *mujhiks* one is acquainted with from Russian historical films. They rush up and down stairways, they fence by hundreds, they stare, feast, dance and mourn with an unquenchable agility and vehemence. Seen close up, they ham an emotion with a capital letter. They do a little classic dancing too, and tie it in by heavy character acting. They are completely convinced, if not completely convincing. You can't miss any point they make, but you do miss a delicacy of implication. The action hasn't that aura, or overtone, of grace and human sweetness that in Shakespeare or in classic ballet lets the wonderful side of a meaning appear as if of its own accord. Instead, the film has a great deal of energetic obviousness, the enthusiastic conventionality we are used to in the ballets of our screen musicals. On that level *Romeo* does very well.

But one expected another level. This *Romeo* is intended to show Russian ballet at its best. It has been adapted from one of the best post-war stage productions, the *Romeo and Juliet* of the Bolshoi of Moscow. It has been choreographed and co-directed by [Leonid] Lavrovsky, the choreographer of the theatre version. The original ballet score by Prokofiev is the film score. It is danced by Bolshoi Ballet, headed by the most celebrated of Soviet

213

ballerinas, Galina Ulanova, who created the same Juliet in Moscow. Very likely the film keeps the style, the general plan and many of the best moments of the stage version; certainly it shows every sign of care and devotion in its realization. And on this level one looks for a general effect much more interesting, and for a show with more sparkle.

But a local ballet fan is too curious about Soviet ballet to leave it at that. He comes to the film delighted with the chance to see the differences in style between these dancers and ours. He watches the detail for moments when what they do will show the kind of force the style has.

And he does see effects that communicate. Juliet, with the Friar's potion in her bodice, as she begins to dance with County Paris, has a moment when she thinks she is dancing with Romeo; the insane flash of it is real, though the style is melodramatic. Romeo has a strange rushing entrance in the tomb scene, and he lifts high what he believes is Juliet's corpse with a gesture that brings back the grandeur of the verse. Mercutio in the midst of the sword fight in which he is to die has a rush of darting and twisting leaps that makes one see his spirit all quickness and no venom. Two acrobats leap through the carnival crowd with a vivid gusto. And when the whole population of Verona is dancing its stamped and Slavic step in the carnival square, in the general enthusiasm the remoter groups can't hear the beat and gradually shift to a later one of their own; this shift is so real it pulls you right into the crush of the crowd. These moments are not effects of classic dancing, they are effects of acting, of mime. And I was delighted as by a sort of virtuoso mime specialty, when Tybalt made his face look the absolute peak of fury, and then slowly altered it to look twice as furious.

But the local fan keeps thinking, what about showing us some choreography? There are groups strolling, crowds milling, pretty girls in tears, people running very fast or standing still, cutting capers, feasting, brawling and constantly making faces and violent gestures. At the ball there is lots of genial ogling and drunken lurching, and with this motivation, slices of four or five dance numbers. But as far as their choreography goes, that turns out to be surprisingly commonplace; uninteresting in its material or in its development to the score. The big folk dance in the square, choreographically speaking, is nothing at all. But the unimaginative choreography of the two decisive *pas de deux* is what astonishes the fan most. The situations are the greatest—those of the balcony and of the bedroom scenes; the dancers are the best. And here at the poetic climax Juliet's dances have no brilliance of choreographic invention, no power of choreographic expression at all. They are elementary. While Romeo's part consists of giving his partner support with now and then the crumb of a leap thrown in. The dancers carry the situation by mime, like fine actors putting across a decisive scene in which they have only a banal text to work with.

The choreographic text is consistently elementary so as not to distract from the mime expression. Very likely the point of our best ballets would be lost on them if they saw them. They would take them for exercises in virtuosity. How could they know that they were meaningful when all the dancers looked so pleasant and so civil?

One comes to see that these Russians don't try for the same lucidity of dance action and of dance rhythm that we are used to, and that an interesting choreographic text calls for. They like to be off the measure. They prefer to fling out a whole step sequence to the general rush of a musical phrase or two, as if they heard in the music only its rhetoric or drive. They prefer to let the mime element—the acted emotion—blur the shape of the step and the classic carriage of the body. There is an exception in the classic-style group dance with mandolins, but the discipline here is meant to register as nice party manners. Only Ulanova shows a consistent powerful exactness of line in feet and legs, but even with her the mime emphasis makes the shoulders rise, the wrists tense, the floor-contact thicken. And the habitually lifted rib-cage (the habitual pouter-pigeon silhouette of Soviet ballerinas, which means "Here is my heart") breaks the line of her back and shortens her neck.

Once a local fan gives up looking for what we call choreography and classic style, he can see that the whole of this *Romeo*—dancing and mime—is keyed to a dominant mime image, a melodramatically violent one intended to characterize the environment of the brawling Capulets and Montagues. That the violence is a Slavic one, and not an Italian, is natural enough. But Shakespeare uses the brutal families as a foil for the marvelously civilized lovers—whose strength and delicacy suddenly become a wonderful and growing power that gives to the tragedy its joyous radiance. The kind of point Shakespeare makes can be and has been made by classic ballet when the piece (as in Petipa) takes its key from its lucidly dazzling grand pas de deux; just as the English play takes its key from its most dazzling sweet moments of verse.

But the Russian choreographer has turned the foil into the protagonist, and has taken his key from the rude and heavy mime motions that signify brutality. Everything in the ballet is oppressed by some reflection of the key. And the insistent intentionalness of the mime key has a depressing effect in another way. The effect is that the only human relations left in the piece are intentional ones.

Anyway the heavy mime style bores you. So when Lady Capulet, with an awesome gesture, rends her bodice in grief over Tybalt, you find yourself peeking at her underwear to see if that too is in period. When Juliet in the bedroom scene keeps falling agonized to her knees, you notice that it isn't in front of the Madonna that she drops but in front of a full-length mirror—and you see Ulanova-Juliet with a ballerina's practice mirror in her bedroom.

But after an irreverent breather, the fan can watch again. Not the acting, but the movement. And how beautifully Ulanova runs. How handsomely they all run. And the fan is struck by how the men sail through the air, all of them, with a fine sustained stretch that few of our boys achieve. They sustain the extension through the powerful middle of the body, they don't hold it as well in the ankles, knees and nape, classic style. So they increase the effect of a weight that sails. The weight the dancers suggest in their action becomes the men better than it does the women. And the men's strong stance is a pleasure. And as the fan watches, he gets to see that the expressive vigor of their action comes from the dynamic sforzando attack they give to a stretching motion, a sforzando that comes from the midriff, and that has been trained in many gradations. Ulanova is a virtuoso of both the attack and the development that follows.

And one can well imagine—when a stage is full of heavy men and women dancing with this kind of powerful sforzando thrust and leaping up with a powerfully sustained extension in the air, so that a continuous pulse of ferocious energy pours out over the audience while the orchestra blares full strength—that the theatre effect becomes so overwhelming one doesn't so much watch the dance as abandon one's self to the orgiastic discharge of it. One can well imagine the mass scenes of *Romeo* or any other piece creating such an effect, so that when Ulanova appears, so slight and small compared to the rest of the cast but so rapid and decisive and so occupied with a particular inner life, the shock of seeing an individual again is shattering. One doesn't ask for more, one sees her through tears of gratitude. One can well imagine it, but the film doesn't show anything like it.

Nor could it. A large stationary stage accumulates energy (or else lucidity) in a way that the swiveling narrow field of a camera can't. A camera can't keep its mind on dancing. In a mass scene its eye catches a hardness of strain in a movement and reminds you that the dancers have been repeating this take so often they are past their best form. The camera eye looks at a few steps of Ulanova's and observes that her waist is not a pretty one. It also observes her worn face, but after a few moments that turns out to be in its own way quite pretty. Of all her many dance qualities, it is her lovely airiness in lifts and supported leaps that best keeps a trace of its stage magic in this film.

It has been a long film but it is over now. The fan has caught the copious visceral vitality of these dancers which would make them a stage success anywhere. Their style

217

has less visual and musical continuity than it has visceral. Conventional ideas when they take this expression become what some of us call vital, human and earthy. What a wow this company would make of *Shéhérazade*. The expression of their style is strongest just where that of our ballet is weakest, and vice versa. When they come to New York, what fun it will be to see the contrast. As for myself, as I went down into the subway on my way home, I began to wonder what Rubens would have done if he had been a Russian choreographer. (*1956*)

Brief Reports

TO LONDON: THE ROYAL BALLET

1. Sleeping Beauty

The Royal Ballet's first night at the Metropolitan Opera House was, as usual, a success—a gala for those members of the New York public who feel at home with English manners.

They welcomed the company, Fonteyn in particular, with a solid warmth; they stayed on at the end to show their solid friendliness by many curtain-calls; and finally they drifted out into the drizzle of an incipient hurricane with a thoughtful glow of approbation.

The Sleeping Beauty, as the company gives it, engenders a comforting glow one is grateful for. Fonteyn, sweetly reasonable, sweetly lucid in every motion, looked lovely; she danced better and better as the evening went on, and was in her full glory in the final fish-dives. As at every point in her career she carried the whole company, the whole drama steadily to a climax.

The Bluebirds (Page and Shaw) thrilled; Powell's Wicked Fairy and Grant's dance timing were extraordinary; Farron's mime as the Countess, and Larsen's as the Queen, excellent; Bergsma's mime as the Lilac Fairy, and Somes's as the Prince, very attractive. The costumes were opulent in colors like good British food; the scenery enormous, wishy washy; the divine music a bit tight and sour.

But the second night, the music opened and sweetened. The young Lilac Fairy, determined to do it right this time, danced beautifully. In the next act, after a slightly forced Rose adagio, Fonteyn's dancing quickly recovered all the gleaming freshness of Aurora. It rose from there to the marmoreal suavity of the Vision, and rose again to the magnificence of the final pas de deux. The company rose with her. A beautiful evening.

2. Ondine

In Ashton's *Ondine* everybody loved the magically liquid sparkle of Fonteyn. She was bewitching endlessly and with ease. Every action seemed the spontaneous one of the character she was playing. Of her last-act swim, in itself a stage trick, she made a beautiful dramatic image; the fatal kiss-of-death pas de deux she filled with grandeur. All evening she was a supreme artist at her greatest, and simplest.

The ballet surrounds her with an expensive spectacle and, much more valuable, with a devoted company. Ashton keeps her on stage most of the evening; what he invents for her is never unbecoming or forced, and now and then it turns excellent.

A delight, too, is Grant's fantastic running, sometimes spinning upward in full career, or at top speed stopping magically. When this sea-god in fury calls on naiads and tritons one is surprised that what happens is a sedate-style stage show. Then and later one is surprised that so marvelous a creature as Ondine should pick her friends from among shoddy people and trivial immortals. The ballet is foolish and everyone noticed it.

3. Antigone, Baiser de la Fée, Giselle

Cranko's tragedy *Antigone* has a dance style that combines American Modern and Greek Modern, both of them at their most pompous and both delivered with a B.B.C. accent. To me it looked like first-rate material for a farce; all it needed was some tourists wandering about. A pity Cranko missed the chance.

In MacMillan's *Baiser de la Fée* the first half of the

Mill Scene showed his striking gift for poetry. Seymour, the Bride, became adorable in an odd way, and the Bridegroom, MacLeary, very promising. But the Fairy (Beriosova), though no woman was ever busier, never became supernatural. Unless she is supernatural, there is no drama.

The Royal Ballet's *Giselle,* now restudied by Ashton, seems to me preferable to the Bolshoi's for style and often for sense. Fonteyn is extraordinarily good, both as a sensitive country girl and as a tender imponderable ghost.

Ashton's peasant pas de deux, delightfully danced by Page and Usher, is a jewel of 1840 pastiche. And his changes have done wonders for the old harvest number. The serious characterizations of Albrecht, Bathilde, Hilarion (Somes, Farron, Edwards) are lively and very touching. Larsen as the Mother becomes thrilling in a passage credited to Karsavina. *Giselle* seems to me more direct when it is cut; that question apart, Ashton's version is the best, and the company does it handsomely.

4. Fille Mal Gardée

La Fille Mal Gardée had a very big success on its first night, on Wednesday, though the leisurely pace of the ballet seemed several times, particularly toward the end, in danger of losing the public. However, they responded happily to all other elements—the sunniness and summeriness, gentle as in England; the good nature, good health, good humor of a mild countryside; the pleasant country dances attractively reinvented, gracefully interwoven with classic and with music-hall numbers; the many amusing finds in steps, in ribbons, in props, in lifts—an adagio supported through a window, for instance, was quite miraculous.

Most of all the public responded to the sweet-temperedness of stars and ensemble (including a white pony)—a company in which no one ever insistently pushed a motion or a gag or a character projection. Neither an American nor a Russian company could have sustained for so long, so airy, childlike and unemphatic a good time.

The stars, Nerina and Blair, were perfect in step and gesture. Holden, the farcical widow, excellent everywhere, in a clog-dance gained a sweet radiance that was adorable.

Grant as Alain was even more extraordinary. In dance and mime he made the full foil for a whole evening of blandness, without the least hint of intending to. No other dancer in the world could have done it.

For all this that Ashton has so happily evoked, guided and invented, he cannot be praised too highly. His idyll passes, for me, too blandly and too evenly. But now that I know the kind of piece it is and the kind it is not, I am curious to see it again. (*1960*)

THE NEW YORK CITY BALLET

5. Liebeslieder Walzer

Liebeslieder Walzer, a ballet by Balanchine, was the peculiar glory of the New York City Ballet's recent season. Peculiar, to put it mildly, is the set-up of this piece. Duration an hour; no orchestra, no story; the music, two Brahms song-cycles all in waltz time with German text; eight dancers. Evidently the master had gone mad.

The curtain rises on a lamp-lit garden room; a summer night at a *Schloss*. The women are in pale, long, voluminous gowns, the men in tails. A group has gathered at the piano, intent on the score, ready to sing in four voices and accompany four-handed. The other guests, four couples, stand in the room about to dance. And in a moment they all begin.

At first one listens more than one looks; the dances begin with graceful Victorian ballroom forms. Then deeper in the music these waltz forms begin to tell what they know. The sensuousness isn't adolescent, the dancing has a boldness of romantic fervor and intimacy one recognizes with astonishment the range of, as much as the grace. There has been no impropriety: nothing, so to speak, has occurred. The dancers open doors into the moonlight and go out.

The curtain falls; when it rises again the company at the piano remains. But the room, moonlit and starlit, has turned mysteriously transparent; the dancers stand poised in it, but the women, now in dresses of transparent gauze, have become ballerinas.

At the first phrase of the music they soar weightlessly high into air, lifted by their cavaliers. The dances, set angelically to the richness of the music, have an unearthly brilliance, a buoyancy in which images, gay or seductive or tragic, float or flash at play. Not that it is possible, but that one believes it is happening.

The dancers have vanished. At their corner of the empty moonlit stage the musicians begin a last song. And the full force of one's feeling listens. In the shadows the dancers return, the ladies in their voluminous evening gowns now sit listening, the beautiful song ceases, the curtain falls.

Liebeslieder Walzer is Balanchine at his most glorious. Adams, Hayden, Jillana, Verdy, Carter, Ludlow, Magallanes, Watts all outdid themselves.

Balanchine made four more pieces, each quite different. *Monumentum* to the recent Stravinsky-Gesualdo score, *Ragtime* to Stravinsky too, *Don Sebastian* to Donizetti and *Variants* to Gunther Schuller. The last was jazz at its most long-hair, and I never saw jazz-derived dancing develop so much concentrated power. We also had new works by Bolender, Moncion, Taras. A busy season, and the company flourished on it. As usual, nobody knows what will happen next. (*1960*)

6. Electronics

Electronics, Balanchine's latest, is Radio City-type art. It takes place in a cellophane cavern of ice to an electronic score. There are some people in long white underwear with cute horns who are a bit squirmy. Creatures in black underwear, almost invisible, come in; they want to do something to the white ones, but can't think of much, and it's too dark to see anyway; so everybody leaves. Some cellophane columns jerk around, semi-tumescent. At the end, the chief white-underwear couple make a very odd ball of themselves and roll around awhile.

This may suggest science fiction, spookily funny and horrid. But what *Electronics* looks like is Sundayfied abstract ballet. It looks like an undertaker. It achieves an impeccably fatuous banality. Balanchine's workmanship is there, his imagination isn't. Not worth making an exception for some details.

The come-on of the piece is the score (Gassman-Sala). It is a tape of electronically produced noises, but it has nothing to do imaginatively with electronic music. It sounds like gems from Sinding played on a Hammond organ by a flustered maiden aunt. Because it sounds like sentimental parlor music, it would be perfect for slapstick on stage. Instead of having fun with the score's maiden-auntieness, Balanchine solemnly mirrors it.

Electronics is not a ballet to be proud of. It puts on a highbrow act, but what it delivers is middlebrow Radio City corn. And it has the success of that kind of a fake—it is a big hit with press and public. I hope it moves to Radio City.

Nothing fake about the dancing of the piece, or about the dancing of the company generally. An old curmudgeon who sits in the last row because from there you can see the feet, I notice that the New York City dancers are extraordinary. (*1961*)

TO SPOLETO

7. Paul Taylor

Taylor's choreography at his first recital ten years back was anti-dance and avantgarde. For example, in the opening number a man in street clothes took a great many instantaneous non-dance poses that had no mime meaning, usually taking a few steps between; this action was set to a tape of the voice on the telephone, "When you hear the tone, the time will be—" a tape that kept telling the actual time every ten seconds for twenty minutes. To another tape, fifteen minutes long—this one of rain noises—two girls stood or ran in curves, nothing else. And to a three minute score by John Cage, a sitting girl and a boy standing beside her, both in street clothes, did not move.

Ten years later, Taylor is choreographing to Ives, Schuller, Haendel, Haieff. The action, though different from classic ballet, is no more avantgarde than the music. Today's avantgarde is as engaged, now as in the past, with anti-music, anti-dance, anti-theatre, and everybody agrees it is a good thing to have around.

Taylor's first choreography was anti-dance with a beautiful clarity and ingenuousness. He admired more than anything the shoreless beauty of Cunningham's dancing anti-dance, and he still does. But the more he danced and choreographed, the more a powerful and complexly fluid dance momentum engaged him. His gift defined itself as one not for anti-dance but for pro-dance. What he has been doing since 1960 is new in the sense that such dance momentum had not existed before in the modern dance (i.e. in non-classic technique). The technical as well as the creative discovery is his.

Taylor is one of the few choreographers who can sustain a large-scale dance with only from five to eight dancers. He is the first New York choreographer since Robbins who has taken the trouble to teach himself the continuous clarity of a wellmade ballet. He has given the modern dance a new resource, one equivalent to (but not identical with) the classic dance-step phrase. (*1964*)

The Opening of
The New York State Theatre

THE NEW YORK STATE THEATRE is a beauty. In the first place, you can see everything and you can hear everything. The stage is large, and the proportions of the proscenium give it airiness. In addition the proportions of the house and of the lobby give you a lift. Space is normally a tunnel in New York. At the Philharmonic you are still in some sort of tunnel—it doesn't have enough shape for its size. At the New York State Theatre the height of the house and of the lobby relate to the room.

The seven-story house is horseshoe shaped and plum-colored, with a chandelier resembling no other theatre's. The cream-colored lobby doesn't either resemble any other lobby. It is a vast promenade with three tiers of airy balconies running round it. They appear suspended by thin strips of brass and seem to have a light matting of metal twigs in place of balustrades. One long four-story wall is glass, with a curtain of brass beads hung from the ceiling to the floor; the opposite wall bulges forward a trifle, accommodating the rear curve of the house. Light is reflected from cream-carpeted walls, and from the beautiful plain ceiling that looks like a deep golden sky. Downstairs on the handsome stone floor people walk about in a light like that of early dusk. That's the main effect. "Does it remind you of anything?" I asked a delighted artist. "The Piazza San Marco." The pair of floodlit statues—so sweetly comic in their enormity—add to the fantasy of a sociable city square. Their joke of scale resembles that of the chandelier in the house. And so it may occur to you that the airiness of both house and lobby derive from the proportions of the proscenium.

In the house, the best seats are downstairs between rows D and M. The size of the orchestra makes the back of the house a bit remote. But at the back of the house, sightlines in all rows at all levels are excellent. Not good are the seats way at the side. Very bad are the second row seats in all side rings. The gallery (once you adjust to the distance) is fine. At the top of the house standing room costs 75 cents. I found Mr. Taras there, watching for faults. Acoustics are perfect everywhere.

Many fans find that, seen from the back of the house, the dancers look too far off and too small. But I found that after watching from the gallery and from standing room, when you return to seats in the lower rings, the seats have moved a good deal closer to the stage. By measurement the back of the house is nearer the stage than the back of the house at the Met, but everybody has long ago adjusted to the Met. As for the City Center, it took years to adjust even to the best seats. Harder to adjust to at the New York State is the absence of memories, the loss for the fans of a place they belonged to.

During the first two weeks at the New York State (which is as far as this report goes) the company added two pieces to its repertory, Balanchine's *Clarinade* and a revival of Tudor's *Dim Lustre*. It also presented *Midsummer Night's Dream*, and twenty-six other ballets, most of them respaced for the much larger stage. The house has always been full, and has become more and more lively. The company started well, and hit its stride in a week. Now the dancers are dancing their heads off. I wouldn't have thought it possible, but with more space to cover to the same musical phrase they have stepped up their speed and sweep of style. They love their new theatre.

Not that the fans didn't notice some victories won by sheer nerve and the grace of God; and a few not won. But the fans knew some of the disasters while the season was being prepared—rehearsal room troubles, lighting troubles. Just before opening, Hayden and Verdy were injured. At Ballet Society's pre-opening Benefit, the nervousness was equal on both sides of the footlights. Then *Serenade* began, sounding heavenly, and gave the fans their first glimpse of the company's new speed and sweep. Wilde was at her greatest. There was a new finale, too, for the third section, very good. *Serenade* was followed by *Tarantella* (McBride, Villella), its happy spirit and wit never so distinctly seen and heard. To everyone's surprise, it was *Agon, Agon* of all pieces, that misfired. A couple of nights later came the Governor's Gala with speeches and TV. The next night, the season opened with *Midsummer Night's Dream.* Certainly George Balanchine and his dancers deserve the theatre; but it wouldn't be here—nor the performing fountain—if Rockefeller hadn't happened to be governor. Architectural risks had to be taken, and political ones, too. Then the general public came. Within two weeks, it had fallen madly in love with the place.

Some fans will remember how, ten years ago, they used to applaud demonstratively after *Four Temperaments,* to save it from being taken out of repertory. It has always been a key piece by which to judge the company. On the new stage it is gloriously danced by everyone, each and all. A particular delight at one performance was seeing Tallchief dancing at top speed with marvelous musical details of phrasing. D'Amboise too was at his grandest.

Grand too was the first *Apollo,* on stage and in the pit. This beautiful ballet has come to be danced with a devoted concentration, each move done on the largest possible scale. The intensity resembles that of a modern-dance ritual. When the score and the choreography now and then exchange a smile, the dancers don't presume to be in on the joke, they are attending to the powerful dance forces present. For me, I would prefer an interpretation less solemn; but this time the solemnity was not so insistent. Govrin and Neary, dancing full force, made unusually clear the gesture incorporated into their variations (gesture like that of folding a private secret into the hand, and then revealing it to Apollo, who is disgusted).

It is a pleasure that Farrell, Govrin, McBride, Neary

and Paul, each of them a phenomenal young dancer, are each so strikingly different. Lovely Farrell is at her loveliest in *Meditation*. You see her yield completely, fainting with a soft abandon in a supported deep back bend, and before you see the recovery, she is already standing apart, mild and free, as if in thought. *Meditation* (like Hermia's variation in *Dream*) is a dance you "read" as a dramatic situation. The more you look and listen, the more absorbing the timing becomes. D'Amboise, the hero, is excellent, except for his last slurpy steps.

McBride, a beautiful woman in every style of ballet, and with the extra gift of a perfect stage smile, has been the season's all purpose heroine. Her triumph came however in an anti-beauty part, the Novice in *The Cage*. Robbins had rehearsed the company move by move, note by note; the larger stage enhanced the piece's horrifying succinctness.

Dim Lustre and *Clarinade,* the novelties, are weak compared to *The Cage*. They were warmly applauded. They are no disgrace to their choreographers or to the company, but they miss. Tudor's *Dim Lustre* is one of those vague English ballroom flirtations. It keeps being stopped for blackouts and flashbacks. Everybody on stage has to freeze, because the hero and the heroine is about to think. What they think is rather silly. The exception is the "white tie" episode, a real whirl (McBride, Rapp). *Lustre* is a charm number—it doesn't call for dancing, it calls for principals who exude charm like a pair of broody sexpots. Villella hadn't figured out what he was there for. The set and costumes by Beni Montresor couldn't have been prettier.

The costumes for Balanchine's *Clarinade,* by contrast might have been borrowed from the Snowflake, Ariz. Ballet. The piece is virtuoso ballet-holds making like a teenage jazz party. The first section is fun; the second super-anatomical with a sweet exit; the last two sections start flickering in front of your eyes, and keep that up till the curtain falls. The Morton Gould score (for Benny Goodman) makes cozy noises, but no remarkable ones; it's good music division music. On stage Farrell and Blum performed their upsidedown absurdities with a sweetly pensive air; Govrin and Mitchell were tops—from all out hot to all cool in an unpredictable flash, ignoring beats like mad without dropping one. A pity Mr. B didn't give them the stage a bit more. In an *Agon* I saw (two weeks after the season had opened), glorious in every way, the pas de deux by Farrell and Mitchell was heaven.

An adorable company. And what an orchestra. There's a great deal more to tell, dear dance fan. Changes good and less good in *Dream*—well nothing that won't keep. The new *Swan Lake* set looked to me like a very expensive, dark ditch on top of a high mountain, but maybe it's the end in elegance.

Part Four

On Painting

The Thirties

PAT PASLOFF ASKED ME to write something for the show about New York painting in the thirties, how it seemed at the time. The part I knew, I saw as a neighbor. I met Willem de Kooning on the fire escape, because a black kitten lost in the rain cried at my fire door, and after the rain it turned out to be his kitten. He was painting on a dark eight-foot high picture that had sweeps of black across it and a big look. That was early in '36. Soon Rudy Burckhardt and I kept meeting Bill at midnight at the local Stewart's, and having a coffee together. Friends of his often showed up, and when the cafeteria closed we would go to Bill's loft in the next street and talk some more and make coffee. I remember people talking intently and listening intently and then everybody burst out laughing and started off intent on another tack. Seeing the pictures more or less every day, they slowly became beautiful, and then they stayed beautiful. I didn't think of them as painting of the New York School, I thought of them as Bill's pictures.

These early ones are easy to get into now from the later point of view of the New York School. At the time, from the point of view of the School of Paris, they were impenetrable. The resemblances to Picasso and Miro were misleading, because where they led one to expect seduction and climax, one saw instead a vibration. To start from Mondrian might have helped. One could not get into the picture by way of any detail, one had to get into it all at once, so to speak. It often took me several months to be able to.

I remember walking at night in Chelsea with Bill during the depression, and his pointing out to me on the pavement the dispersed compositions—spots and cracks and bits of wrappers and reflections of neon-light—neon-signs were few then—and I remember the scale in the compositions was too big for me to see it. Luckily I could imagine it. At the time Rudy Burckhardt was taking photographs of New York that keep open the moment its transient buildings spread their unknown and unequalled harmonies of scale. I could watch that scale like a magnanimous motion on these undistorted photographs; but in everyday looking about, it kept spreading beyond the field of sight. At the time we all talked a great deal about scale in New York, and about the difference of instinctive scale in signs, painted color, clothes, gestures, everyday expressions between Europe and America. We were happy to be in a city the beauty of which was unknown, uncozy, and not small scale.

While we were talking twenty years ago, I remembered someone saying, "Bill, you haven't said a word for half an hour." "Yes," he answered, his voice rising like a New Yorker's to falsetto with surprise, "I was just noticing that, too." He was likely to join in the talk by vehemently embracing a suggestion or vehemently rejecting it. Right off he imagined what it would be like to act on it and go on acting on it. He didn't, like a wit, imitate the appearance of acting on it; he committed himself full force to what he was imagining. As he went on, characteristic situations in his life or those of friends came back to him as vividly as if they had just happened. He invented others. Objections he accepted, or circumvented, or shouted his opposition to. He kept heading for the image in which a spontaneous action had the force of the general ideas involved. And there he found the energy of contradictory actions. The laugh wasn't ridiculousness, but the fun of being committed to the contrary. He was just as interested in the contrary energy. Self protection bored him.

In the talk then about painting, no doctrine of style was

settled at Bill's. He belligerently brought out the mysterious paradoxes left over. In any style he kept watching the action of the visual paradoxes of painting—the opposition of interchangeable centers, or a volume continued as a space, a value balancing a color. He seemed to consider in them a craft by which the picture seen as an image unpredictably came loose, moved forward and spread. On the other hand, his working idea at the time was to master the plainest problems of painting. I often heard him say that he was beating his brains out about connecting a figure and a background. The basic connection he meant seemed to me a motion from inside them that they interchanged and that continued throughout. He insisted on it during those years stroke by stroke and gained a virtuoso's eye and hand. But he wanted everything in the picture out of equilibrium except spontaneously all of it. That to him was one objective professional standard. That was form the way the standard masterpieces had form—a miraculous force and weight of presence moving from all over the canvas at once.

Later, I saw in some Greek temples contradictory forces operating publicly at full speed. Reading the *Iliad,* the poem at the height of reason presented the irrational and subjective, self-contradictory sweep of action under inspiration. I had missed the point in the talks in 22nd Street. The question Bill was keeping open with an enduring impatience had been that of professional responsibility toward the force of inspiration. That force or scale is there every day here where everybody is. Whose responsibility is it, if not your own? What he said, was "All an artist has left to work with is his self-consciousness."

From such a point of view the Marxist talk of the thirties was one-track. The generous feeling in it was stopped by a rigid perspective, a single center of action, and by jokes with only one side to them. If one overlooked that, what was interesting was the peremptoriness and the paranoia of Marxism as a ferment or method of rhetoric. But artists who looked at painting were used to a brilliance in such a method on the part of the Paris surrealists and to a surrealist humor that the political talk

234

did not have. Politically everybody downtown was anti-fascist, and the talk went on peacefully. Then when friends who had fought in Spain returned, their silence made an impression so direct that the subject was dropped. Against everybody's intention it had become shameless.

In the presence of New York at the end of the thirties, the paranoia of surrealism looked parlor-sized or arch. But during the war Bill told me he had been walking uptown one afternoon and at the corner of 53rd and 7th he had noticed a man across the street who was making peculiar gestures in front of his face. It was Breton and he was fighting off a butterfly. A butterfly had attacked the Parisian poet in the middle of New York. So hospitable nature is to a man of genius.

Talking to Bill and to Rudy for many years, I found I did not see with a painter's eye. For me the after-image (as Elaine de Kooning has called it) became one of the ways people behave together, that is, a moral image. The beauty Bill's depression pictures have kept reminds me of the beauty that instinctive behavior in a complex situation can have—mutual actions one has noticed that do not make one ashamed of one's self, or others, or of one's surroundings either. I am assuming that one knows what it is to be ashamed. The joke of art in this sense is a magnanimity more steady than one notices in everyday life, and no better justified. Bill's early pictures resemble the later ones in that the expression of character the picture has seems to me of the same kind in early and later ones, though the scope of it and the performance in later ones becomes prodigious.

The general look of painting today strikes me as seductive. It makes the miles of New York galleries as luxurious to wander through as a slave market. Room after room, native or imported, the young prosperity pictures lift their intelligent eyes to the buyer and tempt him with an independent personality. The honest critics, as they pass close to a particularly luscious one, give it a tweak in the soft spots. The picture pinches them in return. At the end of a day's work, a critic's after-images are black and blue. It takes more character to be serious now.

Twenty years ago Bill's great friend was Gorky. I knew they talked together about painting more than anyone else. But when other people were at Bill's, Gorky said so little that he was often forgotten. At one party the talk turned to the condition of the painter in America, the bitterness and unfairness of his poverty and disregard. People had a great deal to say on the subject, and they said it, but the talk ended in a gloomy silence. In the pause, Gorky's deep voice came from under a table. "Nineteen miserable years have I lived in America." Everybody burst out laughing. There was no whine left. Gorky had not spoken of justice, but of fate, and everybody laughed open-hearted.

At a WPA art occasion, I heard that LaGuardia had made a liberal speech about art and society. After the applause, Gorky who was on the reception committee stepped forward unexpectedly and began, "Your Honor, you know about government, and I know about art." Short LaGuardia looked at tall Gorky, who was earnestly contradicting him in a few sentences. I imagine he saw Gorky's seedy sport-clothes and the exhilarating nobility of his point of view and valued them. Maybe he felt like laughing happily the way we did. The last time I saw Gorky, not long after the war, he was sitting with Bill and Elaine in the diner that used to be at Sixth Avenue across from 8th Street, and I went in and joined them for a coffee. I told them I had just read in a paper that when the war was over there were 175 million more people in the world than before it began. He looked at me with those magnificent eyes of his and said quietly, "That is the most terrible thing I have heard." The beauty of Gorky's painting I understood only last year.

I began this train of thought wondering at the cliche about downtown painting in the depression—the accepted idea that everybody had doubts and imitated Picasso and talked politics. None of these features seemed to me remarkable at the time, and they don't now. Downtown everybody loved Picasso then, and why not. But what they painted made no sense as an imitation of him. For myself, something in his steady wide light reminded me then of the light in the streets and lofts we lived in. At that time Tchelitchev was the uptown master, and he had a flickering light. The current painters seem for their part to tend toward a flickering light. The difference that strikes me between downtown then and now is that then everybody drank coffee and nobody had shows. Private life goes on regardless.

Willem de Kooning

WILLEM DE KOONING was stopped on the street by a young man he hadn't seen before who said bitterly, "Doesn't it bother you to be so famous?" "No," de Kooning said, "but it seems to bother you." De Kooning's fame has been spreading steadily for a decade; there have been complaints about it in the papers.

At the benefit show for Nell Blaine two years ago, I saw on the wall a drawing of his—no larger than a Lucky Strike package—a drawing of a seated woman, as absorbing to look at as a drawing by a Renaissance master, it had that force of volume. Elaine de Kooning told me that when he did it, in the early forties, he said he wasn't going to do any more of those, you could lose your mind doing them. She had picked it up from among the week's litter on the studio floor.

At the time, Bill and Elaine were living on 22nd Street. It was a top floor loft, spacious and high-ceilinged, sunny at the back. When he took it, it had long stood empty. He patched the walls, straightened the pipes, installed kitchen and bath, made painting racks, closets and tables; the floor he covered with heavy linoleum, painting it grey and the walls and ceiling white. In the middle of the place, he built a room, open on top, with walls a bit over six feet high. The bed and bureau fitted into it; a window looked out into the studio. The small bedroom white outside and pink inside seemed to float or be moored in the loft. All of it was Elaine's wedding present. The six months he spent getting it ready were the only time during many years before or later that he put off painting for longer than a couple of days. While they lived there, Saturday afternoons he stopped whatever he was doing and washed the place down.

They didn't live there very long. They were often fifty or a hundred dollars in arrears with the rent. Bill had been a steady tenant of another loft in the same building for several years previous. But now the landlord took to pounding on their door. The dispossess notice went up. The landlord climbed up by the fire-escape and pleaded for the rent through the window. They asked him in for coffee. He told them that he liked them both, but that he had a heart-condition and couldn't stand arrears in the rent. After the loft, they went to live in a tenement on Carmine Street.

Two or three pictures of his had been shown at the Bignou Gallery. They made no stir, but after awhile the Modern Museum invited him to bring photographs of his work. At the door he bought a ticket to get to the office for the interview; and after a friendly chat, since he didn't have carfare left, he walked back to Carmine Street. By the middle forties, though his pictures were extraordinary, he was poorer than ever. His first show was in '48, at the Egan Gallery. In '50, the Modern Museum sent pictures of his to the Venice Biennale, giving him a place of honor together with his friends Gorky and Pollock. Several years later, in his 10th Street loft, he opened a box to show me a handsome suit that had just arrived. He seemed to be wearing, as he had been during the twenty years I had known him then, a hand-me-down given him by a friend. This was his first suit. His fortunes were mending; for some time he had been paying his rent and his color bill; in fact he had been helping out friends in trouble, and standing everybody to drinks and dinner, and often quite a number were around. In '53 his third show, the first at the Janis Gallery, was crowded day after day; the elevator man said, "The way people are coming to this show, that man must be dead." The show ended with de Kooning in debt to his dealer.

A year ago he came back with a dozen suits from Rome, where he had taken a three months vacation. He came back to a new loft near 12th Street, wonderfully airy and light with slender cast-iron columns, that in the seventies might have been the floor of a department store. The landlord had reconditioned it to suit his tenant, and it was even nearly ready. A little later Bill said, "I thought that now I had this wonderful loft, and some money, and all this experience, and had had this nice vacation, when I started to paint again, it would be easier. It was for two days. Now it's the same it used to be, I don't know how to do it."

I knew how it had been twenty years ago in one or the other loft on 22nd Street, when I used to see him several times a week. A new picture of his, a day or two after he had started it, had a striking, lively beauty; one such sketch that he gave to Rudy Burckhardt who asked him for it at the time, still has it. But at that point Bill would look at his picture sharply, like a choreographer at a talented dancer, and say bitterly, "Too easy." A few days later the picture looked puzzled; where before there had been a quiet place for it to get its balance, now a lot was happening that belonged to some other image than the first. Soon the unfinished second picture began to be pushed into by a third. After a while a series of rejected pictures lay one over the other. One day the accumulated paint was sandpapered down, leaving hints of contradictory outline in a jewel-like haze of iridescence—a young painter recently found such a de Kooning on the street—and then on the sandpapered surface Bill started to build up the picture over again. I can hear his light, tense voice saying as we walked at night, "I'm struggling with my picture, I'm beating my brains out, I'm stuck." Next time I asked about it, "I've an idea I'm trying out, I think I'm getting it," he said shortly. Once or twice after weeks of that, he kicked or slashed the canvas to bits; usually he stowed it on the rack, saying he couldn't finish it. When at the time Mr. Keller of the Bignou Gallery came to see what he had put aside, and offered him a show, Bill was delighted, and worked harder than ever, but in the end there were only two canvases he was ready to show. His friends would say, "Listen, Bill, you have a psychological block about finishing; you're being very self-destructive, you ought to see an analyst." He burst out laughing, "Sure, the analyst needs me for his material, the way I need my pictures for mine." Those of that time that then looked unintelligible now look beautifully alive and clear all over.

While these pictures were wearing him out, he was day by day for the people who came to see him the most generous and perceptive of friends. He came to a hospital bed where I lay seriously wounded from a drunken brawl the night before, took a sharp look at me and said in a low voice vehemently, "If I could find the man who did that to you, I'd kill him." The same day another friend, an extremely brilliant man, too, came to see me. "Oh, I'm so sorry for what happened," he said smiling, "but tell me, Edwin, didn't you provoke it a little, I don't mean consciously."

De Kooning when I had met him first five or six years earlier had been a young painter cheerfully in earnest living next door. He readily talked and listened, sitting forward on a chair. He admired Picasso enthusiastically. After a while one realized what it meant to him to be a painter. It didn't mean being one of the boys, making the scene or leading a movement, it meant meeting full force the professional standard set by the great Western painters old and new. He wasn't naive, he was undesigning. This was also the time—the mid-thirties—when he met Gorky first. After Gorky's death, to a critic who said Gorky had been influenced by him he wrote, " . . . When about fifteen years ago I walked into Arshile's studio for the first time, the atmosphere was so beautiful that I got a little dizzy, and when I came to, I was bright enough to take the hint immediately . . . I am glad that it is about impossible to get away from his influence. As long as I keep it with myself, I'll be doing all right. Sweet Arshile, bless your dear heart."

As he in the early forties struggled with his unfinishable pictures, day by day de Kooning was also finding out

241

what further try some other theory could suggest to him. Pressed to join a cause, "That's your status quo," he shouted. "I'm not supporting anybody's status quo." He described an ordinary looking person or incident, and without explanation as he told the facts, the particular gesture he was recognizing in a theory or ideology became so clear everybody laughed. He talked about how a masterpiece made the figures active and the voids around them active as well, as active as possible, it squeezed everything dramatically but somehow the picture opened itself way out, changing the center and the frame. He thought it opened where the eye believed it saw one thing, but knew it saw another, like near and far, resemblance and form, both at once, or funny and fatal, like in a Primitive. He spoke to me about the trouble he had with the projecting thighs of a fullface seated figure. I pointed out that he avoided foreshortening. He said vehemently that it made him sick to his stomach, not in other people's pictures, but when he did it himself. He pointed out the landscape-type scale in the shoulders of a Raphael Madonna in Washington. We talked about the mysteriously powerful nastiness in the hair of a Raphael youth there, who looks at you over his shoulder. A few times as we walked in our neighborhood he pointed to instances —a gesture, a crack, some refuse, a glow—where for a moment nature did it, the mysteriousness you recognize in a masterpiece. I couldn't see it where he pointed to, but for that matter like everybody, I knew the kind of perception he was referring to, the flash called beauty, which is actual. He looked hard to catch exactly what was there. Walking at night with a friend, he suddenly went back a few steps and stood peering intently at the pavement. The other man saw that there was a child's scribble there. De Kooning returned to him, head down, muttering, "They shouldn't be able to." The friend burst out laughing. Bill looked up suspiciously, then burst out laughing too, shouting angrily as he laughed, "But art isn't meant for children." Another night he was walking with Elaine and her teenage brother down dark Sixth Avenue. Across the Avenue he saw a group of youths come running and laughing out of a side street, knock down one among them, kick him, and still running and laughing, disappear again. Then he saw another boy bend over the victim, and begin to lift him to his feet. As he held him, running and laughing the gang was back, knocked the Samaritan down, kicked him, and ran off laughing around the corner. As Bill looked across at the two bodies, he realized that the second was that of Elaine's brother, who he thought standing beside her.

In 1950, nearly a decade later, I had been abroad and out of touch for several years, when I heard that several pictures of his painted since I left hung at the Venice Biennale. I was eager to see them. But after reaching Venice a week and more passed before I got to the Biennale Park. I had been walking through the exhibit in a stupefied state for two hours when I entered an empty room hung with de Koonings, Gorkys and Pollocks. I stood glancing around with a smile, ready to have them take me back to the New York that was home, expecting Bill and I would go down to the corner for a coffee. Not at all. The pictures looked at me with no recognition whatever, not even Bill's. I had no private access to them. Standing there as a stranger, I saw the lively weight the color had, the force and sudden grace the excitement had. I realized that the buoyancy around me was that of heroism in painting. That I could see it was due to luck. A week earlier, sitting in front of the Titian Pieta in the Accademia, exasperated by the seasickness Titian was insisting I endure, I angrily looked away from the canvas and happened to recognize the painter Kokoshka, standing to one side, watching with delight the same heaving and crashing storm of gold and silver that I found too rough. I was furious. Ashamed of my squeamishness I had stuck it out with Titian and the Titian-side of his younger competitors, like gales at sea, for a week all over Venice, and had gotten my sealegs. Because my eyes had become adjusted to that range in painting, they could tell me what the New York School was up to. That was how I discovered it; it wasn't through knowing Bill's honesty in daily life. But when I saw it I thought that the Europeans, more used to

243

great painting than I, would see it quicker than I had. Wrong again. It took them seven or eight years more.

Fairfield Porter, himself a leader among New York representational painters, reviewing in 1959 de Kooning's fifth and most recent show, wrote in *The Nation,* ". . . A painting by de Kooning has a certain superiority to one by any other painter, which is that it is first-hand, deep and clear . . . In the same way that the colors are intensely themselves, so is the apparent velocity always exactly believable and appropriate. There is that elementary principle of organization in any art that nothing gets in anything else's way, that everything is at its own limit of possibilities. What does this do to the person who looks at the paintings? This: the picture presented of released possibilities, of ordinary qualities existing at their fullest limits and acting harmoniously together—this picture is exalting. . . . Nor is there in de Kooning's paintings the idea that abstraction is the historically most valid form today . . . Once music was not abstract, but representational . . . In this way de Kooning's abstractions, which are in terms of the instrument, release human significances that cannot be expressed verbally. It is as though his painting reached a different level of consciousness than painting that refers to any sort of program . . . No one else whose paintings can be in any way considered to resemble his reaches his level."

As a professional, de Kooning has developed a number of virtuoso procedures of brush-stroke, of drawing and of composition that other painters here and abroad have taken up. His most recent technical invention has to do with a way of bypassing the earth-colors which equalizes the rate of drying everywhere on the picture; his most recent compositional one seems to me to have to do with color also.

De Kooning was born in Rotterdam. His father remarried. His mother, a woman of vigorously upright character, kept a bar. At twelve years old he was apprenticed to a housepainting and decorating firm with, to start with, a nominal twelve-hour working day. Later however, and for seven years, he went to evening classes at the

244

Academy. When his sailor friends heard he wanted to go to America, they found him a job as wiper in the engineroom, and showed him how to jump ship over here. Here he was first a house-painter in Hoboken, then a window display man in Manhattan and helped decorating speakeasies. A few pictures of his painted around 1930 are curious but not particularly promising. Twenty years later on 10th Street he was beginning the picture later called "Woman," which became the most widely reproduced painting of the post-war. And by then in intellectual dispute at the Painters Club, like with a blow of a lion's paw, he could tear an opponent's heart out, so fairly everybody else laughed.

About then, back from Italy, I was telling him about the Sistine Chapel ceiling, the smell of shoes where it is, and as you go on looking it makes you so marvelously happy you can see that every way the centuries praise it is reasonable. Not that Michelangelo's mistakes aren't obvious, and I spoke of them. When I stopped, he said, still listening intently, "Yes, right, wrong, right, wrong, right, wrong," striking each with the same hit of his fist like a carpenter driving a heavy nail. Two talks of his on art printed around 1950 belong to the most graphic a painter has offered. In one, near the start, he says, "It is very interesting to notice that a lot of people who want to take the talking out of painting do nothing but talk about it. That is no contradiction however. The art in it is the eternally mute part you can talk about forever. For me, only one point comes into my field of vision. That narrow, biased point gets very clear sometimes. I didn't invent it. It was here already. Everything that passes me I can see only a little of, but I am always looking. And I can see an awful lot sometimes."

Nowadays, when a new picture of his is exhibited, young painters sit around chin in hand scrutinizing it. One of them pointed to a detail and said to another, "Look at this, he's faking his style." "I saw that," the other answered, "so it's not pure—as far as I can see he's not making style, he's making a picture. As far as I can see, he's way ahead of the field."

245

Recently a young painter walking at night down Third Avenue near 10th Street, saw him running fast. The young man wondered why de Kooning was running so fast at night. Then he saw Lisbeth, de Kooning's little daughter. They were playing hide-and-seek.

"I'm not so crazy about my style," he said to me recently, "I'd just as soon paint some other way." When he was in Rome last autumn, he told me, he met at a party an American painter of his age, dignified and well dressed, with a nice wife and college son. They were making the rounds of museums and the ruins, they knew about all there was to see, and enjoyed looking at it intelligently. Bill said that when he was young he expected he would later turn into a man such as that, but somehow it hadn't happened.

Postscript

THE BALLETS here reviewed at length are described in their first versions; those kept in repertory have been reworked since, more or less.

I have not reworked these articles. I am astonished that I ever thought *Serenade* would be better danced in a demi-charactère way. Astonished, too, that the thrill I remember so distinctly of LeClercq's climax in *La Valse*—throwing her head back as she plunges her hand into the black glove—is not mentioned here. Her solitary pacing that made the last minute of *Opus 34* so marvelous is mentioned but without naming her. Not mentioned is her leading part in developing the company's current dance style.

Here is a lively review of a matinee *Firebird* at the City Center. It was dictated to his mother by a seven-year-old friend of mine.

First he was walking around—the prince. And then he started to see a little shiny dot like gold and then it got bigger and bigger and suddenly it had a face and then see—the prince danced with Firebird. Now comes the place where the prince goes to church to be married and then he sees it again. We forgot—about the demons, they come and fight. And he calls Firebird and it comes as fast as a jetplane, see—and the wing is sharp and even stronger than a sword and he throws it at the demon king's head so he falls down. Then it flies away and goes to church, and there is a lot of firecrackers and he sees Firebird lighting the candles and he does something funny, he runs out of the house, appears in a tree, disappears in the tree, and there he is back in church! The whole thing—it was painted and it was standing pretend not to be real on top of the cross. And the prince knew it was real. And two bangs came that were firecrackers and then something else funny, he changed into a dragon who could talk, then he changed into a human being, then back into Firebird. I think maybe that's all. I don't know, or don't write that.—One more thing: he went into a basket and into a piece of paper and came out with a handkerchief over his face and the handkerchief flies off and it is Firebird. But now there is no more. At the end write under it Firebird and Princess.

INDEX

INDEX

252

253

254

FREE
Fawcett Books Listing

There is Romance, Mystery, Suspense, and Adventure waiting for you inside the Fawcett Books Order Form. And it's yours to browse through and use to get all the books you've been wanting . . . but possibly couldn't find in your bookstore.

This easy-to-use order form is divided into categories and contains over 1500 titles by your favorite authors.

So don't delay—take advantage of this special opportunity to increase your reading pleasure.

Just send us your name and address and 35¢ (to help defray postage and handling costs).

FAWCETT BOOKS GROUP
P.O. Box C730, 524 Myrtle Ave., Pratt Station, Brooklyn, N.Y. 11205

Name_____
(please print)

Address_____
City_____ State_____ Zip_____
Do you know someone who enjoys books? Just give us their names and addresses and we'll send them an order form too!

Name_____
Address_____
City_____ State_____ Zip_____

Name_____
Address_____
City_____ State_____ Zip_____